William H. Russell

My Diary in India in the Year 1858-9

Vol. 1

William H. Russell

My Diary in India in the Year 1858-9
Vol. 1

ISBN/EAN: 9783337043995

Printed in Europe, USA, Canada, Australia, Japan

Cover: Foto ©Andreas Hilbeck / pixelio.de

More available books at **www.hansebooks.com**

MY DIARY IN INDIA,

IN THE YEAR 1858-9.

BY

WILLIAM HOWARD RUSSELL, LL.D.,

SPECIAL CORRESPONDENT OF "THE TIMES."

With Illustrations.

IN TWO VOLUMES.—VOL. I.

LONDON:
ROUTLEDGE, WARNE, AND ROUTLEDGE,
FARRINGDON STREET.
1860.

[*The Right of Translation is reserved.*]

PREFACE.

ON looking over the pages of a Diary which was assiduously kept as long as my health permitted me to write it, I found many subjects entered and alluded to therein which were not mentioned in my letters to *The Times*, but which might nevertheless be interesting to general readers. In the belief that the incidents of Indian life and personal adventures in the field may not be altogether destitute of attraction, I have prepared my journal for publication. It is with much diffidence I ask my readers to remember that a diary is essentially an egotistical work, and that one who is lord of himself, in his memorandum book, is apt to rule it over his heritage in a very despotic and narrow spirit which shuts him up in the prison of his own thoughts, and looks very little beyond it for treaties of friendship and alliance. The frequent use of the first personal pronoun is the necessary consequence of a personal narrative, written from day to day, of the impressions made by passing events on the senses of the spectator. To the text of the Diary I have added a few notes and observations not originally incorporated with it; but with this modification, and with the exception of omissions of conversations and occurrences of a private or confidential character, and of purely domestic and personal references, the MS. is printed almost as it was penned. I shall betray no confidences, I shall violate no trusts; and if in observing that condition I may be compelled sometimes to be silent, I shall tell, at all events, when I do speak, the truth, and nothing but the truth. Whilst I was in India I had no authors to consult, no books to read, and I had no guides but my own perceptions; but neither had I any prejudices to overcome, nor theories to support. It may so have happened that, like the traveller who stands for the first time in a great city, I have been struck by objects which to the inhabitants had no significance or value. I may have detected a crack in the wall of the capitol which they believe to be secure because they have been looking at it so long that it ceases to cause any apprehension. Things familiar to, or unnoticed by, them, to me may have had a remarkable aspect and importance.

The temples, which to my eyes seemed foul with smoke, may be under the care of cunning workmen, who, as the good citizens know, will soon restore the walls to more than pristine whiteness. The bridges, which appeared to me sinking and gaping wide, may have some secret props that give confidence to all the habituated that cross them. The stream, that filled me with alarm as it rolled sullenly on, may have rolled on thus for centuries and done no harm, but, passing smoothly along, have borne quiet generations to eternity. Ignorant of those hidden sources of knowledge, I stand and look around, and say, "thus does it appear to me, and thus I seem to see." In saying so I always bear in mind and fully acknowledge the liability to errors into which one may fall, who allows himself to be led by first impressions. I think it is Sir Gardner Wilkinson who tells a story in one of his books respecting a learned German who came to London, and at once went forth to generalize his remarks. He walked into Grosvenor Square, and observed an escutcheon on the walls of a house, which he duly considered for some time, and noted as an object to be inquired into. On going into Berkeley Square, he saw another escutcheon on the walls. "Ha!" quoth he, "I see it now," and forthwith he proceeded to write: "Each square in London has its distinct coat of arms, which is placed in a conspicuous place on one of the houses, and is generally identical with the arms of the principal proprietor."

Have you ever passed through the Strand, or Fleet Street, at dawn on a summer's morning? If so, you will have seen a street unknown to you by day—sharp gables, quaint angles, odd signs and sculptures, strange shops, new alleys—a curious old carved and irregular continental street, with antique spires peering over a toppling sea of roofs, as unlike the street that the good citizen sees when he takes down his shutters as Venice is to Bermondsey. I saw India in mourning, lighted up by a blood-red conflagration, and in her misery she appeared very different indeed from the pictures which had been drawn of her, but they may have been, nevertheless, accurate representations of her former state. I know not if I have seen aright or can describe the objects which I beheld; but such as India appeared to me, it shall be, to the best of my poor ability, portrayed in pen and ink.

Into the history of the Mutiny I do not pretend to

go—nor will I, except incidentally, touch upon the revolt which followed it, and which was, in certain places, more or less popular in its character; but I trust the reader will find a recompense for the absence of such disquisitions in what I would fain hope to be truthful details in reference to some scenes of the revolt, and more particularly to portions of the glorious efforts which crushed it. If there is something to be extenuated, surely nought shall be set down in malice. If I mention names, the owners will, I trust, take it not amiss, and if they do I shall gladly make amends hereafter and erase any index to their identity.

I have to express my obligations to Mr. Lundgren, to whose well-skilled pencil I am indebted for the illustrations.

WILLIAM HOWARD RUSSELL.

London, December, 1859.

CONTENTS.

CHAPTER I.

Departure for the East.—Scant time for preparation.—My fellow-passengers.—Marine cookery.—Daily life in an oriental steamer 1

CHAPTER II.

Arrival at Malta.—Sir Edmund Lyons and Balaklava.—Proposed bombardment of Odessa.—General Pennefather.—The fortifications at Malta.—Characteristics of the Maltese.—Alexandria.—One-eyed pilot and boatmen—News from Lucknow and Cawnpore.—Havelock's death.—The landing-place at Alexandria.—The railway station.—Arrival at Cairo.—The Hotel du Nil . . . 11

CHAPTER III.

The bazaar of Cairo.—Felicitous arrangements for passengers.—A "gentleman."—French influences.—English behaviour.—Oriental gravity.—The Desert.—Arabian Navvies.—Lost in darkness.—The Hotel at Suez.—The "American System."—Picturesque dirtiness.—Arab Crafts and their crews.—Exhausting heat . . . 31

CHAPTER IV.

A vow.—An appeal on behalf of the ladies.—The surgeons' and officers' cabins.—Learned pundits.—The walnut stage of argument.—La race blanche.—Why are we in India ?—The hottest place in the world.—Flying fish.—The French at Pondicherry.—Mistake imputed to the English.—Is our French friend right ?—A novel resting-place.—Astronomical contemplatious.—Washing decks . . . 46

CHAPTER V.

Music.—Pirates or pilgrims ?—Miss Telle and Mr. Quel.—Flying-fish or sandlarks ?—A doctrine both new and old.—Traditional Nabobs.—Eagles and eaglets.—The Isle of Perimm.—Aden.—Simawlees and Arabs.—The "Prince of Wales" hotel.—Cowasjee's shop.—Athletic sports.—A souvenir of the Crimea.—The Nubians and the Almaites.—A Calvinistic sermon.—Sea-serpents and sea-snakes.—The harbour of Galle 61

CHAPTER VI.

Point de Galle.—Lorette's Hotel.—O'Dwyer, the waiter.—A slice of old Europe.—Old friends and old times.—Cricket with thermometer at 98°.—Real tropical vegetation.—Departure from Ceylon.—Native habit of hoarding.—Our ignorance of Indian social life.—Approaching the land.—The pilot, and his letter-bag.—Startling news.—Corporal Brown.—India safer than Ireland 79

CHAPTER VII.

The Hooghly.—Hindoo Temples.—Garden Reach.—Floating Hindoo corpses.—The Bengal Club.—The city of palaces.—The Fort.—Simon, once Allagapah.—The Esplanade.—A drive in the dark.—Europeans and Indians.—The Auckland hotel.—Proposed objects for investigation.—Musquitoes and jackals 93

CHAPTER VIII.

A delightful rush at clear, clean cold water.—Black washerman.—The Ochterlony monument.—Government House.—Absence of English domestics.—Interview with Lord Canning.—Hospital for sick and wounded officers.—Kindness of the ladies of Calcutta.—The "upper ten" at Lucknow.—The Southwark of Calcutta.—Paucity of white faces.—A row by moonlight.—Burning ghauts.—Indian official papers.—General Dupuis.—A ball at Fort William 110

CHAPTER IX.

Preparing for a start.—The king of Oude's menagerie.—Simon and Sally Bridget.—My fellow-traveller, Dr. Mouat.—The rajah of Pachete.—Raneegunj.—A mess-dinner.—Camp of Government elephants.—Locomotion by gharry.—A shattered wheel and its consequences.—Fording a river.—Numerous tanks, birds and squirrels.—Bungalows.—Theory and practice.—" Serry Shrab."—Approach to Benares.—The Holy Ganges. 130

CHAPTER X.

Outside of Benares.—Allahabad : the fort.—A canvas wall.—The Governor-General's tent.—Lieut. P. Stewart.—A colonel of sepoys.—Poor Clarke !—Question and answer.—Railway terminus.—A short walk.—Gharrys for Cawnpore.—Sir Robert Garrett's tongue.—Hall at Futtehpore . 149

CHAPTER XI.

Look at Cawnpore !—Its atrocities paralleled in History.—Azimoola Khan.—Strange curiosity in an Asiatic.—Barracks.—Miserable defensive position.—Camp of Sir Colin Campbell.—A compact.—The Highland bonnet.—Headquarters' staff-mess.—General Mansfield.—My tent and its attendants.—Dinner with the Commander-in-Chief.—The French General, Vinoy 163

CHAPTER XII.

PAGE

Wheeler's intrenchment.—Windham's position.—The two parts of an Indian station.—An imaginary review.—The Cutchery.—A Bedouin of the Press.—Generals cannot "do the graphic."—Bottled beer.—Members of our mess.—School of dialectics.—Improved life of Europeans.—Want of sympathy for natives.—Up-country life and Calcutta life.—Sir Hugh Wheeler's ayah.—Sir Archdale Wilson.—Captain Peel and his blue jackets.—Cawnpore dust.—"A shave of old Smith's."—Cawnpore in its palmy days.—Beggars and wigwam villages . . . 178

CHAPTER XIII.

Action at Meeangunj.—Sir Colin Campbell and Jung Bahadoor.—Hindoo temples mined.—Moonlight walk with Sir Colin.—Notes on the birds.—A bad day for quadrupeds.—Fishing in the Ganges.—Morning devotions.—Our first haul.—Plan of attack on Lucknow.—General notion of our plan of attack.—Astonishment of an old Sikh.—Scene of the Cawnpore tragedy.—Divine service in the ruined church.—A distant cannonade.—Reports of spies.—The enemy in immense force.—The Adjutant-General.—A near approach to ubiquity.—Camp of the Agra convoy.—Rotting corpses 196

CHAPTER XIV.

The army massing itself.—A living *corpus delicti.*—Sir J. Outram attacked.—Buy a gharry, a horse, and coachman.—Our army on the move.—Destruction of Hindoo temples.—Reply to a priest's intercession.—War, and no quarter given.—Indiscriminate executions.—Striking tents.—Camels and their burdens.—A welcome invitation.—Cross the Ganges into Oude.—An apparently illimitable procession.—A notion of Old World times.—"Master's mess buckree."—Ruined villages.—Orders for marching . 215

CONTENTS.

CHAPTER XV.

The first bugle.—The head of the column.—Sunrise.—Bullocks, camels, and elephants.—The white mare.—Sinking down into a gulf.—"Are you kilt, sir?"—A fast-trotting camel.—False alarm.—Camp grass-cutters.—Sir William Peel and his heavy guns.—Left behind.—Kavanagh.—A joyful surprise.—Orders to march 232

CHAPTER XVI.

March for Lucknow.—A vision.—Jellalabad.—Sepoy skeletons.—An old Sikh officer.—Sergeant Gillespie.—Site of our new camp.—The Martinière.—The Dilkoosha.—A breach of etiquette.—View from the roof of the Dilkoosha. —The enemy's trenches.—A round shot.—Striking beauty of Lucknow.—A young langour.—Visitors and guests . 245

CHAPTER XVII.

A narrow escape.—Under fire.—A kind of club-meeting.— Horsford and the yellow eunuch.—*Personnel* of our officers. —Reconnoitring.—A prettily-adjusted brass shell.—Sepoys' courage.—The yellow eunuch again.—Floating bridge across the Goomtee.—Habitual use of a telescope.—Advance of the enemy.—A brisk cannonade.—Brijeis Kuddr. —Daily avocations.—General order from Bahadoor Khan. —Fly-fishing.—A dignified retreat 260

CHAPTER XVIII.

Sir Colin Campbell's plan of operations.—A beautiful sight.— Unjust estimate of men's actions.—The enemy swarm.— The Bays, the Artillery, and the Rifles.—The day's work done.—Outram's camp.—The enemy active and unhappy. —Little Miss Orr.—Preparations for Outram's advance.— Kite-flying.—Warfare and cruelty.—Native milk-women. —Outram's advance.—My Caubulee pony.—A terrible game of cricket.—The storming party.—"Pandy" and "Smith."—Assault of the Martinière.—A canter to the newly-gained post.—Butler, of the Bengal Fusileers.—Pandy's deserted trenches.—Sikh barbarity.—The Begum still undaunted 278

CHAPTER XIX.

Outram's great success.—Jung Bahadoor's arrival announced.—Poor Garvey!—The Begum Kothie.—The Maharajah's reception.—The Begum Kothie taken.—The rush of the 93rd.—Horrors ineffable.—The Secunderbagh.—General Outram's camp.—"The Bayard of India."—The Badshahbagh.—Cunoujee Lall.—An old curiosity shop.—Death of Hodson.—Tremendous bombardment . . . 304

CHAPTER XX.

Capture of the Kaiserbagh.—The camp in commotion.—Voilà la différence!—Marks of shot and shell.—Poor Da Costa! —The Huzrutgunj.—Sappers at work.—Discipline after an assault.—Drunk with plunder.—A camel-load of curiosities.—Ready money transactions.—Presents of jewelry.—Camp followers.—Simon and his scales.—Telegraphic messages.—Plundering stopped.—A zenana.—Dinner with General Outram 322

CHAPTER XXI.

No rest for the rebels.—The shattered Residency.—A pleasant chat.—A capful of grape.—Street-fighting.—The great Imambarra.—View from one of its minarets.—Shots from all quarters.—A draught of nectar.—Barbarous act of an officer.—Awful accident.—News from Jung Bahadoor.—Pertinacity and Vacillation.—The Moosabagh.—Napier in distress.—Lord Canning's Proclamation.—Rev. Mr. McKay's sermons 340

CHAPTER XXII.

Lord Canning's Proclamation.—Visit to the begums.—Mrs. Orr and Miss Jackson.—Frightful wounds of poor Bankes. —The camp of the Seventh Hussars.—Sir James Outram and Lord Canning.—Visit to Sir William Peel.—Munoora-ood-dowlah.—Our aides-de-camps.—The Chief Commissioner of Oude.—My palkee and appurtenances sold.— Sir James Outram's departure.—Doggerel verses and charcoal sketches.—Routed by an elephant.—Sales of captured property 357

CHAPTER XXIII.

My last days in Lucknow.—The soldier's goods and chattels. —A palpable obstruction.—A night of great pain.—A melancholy mode of progression.—Lord Clinton ill at Cawnpore.—The whole art of war.—Welcome repose.—A Drive through Cawnpore.—Death of Adrian Hope.—Discomfort of night-marches.—Joy to reach the camping-ground.—The lost tent.—The ruins of Kunouj.—Futtehguhr.—Brigadier Seaton 373

CHAPTER XXIV.

Dhuleep Sing's bath.—A savage, beastly, and degrading custom.—The column filing off.—Told off to an elephant.— Fields strewed with skeletons.—Junction with Walpole.— An Indian storm.—A short but grateful sleep.—Difficulty of keeping Highlanders back.—Sir William Peel no more! —An English soldier and his "presner."—Desperate kick from a horse.—Mounted on a tumbril.—A day of drowsy pain.—More dooly travelling.—General Penny killed.— Disaster at Kukrowlee.—Halt near Shahjehanpore.—Ride through the city.—Sea of mango groves.—Conflicting reports from Bareilly.—Bamboo backsheesh.—Expected engagements 389

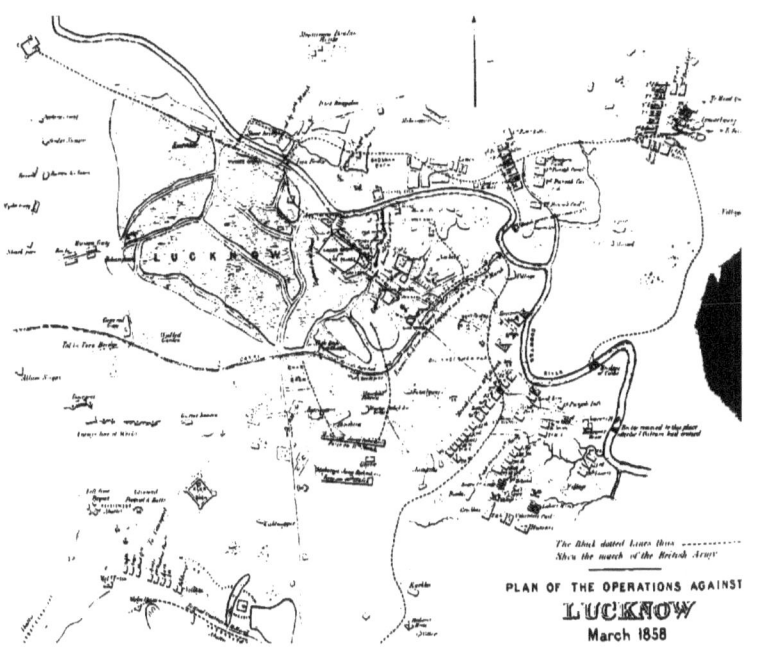

PLAN OF THE OPERATIONS AGAINST
LUCKNOW
March 1858

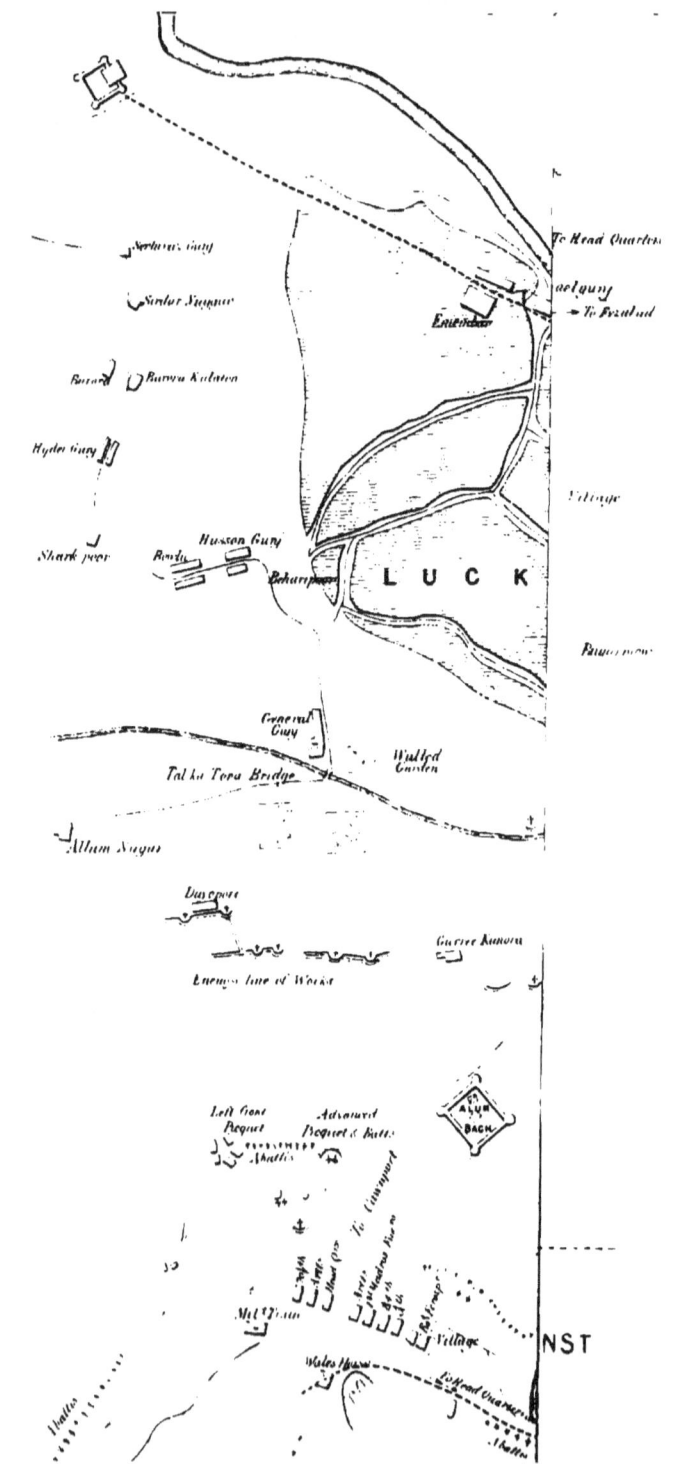

MY DIARY IN INDIA.

CHAPTER I.

Departure for the East.—Scant time for preparation.—My fellow passengers.—Marine cookery.—Daily life in an oriental steamer.

NOT one year home from the Crimea and I am once more on my way to the East—another and a farther East. Landing with the first British soldiers who set foot on the soil of Turkey I had accompanied the advanced guards of the British army to Gallipoli, to Scutari, to Varna, and to Old Fort, and, in 1856, had quitted the camp before Sebastopol only when I was left alone in the front with the rats and the Cossacks. Then, after a visit of just ten days to England, I went once more to Russia, witnessed the coronation of the Emperor at Moscow, the "barbaric pearl and gold" of the most magnificent spectacle these later ages of ours have ever produced, travelled south to the Crimea, revisited the resting-places of our illustrious dead, and, turning westwards to Odessa, traversed the steppes by Bender, and passing through the much-disputed Bolgrad, in the beginning of winter reached Czernovitch, from which my way homewards lay straight before me, and I arrived in London once more in the spring of 1857. The close of the same year sees me bound to the regions of which the "we" of England know so little, and as to which our carelessness has been an equivalent of our ignorance. But our apathy has been rudely disturbed. It was just as our journalists and statesmen were somewhat feebly glorifying our rule in India, and mildly rebuking the neglect which was allowing the centenary of Plassey and the grandeur of Clive to pass away, that the day of whose advent Metcalfe had prophesied and Napier had warned dawned in Hindostan and cast its blood-red light over the land. Hideous massacres of men, women, and children,—compared with which Sylla's proscriptions, the Sicilian vespers, the great *auto da fè* on Bartholomew's eve, or the Ulster outbreak of 1641, were legitimate acts of judicial punishment,—were reported to us with such seasoning of horrors, made by skilful masters in that sort of cookery, as the imagination had never before devised. I had been deeply impressed by those awful scenes. I was moved to the inner soul by the narratives which came to us by every mail, and I felt that our struggle against those monsters of cruelty and lust must be crowned by Heaven with success. But after a time I began, mail after mail, to seek for evidence of the truth of those disgusting anecdotes glossed with still more revolting insinuations. I never doubted them, but I wanted proof, and none was forthcoming. All the stories we heard emanated from Calcutta, and the people of Calcutta were far from the districts where, no doubt, most treacherous and wholesale murder had been perpetrated. At last I was going out to the very country which had acquired such a fearful interest in our eyes, and I hoped to join my countrymen ere their vengeance was consummated, and India was once more restored, at least, to the tranquillity of conquest.

I had but scant time for preparation, and even that was encroached upon by domestic affairs; but thanks to the resources of those who in London are called upon every hour to provide outfits for every portion of the globe—from the North Pole to Australia—I was in readiness to start within a week, crossed to Calais in a winter gale, managed to arrive in Paris just as the train for Marseilles—the last that could catch the steamer for Alexandria—left it, journeyed express with the officer in charge of the mails, who fortunately was as late as myself, by special engine and carriage till we overtook the mail-train beyond Lyons, and had just a moment at Marseilles to get my permit and embark on board the Valetta, which was soon, with the lively habits of her class, battling the mistral in the Gulf of Lyons, and plunging through head seas like a cormorant in a tide-way. The number of books on the overland route from time to time which have been "done" by various hands would constitute a library *per se*, but all its incidents have been exhausted by him who made that famous trip from Cornhill to Cairo; and, as I have read from an early age in reviews and magazines perpetual remonstrances against the vanity of those who think their eyes are better and their wit brighter than those of others, and who have, therefore, insisted on giving the public their version of the impressions produced by this beaten ground and much-vexed sea, I shall not say one word about the Mediterranean, and but little of the waters which form by far the greater part of what is, by a sort of "dry humour," called the overland route. Our fellow-passengers were, for the most part, either old Indians, returning full of anger, gloom, and vengeance to their former posts, now freed from the enemy, or to others promised or to be gotten by interest and perseverance, or young ones, of whom one alone was preparing himself by studying the language and history of the people for the sphere of his labours. There were also some Queen's officers going out to join their regiments, a few younger men, unposted, who expected to be attached to Queen's regiments, as their own corps were fighting, or trying to fight, against us, and a few civilians; with a poll of wives going to their husbands, and of young ladies going to find husbands in that land where they hang like flocks of the golden fleece, which daring argonauts from the schools may pluck as they will. To trace their destinations from Malta would be to cover the East with a wide-spreading fan. There were men for Australia, for China, the dominions of the Rajah of Sarawak, for Penang, Singapore, Hong Kong, Java, Lahore, Aden, Bombay, Calcutta, Ceylon, Pondicherry, and many unknown places beyond the seas. The little steamer was a turbulent microcosm, and at times, when the Mediterranean gave us a taste of its quality, and the great seas came flying over the bows, sluicing the decks with a mimic ocean, our microcosm became sick and querulous. But even then stood, cigar in mouth, standing stiffly with swaying body, on well-set sea-legs, one bronzed, compact little man, who set an example of appetite, endurance, and good humour that provoked the invalids and attracted the few who could stand the capers of the Valetta. This was a French medical officer of the navy who was going back to his duties as Intendant of Pondicherry, a man full of anecdote, resource, and observation, who had two fixed ideas—that all our naval battles were won by mistake, and that it was the mission of *la race blanche* to make India happy by some process which the English were to begin and fail in, and which the French were finally to accomplish. Of him and his theories we shall hear more by-and-by.

Now, excellent Directors of the great Peninsular and Oriental Company! May I say one word to you? Your ships are good, the service of the mails is excellent, but would you be kind enough to send a travelling director now and then, not of too robust a stomach, to journey overland to India? The complaints of the cooking and of the crowding on board those splendid ships are only too well founded. The claret is some sort of rough Rhine wine, and resembles greatly the liquid sold under the name of Tenedos wine at Gallipoli. The port and sherry must be made on board, as they are never met with out of the ships; and yet I have drunk at the offices in Leadenhall Street very good, pure wine, which I am assured was, and which I am satisfied is believed to be, the same as that given to the passengers on board ship. The tea and coffee *mihi nullo discrimine agentur*. One cannot expect fat poultry on board ship, but at least some attempts might be made to put a little fowl on their bones by plentiful diet. This, however, would be opposed to the traditions of the ships' cooks, who declare—at least one of them did to me in reply to a remark that the creatures seemed very hungry—a plentiful supply of food would be fatal to them. Of the vivacity of the inhabitants of the coops, under the present system, there can be no doubt. They are as lively and discontented as Italians. One curious result of the treatment as it progresses is to give the ships' boys an increase of exercise every morning, for the chickens become so thin that they are able to flutter into liberty through the bars which detained them at first, and they pick desperately at the carpenters' chips or bits of oakum lying about the decks in the early morning. The bill of fare of the passengers, however, is plentiful to redundancy and even coarseness of superfluity; but, making every allowance for the difficulties of the marine Francatellis, the cooking is indifferent. It is true that on board the larger ships the number of passengers to be provided for creates another impediment; but if the good Peninsular and Oriental Company would only condescend to take a page out of the book of cookery followed by the *Messageries Impériales*, they would find, unless one's experience is greatly in error, that they would nearly silence the grumblings which are such an unpleasant substratum of all the dinner and breakfast conversation on board their vessels.

There are two kinds of monopoly, that which is conferred by the State and that which is attained by the perseverance and ability of a corporation, sole or aggregate, in supplying the public wants, by which it has accumulated wealth and resources and advantages that place it above all rivalry or competition. In the enjoyment of the latter monopoly the Peninsular and Oriental now confessedly stands, and I for one do not by any means wish to deprive them of it or its emoluments, for the directors have displayed extraordinary energy, made great sacrifices, and put forth great exertions to the benefit of the country and of the public service in attaining their present position. All I would venture to suggest is, that there might be a little more delicacy in the *ménage* on board. The pursers are gentlemen, attentive and prompt, but they are so used to insinuation and open rebellion on the subject of accommodation and feeding, and are so callous to round-robins, letters to *The Times* and to the Company, that they regard such courses as the normal state of affairs, or as a result of sea-sickness or disordered liver and bile. Indeed they pleasantly draw comparisons between the average tempers of passengers as they happen to be bound outwards or homewards; and it must be admitted "the confounded public," as that large and respectable body is frequently styled in the privacies of official and monopolitical life, is apt to be very eccentric and unreasonable at times; but at least all just grounds of complaint may be reduced to a minimum without any great trouble. Now, on board the *Messageries* and the Austrian Lloyd's boats in the Mediterranean, the cost of provisions per head and the expense of cooking must be far less than in the Peninsular and Oriental ships, and I am bound to say that, having several times travelled in each of all three, I have heard no grumbling, and I have been much better satisfied on board the two former. How the English passengers would like to pay extra for every wine, except the *vin de pays* that is placed on the table, and for their ale, porter, and spirits, I cannot say, but I should think that it would resolve itself into a question of fares. Certainly the *dîner à la Russe* might be introduced with great advantage. Of a hot day the smell of great joints, of liver and bacon, of steaming meat-pies, of roast goose, poultry, duck, and of pea-soup, and its congeners, is most overpowering, and the miseries of the unfortunate gentlemen who preside over favourite dishes, such as an impectoral turkey, the victim of anchylosis in every joint, or a huge plateau of salted beef, are only terminated by a sudden loss of temper, and a hasty aside to the steward—"No! I'm, &c., if I do. Take it away and cut it yourself!"

Could all the pale ale, soda-water, sherry, porter, and *vin ordinaire,* and the feebler bibables be turned into nectar, and all the heavy garniture of the table assume the taste and form of ambrosia, the Homeric deities could desire no better Olympus than one of the Peninsular and Oriental vessels, presided over by some genial Jove of a great sea-captain. Here is one day's life as I find it in my diary: A pint or so of tea and coffee, either plain or mixed, at any hour from six A.M. to eight A.M.; dress (and a bath if the weather permits); a more or less uncomfortable promenade, during which the ladies begin to develope themselves upon the deck. At nine a bell rings, and an avalanche of hungry passengers descends upon the eatables and uneatables, eggs *au plat,* hot rolls, mutton chops, &c., &c. At ten, the deck, which becomes tolerable under the influences of breakfast, a cigar, and a view of some distant headland, or of a passing sail. At twelve another bell, and with unflagging energy the world rushes below again and proceeds to attack cheese, biscuit, and butter, pale ale, porter, spirits and water according to its taste. A dreary indigestible interval of some hours, which in bad weather can only be conqueered by incessant smoking or great internal resources. At four or at five, according to the rule of the ship, the bell again, and the great event of the day—dinner —*exoritur clamor vivorum et* (I am bound to add) *fœminarum*. The stewards in a noble frenzy scuffle up and down the narrow gangway between the backs of the seats and the cabins with piles of plates, or in rough weather swing to and fro and balance themselves onwards with an air of mild dignity, preserving the equilibrium of the soup or gravy. Heat, clatter, and voracity, the latter produced by the sea-air it is said, distinguish the banquet till it is closed by the fiery enjoyments of the port and sherry with Dodoncan nuts and the dessert. Then the company mount to the deck again; and at seven there is a service of tea and bread and butter; and at thirty minutes past eight the last bell rings for the day, and all hands make a final charge at the table, and establish themselves before decanters of wine and spirits, whiskey, gin, brandy, and rum, wherefrom they proceed to various brews, and thence work onwards to a round of *vingt-et-un* or a rubber of whist. "Inextinguishable laughter" prevails for a time, which after a time is mingled with less agreeable sounds, and at ten is quite put out by the extinction of the ship's lights, a process which is never effected without argument on the part of the players, determination on the part of the stewards, and a general expression of opinion that "I never was in such a confounded disobliging ship in all my life." And so we went on day after day, night after night.

Wintry seas around us,. distant views of Corsica and its rugged coast line, backed by mountain ranges, covered with snow, like giant waves crested with creaming surf.—Then Sicily blurred by driving clouds of mist and spray, but revealing its long sea-board, covered with white houses, from time to time, as one of her own nymphs of old might have dazzled a pursuing faun with glimpses of her snowy feet beneath her flowing robes.—Then the great, round, unbroken shield of the sea once more, of which our little bark is the boss with its soup-swilling, love and grog-making, eating, card-playing, and smoking.

CHAPTER II.

Arrival at Malta.—Sir Edmund Lyons and Balaklava.—Proposed bombardment of Odessa.—General Pennefather.—The fortifications at Malta.—Characteristics of the Maltese.—Alexandria. One-eyed pilot and boatmen.—News from Lucknow and Cawnpore.—Havelock's death.—The landing place at Alexandria.—The railway station.—Arrival at Cairo.—The Hotel du Nil.

It was late on a winter's evening as we glided into the smaller harbour of Malta, and cast anchor off the lazaretto. The last time I, outward bound, saw the anchorage, it was full of French and English ships laden with full freightage of gallant soldiers, of whom but very few are now alive. There were the Zouaves, about to commence that great military career in Europe which has made their names famous by every hearth, then unknown warriors of Algerine skirmishes, and the local heroes of obscure victories. There were the Guards, then 2500 strong, the sons of British Anak, who, having added the glorious words "Alma" and "Inkerman" to the roll of their triumphs, left a few poor winter and fever-stricken survivors to march down in sad and scanty file from the front to the refuge of Balaklava. Even of the veterans who did not succumb to pestilence, to battle, to Russian lead and iron, or to the slow process of disease, how small are those in number who can be found in the ranks or in service! The whole of the gaudy flotilla, full of life and tumult, was at present replaced by half-a-dozen coal brigs, and Moorish zebecs, or Sicilian trabocoli, laden with fruit and Marsala wine. As soon as a wise-looking little man, in spectacles, had looked over a paper by the light of his boat's lantern, and had pronounced us to be quite "clean," most of us got afloat and scuffled on shore in the dark to the stairs, where there is a certainty of finding a relay of guides, who are firmly persuaded that the main object of every passenger's existence is to buy gloves, Maltese crapes and lace; or, if not these, to get his hair cut, and to discover the Strada Reale. I had intended to call on Lord Lyons in memory of old days on board the Agamemnon, and more recently up that delightful estuary beyond the Spit of Kinburn, where we were glad to get sea-gulls for dinner, and fancied they were as tender and as *un*-fishy as canvas-backed ducks, but we heard with regret that the gallant old admiral was in great affliction on account of the loss of a near relative. I never saw him more: old as he was, there were no signs of mental or bodily decay in him when last I met with him, and he appeared as if he were likely to live till he might be wanted.

It would be unprofitable and painful to revive an old and almost forgotten controversy — fully four years' old, but one cannot help remembering the great expectations which were entertained from Sir Edmund Lyons' ability and dash when he assumed the command of the fleet before Sebastopol, and how many after a few weeks shook their heads and said, "It's the old story — the second in command is always better than his chief till the change comes." But it would be unjust to the memory of the gallant sailor to forget, even while second in command, what abiding strength he gave to the councils of our army, what life and energy he infused into our operations, what enthusiasm and zeal into the whole naval service. He told me one day, in reply to a question which I founded on a very secret rumour (confidential at the time), that it was quite true he prevented the abandonment of Balaklava by our generals after the action of the 25th October. "The day after," he said, "I was on my way to head-quarters, to see Lord Raglan, when I heard that orders had been given to prepare for the abandonment of Balaklava. I was astonished and incredulous—I went to head-quarters and found it was quite true. I ventured to expostulate, but Lord Raglan said that he, and Airey, and all of them were of opinion the line was too extended and too weak, and that he had ordered everything to be moved so as to evacuate the place. 'Good God,' I exclaimed, ' do reconsider this decision ! Why, if you give up Balaklava, how will you feed your army, or land your ammunition and your siege material?' I urged his lordship strongly; and at last I said that if he let me I would engage to hold Balaklava with my own men, and Lord Raglan yielded—the orders were countermanded, and our position saved." Such, as nearly as I recollect, was his account of a very remarkable transaction, narrated with that fire of utterance, that light of the eye, and expressive action which gave the admiral a peculiar interest when he was excited—it was then that his resemblance to the best portraits of Nelson became exceedingly striking—a resemblance which extended even to the slight and almost meagre figure. He used to complain greatly of the way in which he was hampered by the French, whose vigilance as to joint operation amounted to an annoying surveillance. "I can't so much as send out a gun-boat with my mails but *mon cher amiral* telegraphs to ask me where she is going to, and what her errand is." But when off Odessa for the second time he gave great credit to the Emperor for his sagacity. The admirals telegraphed to their governments for instructions as to a bombardment of Odessa. Sir James Graham telegraphed, "Don't, unless you think you will succeed." The Emperor returned the answer, "I am radically opposed to an attack." "And," said Sir Edmund, " the Emperor's quite right—that's a proper sort of answer. How the deuce is a man to attempt a thing and be sure of succeeding? Who can tell what may happen?" The admiral's opinion, however, was, very decidedly, that a bombardment of Odessa would be a failure. No doubt great damage could be done to parts of the town, but the houses are incombustible, and those parts of the town which could be damaged are private residences or stores, and inconsiderable government stores, whilst from their position it would scarce be possible to silence the guns of the petty defences altogether; and if the Russians could have fired but one gun as we withdrew, they would have claimed the credit of beating us off.

I know more than one ardent admirer and devoted officer of Sir Edmund Lyons who regretted, and still speak with regret of, the evidence he gave before the Chelsea Commission, because in it he seemed to forget the expressions and opinions he had frequently uttered. There is one still living who can bear witness that ere the admiral became Lord Lyons, he once, at all events, entertained very different notions of the nature of the arrangements in 1854-5 and of the management of the army; but whatever may have been the change and the nature of it in that point, none could have taken place in his kindly gallant nature, or in his zeal and devotion to the service, and his thorough English feelings.

I saw Mr. Cleeve, his indefatigable and efficient secretary, who had then received no reward for his laborious services. I hope that he has had reason to be better satisfied long ago. At the best of times the office of admiral's secretary is difficult, laborious, and thankless.

Although our time was short on shore, and the hour was late, I could not leave Malta without seeing General Pennefather. Who can be insensible to that warm Irish welcome that is worth a thousand *cead mille failtha* of the tongue? To the frankness of the soldier the brigadier of the "fighting brigade" of the old second division adds a charm of manner, united with much humour, fine subtlety of apprehension, abundance of anecdote, and allusion, and "love of fun" that give wonderful interest to one who is known to be a stern, sharp officer, resolute and daring in danger, and never so cool as when he is in action. All the General's thoughts were fixed on China, and he was evidently pining for another look at the flowery land. As to India, he regarded the work as done. "Delhi is gone," said he, " and Colin Campbell is sure to relieve Lucknow, and to do it well. The rest is all a work of time, but it is sure to be done." They are strange beings those old soldiers. They tell you war is a dreadful thing; that it is a terrible trade—a curse to the earth; but still they are never so happy as when they are at it. I don't mean that any of those veterans who have seen warfare and its results really would, of their own free will, deliberately do any thing which would cause its advent, but that when war is going on they are all anxious to be engaged in it. "'Tis their vocation, Hal!" And so it was that the good, kind, and Christian General, who was quietly situated at Malta, in command of its peaceable garrison, who would not hurt a fly (and they are very irritating at Malta), and who on Sunday enjoys deeply and wisely the holy repose it brings, was now burning "to see what they were at in China." And surely had he been sent there it may be said, without disparagement to General Straubenzee, that the work would have been done in a much more complete and soldier-like manner; for there was no officer in the service, as I have heard from those who ought to know, who could handle British soldiers with greater skill and *consideration*, or who could temper the most brilliant courage with skill and judgment better than Sir John Pennefather. In his hands Malta ought to be safe, but it must be remembered that, formidable as the works look, and as they undoubtedly were in the days of Napoleon, the armament has not been renovated so as to bring it to a level with the means of attack which could be brought to bear upon the place. General Reid did much to improve the defences. In his time the face of the works, and in some instances, the profile was improved. Light guns were replaced by heavy, and the old and dangerous cast-iron gun-carriages were replaced by improved carriages of wood, but how far the improvements have gone I am not able to say. However, Malta stands in the same category as all our colonies, our fortresses, and even our liberties. Its possession depends on our naval supremacy, on our command of the seas, without which even Gibraltar itself must go in time. The works would scarcely protect a fleet from a bombardment, and a blockade at the sea, and an investment on the land side would reduce the place. It seems to one like myself that it is more open and weak on the side towards Fort Tigné and the Lazaretto than in any other direction; but it is certainly quite strong enough to defy and punish cursory attack, though its permanent possession depends upon our naval preponderance in the Mediterranean.

I have never yet read any description of the town of Valetta, or, indeed, of the island of Malta, which satisfied me. It seems to be our hard fate to be doomed to do ungraceful things in the eyes of those whom we rule and govern, and though it would be a difficult matter indeed for a Protestant State to conciliate the affections of such devout Papalists as the Maltese, we might certainly tread a little more gently on their Catholic corns. Notwithstanding a plethora of priests, which, taken from the male circulation of the island, deprives it of so much vigour and industry, no one can deny the Maltese the glory which belongs to hard work, to thrift, and energy in search of gain. The lower orders are content with our rule, for they have real liberty and full security for life and property. The upper orders are not so well satisfied, for they find the higher walks of social life closed by foreigners, and their religion disposes them to view the heretical *forestieri* with a jealous eye. Besides, they furnish the priesthood with its largest supplies, and now and then conscientious captains and subalterns won't turn out the guard for the passage of the Host, and there is a seven days' ferment thereupon among the High Church people. Our necessities force us to use those stately old albergi as barracks, and in the courts where once trode the Knights of Castile, of France or of Austria, we see the British "awkward squad" undergoing the cruelties of the drill sergeant. Those contrasts are more striking to the natives, who have traditional and indistinctly-grounded reverence for such places, than they are to ourselves, and I wish— without exactly knowing how to effect it—that we were less like a garrison and more like a settlement or affiliated colony than we are at present. Many people give the Maltese a bad name, but naval officers and merchant captains, who have worked with them, are not disposed generally to coincide in an unfavourable view of their character. Poor, they are fond of money—of strong domestic feelings, they hoard every penny to extreme stinginess. Often and often the astonished traveller is left in some remote region by his "Smitch," who suddenly "wants to go home to see mee mother," or "whose brudder sick, saar." In the Russian war they followed the track of an army in some inscrutable manner, and no sooner was the British pendant flying in some obscure water of the Black Sea than Tonio or Giacomo made his appearance with his boat, as if he belonged to the place, and offered to "put master ashore for two shillin'." They briskly competed with the Turk, Greek, and Armenian caiquejees at Gallipoli, at Scutari, and the Golden Horn, and then worked their way up to Varna and across to Kamiesch and Balaklava. They form the staple of the crews engaged in the boats of the Peninsular and Oriental, of the *Messageries Impériales*, and of the Austrian Lloyd's, and not a few of the quartermasters and non-commissioned officers in our fleet hail from the little island, which is buffeted this day by the seas of the Gregale as when St. Paul was driven by its fierceness to take refuge among their savage progenitors.

It was blowing wild and strong on the winter's night when we ran out of the smooth water of the small harbour, and rose to the high seas, which rushed in great battalions past the battlemented rocks of St. Elmo. It has been my fate, for some half-dozen times, to go into and out of Malta in a gale of wind, or something like it. The last occasion but one I was on board a French steamer. The captain, who, in his anxiety to get away, had steamed out of the harbour with his anchor at the bows, sent men forward to cat it properly. As the vessel shot out of the harbour a huge black sea came roaring to meet us. With a mighty leap it sprang upon our bows, and through the hissing of the waters and the howl of the wind, and the wild concert in the rigging, we heard too surely and too well that agonising and dreadful cry which is the first breath of the "man overboard!" It was pitch dark. The lights of the town dotted and flecked a heaving inferno of black sea with their starlike specks, beyond which tumbled the upward avalanches of the breakers. Away went the life-buoy from the taffrail, with its portfire blazing and hissing for a moment, then it disappeared, and once again, through the darkness, we heard the cry under our counter, and again all was silent but the noise of the sea and of the storm. Not one stroke could we relax our engines, for the rocks were close on our lee, and it was then, to their credit be it spoken, that the old quartermaster, one of those despised Italians of Ancona, came forward with four men, one Frenchman and three Maltese, and supplicated the captain to be permitted to lower the quarter-boat on a hopeless errand of mercy. Refused, on the ground of mercy to themselves, the poor fellows almost mutinied in their desire to help their drowning comrades. Alas! they had, whilst their mates were speaking, sunk for ever in the pitiless waters, or had been dashed by the sea-crests into pieces on the jagged rocks!

Three days more brought us in sight of Alexandria, a flat, low, sandy shore like the dunes at Dunkirk or Ostend, studded with as many little windmills as the village heights of the Dardanelles. The "Pharos," which lights no more Roman galleys into those muddy waters, is but of little use to the more adventurous and far-sailing barques which have replaced them, because the port is too dangerous to attempt at night, except under very peculiar and favourable circumstances. Through the glass one could make out Pompey's pillar, which—but no, I am not going to say one word more about Alexandria, or Cleopatra, or ancient Egypt, and shall simply content myself with reporting the arrival of the Egyptian pilot from his boat, at 9·30 on the morning of the 3rd January. He had but one eye. And lo! on looking into his boat,

there were four men with only five eyes between
them, three being monocular likewise. Our Egyptian
was attired in a fez cap, a fur-lined jacket under his
grecco, a vest of many metal buttons, and silk sash,
Greek baggy breeches, naked legs covered with bites,
and carried a long pipe, with the stem of which he
" conned " the ship, whilst the crew of his boat
hooked on aside, immediately lighted their pipes, and
gazed with all their eyes at the smoke. As Alexandria opened upon us—mills, houses, sentry-like trees,
and sands—we beheld an amazing forest of masts;
nearer still, the flags of all nations were visible,
waving from truck and peak in honour of Sunday.
And soon we came to our moorings, close to a double
line of men-of-war, one three-decker, three two-
deckers, and four frigates lying in ordinary, with the
red flag and the white crescent-moon in the centre
flying from their ensign-staffs.

Fast-pulled and vigorous out comes the agent's
boat. There is a rush to the side, and he is almost
mobbed as he gains the deck. " Lucknow is relieved ! " " Hurrah ! bravo ! " from the crowd.
" Windham has been attacked at Cawnpore by the
Gwalior people, and was only saved by Sir Colin's
arrival." " Is it possible ? " " Havelock died of
fatigue after the relief of Lucknow ! " A low mur-
mur, broken by ejaculations of sorrow and astonishment, and rising at length into that strange sort of
utterance which comes from many human beings
when in affliction, followed this announcement. There
were few of us going out to India who did not look
forward with the very keenest desire to see the
soldier who seemed to have started up suddenly in

the midst of the great calamity which had befallen us, to avenge our wrongs. We were all speculating on the pleasures which awaited him on his return to England, and on the honours which would close that long career of quiet service, and now the news was so suddenly communicated to us that all our hopes and our anticipations and speculations had been abruptly buried in his grave, the cry of emotion and of grief which burst from the deck of our steamer was but the prelude of the loud wail that rose from the heart of a nation. It really was some minutes ere the aggregate remembered they were individuals, with individual cares and duties to perform, and broke up to look after baggage, luggage, and preparations for landing.

"As soon as you can for shore, ladies and gentlemen, the train is just off!" A swarm of boats were alongside us, manned by Egyptians imperfectly provided with visual organs, and it was not hard to choose, as all were alike. As soon as a party of four or five of us had entrusted ourselves to the first "*embarcation,*" as the Gallicized native called it, a small Nubian imp, who acted as helmsman, began, with great fervour, to solicit us for "backsheesh," which was immediately given to him, after the playful manner of the Islanders, in the shape of taps on the head and shins from walking-sticks and umbrella ends, but still the imp shouted for "Backsheesh! backsheesh! I say, sar, give backsheesh!" till that horrid word fairly beat us, and with tearful eyes the young wretch clutched a few halfpence, and secreted them somewhere about his all but naked person. Meanwhile we were rapidly nearing the shore by the aid of a large lug-sail, which was so ingeniously managed that, after hopping off the side of a great Yankee clipper, we came squash on the bows of an Englishman, of which the captain had evidently not attended to divine service that morning, judging from the excesses of the language he addressed to the boatman, who merely laughed and said, "You Johnny no good!" a national insult at once resented by one in the boat, who hit the speaker on the head with his hat-box. As those little incidents were always attended by a certain danger of capsizing, and we had all heard of the sharks in the harbour, most of us were very glad to scramble up the unfinished pier, after a wrangle about the fares, and to make our way towards the railway station. But, no! we must not go just yet. One look at the crowd which is waiting on the pier. Did you ever see such a ragged, scarecrow crew? such blear-eyed, pock-pitted, evil-looking *canaille?* Ophthalmia was present among one-half of them, and had blurred or destroyed the eyes of half of the remainder. Surely, in spite of the pure blue sky and balmy air, there must yet remain in Egypt some trace of the plagues wherewith it was afflicted. In every respect, even in energy, the people around me seemed inferior to the Turks. The most imbecile and feeble attempt at labour I ever saw in my life, with the exception of a demonstration at paving Dawson Street, Dublin, which I used to watch from the windows of Morrison's Hotel, in the year of grace 1857, was going on at the end of the pier, where about 100 men were engaged in hauling up small weights to the top of small beams, and letting them fall on sticks stuck in the mud, to the measure of a dreamy, drowsy chorus, and fondly believed they were pile-driving. The blocks, the timber, the tackle, and the workmen, who, by the bye, wore nicely-polished steel rings round their legs, and were properly equipped for dancing the hornpipe in fetters, if so minded, were all alike miserable. Their exertions were superintended by six or seven overseers, who were busily engaged in watching the smoke curl from their pipes, and seemed quite satisfied with the turn things were taking.

Around us, as we made our way slowly on, sometimes by dint of hard blows and a shower of umbrella cuts, swarmed the crowd, which was accompanied by clouds of clammy-footed flies hungering after their watery eyes. All the naked, dirty little heathens, diverse-bearded, various-haired, and multi-coloured Nubians, Copts, Fellahs, Arabic intermixtures—jabbered English variations on the theme "Backsheesh." Hot and furious as a routed army pursued by the enemy's horse, we rush to the railway station; a big white flag, of the usual architecture invented for those structures, stands starkly out in the sunshine on the outskirts of the town, a good two miles from the pier. My feeble remains of Turkish were of no use, but French and English made rapid way among the dragomanish officials of the rail, and we heard with little regret that the train would start at once for Cairo. Why this haste was manifested, only those in the secrets of the Transit Mal-Administration can guess; but of a surety we were pressed and rammed into first and second class carriages, and, swollen by the passengers of the Pera from Southampton, who had just landed before us, we filled a most formidable train.

On the production of our Peninsular and Oriental

ickets, each passenger received two—one for the
railway, the other for refreshments on the Desert line.
The excitement of looking after luggage and keeping
your place against all comers was diversified by skirmishes between the Egyptian policemen, or station
cavasses, and the orange and beggar boys, who made
razzias through the open doors and from behind pillars
at the carriages, and had just time to squeak out, "I
say, John!—Buy orange? buy orange?—I say, Backsheesh!" when the cowhide, whistling through the
air, came down on head or stern.—As well try to keep
off flies with a broadsword. Hurrah! we're off at
last—away from all our persecuters, except the flies,
which haunt us yet; and which, remembering their
diet, we fight fiercely with tobacco-smoke and pocket-
handkerchiefs. It is a tradition—beyond which I
know nothing, and answer for nothing—that the flies
aforesaid do give people ophthalmia by settling at the
edge of the eyelids with their feet still steeped in con-
tagious matter, and therefore it is recommended that
travellers should use gauze wire spectacles in going
through Egypt. Certes, whether true or not, I would
recommend those who dislike flies, and especially
flies accustomed to live as we see these, where-
ever ophthalmic natives are asleep, to wear some such
contrivance to keep off their polluting touch.

The train moves off under a smart fire of oranges
from some young gentlemen of the Army Medical
Department, who think that the railway people would
regard them very unfavourably if they did not do
something "fast," and who repeat the process at
various stations, till we all sincerely hope the police
will lay hold of them. Away we went, palpitating

with the heat even in this month of January, by the side of the great lake—a veritable palus covered with duck, widgeon, and teal, various and innumerable, with snipe-haunted borders, whereon, too, ran myriads of dotterel, sandlarks, and sandpipers, and curlew. And soon we passed by villages and people, which made those who had never been in poor Ireland and visited the far West, raise up hands and eyes in special wonder. Shall I describe them? No. Are they not described from foundation to rooftree, and from toe to top-knot in many books; and is not their aspect familiar to every reading Englishman, and to those of them almost as numerous—every travelling Briton? We were started off, as it appeared, in mad haste; but when we were half way to Cairo the train stopped, and, to make a two hours' story short, there we remained for that time, till it should please His Highness the Pasha to pass us. But he did not come at all, and somehow or other we all felt greatly relieved when the young surgeons, apothecaries, and hospital dressers began to pelt the guards and the bystanding natives with oranges—an operation which had nigh come, in one instance, to an unfortunate end, inasmuch as a light-haired blue-eyed Egyptian with a Fez cap, who received "one in the eye" as he was descending from the engine, with much impetuosity dashed at one of the carriages, and exclaimed, "Darn my buttons if I haven't jest a mind to take you neck and crop and chuck the whole bunch of ye down the 'bankment: whoy doan't ye go to skule and larn manners?" A solemn menace and demand, which produced a great effect on their youthful spirits.

At last the Pasha sent word by electric telegraph to say he was not coming, and a messenger on foot carried the message from some distant station to the conductor, whereupon we rolled on till we stopped on the banks of the Nile—where, at the temporary station —near which, by the way, stands a stone or wooden hut in solitary dignity, with a board, thereupon inscribed, "Mat. Jackson—Entertainment—Ale, Porter, Tobacco—Gin and Whiskey—English Cheese"—we had a Barmecide banquet, at which the flies assisted in overwhelming columns, and where a bottle of Bordeaux cost 8s. I had much to say about the Nile, but for the same reasons which compel me to suppress myself about Egypt, I gave up all my emotions and sensations respecting the sandy, dirty, Thames-coloured, sacred old river, to which railway bridges, steamboats, and canals give a most unnatural aspect—just as if one were to dress the Sphynx in a French bonnet and crinoline. It was late at night when the train reached the station at Cairo, and we were disembogued through the portals amid a wilderness of donkeys and Egyptian hackney-coachmen. Every voice cried, "To Shepherd's Hotel!" but all the donkey-boys, and all the dragomans and hackney-coachmen shook their heads, and their fezzes, and turbans, and said, "No good! Shepherd's all full!" Not to be imposed on by this transparent artifice, everyone drove to Shepherd's, or rode there, and was duly informed that there was not standing room, inasmuch as the passengers by the steamer which preceded the Pera from Southampton could not get on, as the steamer which should have carried them on from Suez had broken down. We now fully appreciated the excellence of the administration which had hurried us on from Alexandria, where we could have got room, to this place where it was quite impossible to do so without assistance and local knowledge, neither of which we possessed. Not only were the Alma's passengers in Cairo, but the overland people from India had, with that precision of mal-administration which distinguishes the transit through Egypt, been carried on from Suez and thrust into the city the day the overland outward bound had arrived. In the dark, among the dogs, through lanes and alleys of infinite closeness, nastiness, and irregularity, we stumbled deviously, the playthings of dragomans and donkey-boys, till some of us disappeared in one hole or other, were swallowed up in a gateway, or were absorbed round a corner, and I and a few more ran to earth in a mansion apparently situated among quarries and lime-kilns. It was called the Hotel du Nil, and it well deserved the name, for we could get nothing to eat, not even a piece of bread, when we arrived. In a long, ill-lighted room, at a lanky table covered with a dirty cloth, sat three men smoking vigorously and talking in lingua Franca about "solde," and "argento," and "negoziante," one of whom told us "*Signori ! avete patienza e averete qualche cose subito.*" *Subito* meant just two hours, at the end of which time the council of three resolved themselves into waiters, and appeared with the very smallest and mouldiest chickens I ever beheld, hatched evidently by ill-humoured ovens in unpleasant places. These were supported by omelettes made of eggs, which were just about to make chickens, and by cakes for "*non 'che pane adesso, ma domane!* do-

mane!" but our appetites were better than the food, and washing the meal down with copious draughts of a wine which tasted like writing fluid, we stretched ourselves on chairs, tables, and sofas, and sunk into a sleep which relieved the musquitoes from the smallest anxiety of interference in their assiduous labours. Wah! Wah! The waking that morning! Eyes half closed, hands, wrists, forehead, insteps, ancles, devoured, blotched, and blurred by the venomous bloodsuckers. We were awakened by a bell at 5 o'clock to announce that the train would start at 6·30. The promise of bread was not kept, for some hours at least; and, to put us all in good humour, a message was sent from the transit to say the train would not start till 9·30. Under any circumstances it was expected of us to mount donkeys and go to the Ezbekeyah, and we bowed to necessity and precedent and mounted our donkeys—some of which, if they live, must remember that morning well. The great advantage of seeing the Bazaar at this early hour is, that you can get nothing to buy, as the shops are all shut, so that you save your money, and have the fun of riding full tilt down the narrow streets, of spilling people, and getting "spilt" yourself, and of chastising donkey-boys without any outlay. The delusions which our good nature fosters abroad are very preposterous. In Cairo every inhabitant firmly believes that every Englishman wants to buy slippers, to lay in a life-long stock of latakia, to purchase pipe-stems, and to invest in little marble eggs, tarbooshes, and Egyptian whips, and no one will take the trouble to undeceive them.

Having contributed rather to the corroboration of

those notions, we returned to the Hotel du Nil, where we actually found bread and coffee, and made a good breakfast. Some of our fellow-passengers, greatly flea and mosquito bitten, passed a high eulogium on the rooms; but those who slept in the gardens were quite delighted with the mildness of the night, though one of them did admit he got rather uneasy at finding a hideous marble deity (which was for sale on the premises) staring at him rigidly in the moonlight, particularly when he discovered that his chairs were flanked on each side by mummy cases.

CHAPTER III.

The bazaar of Cairo.—Felicitous arrangements for passengers.—
A "gentleman."—French influences.—English behaviour.—
Oriental gravity.—The Desert.—Arabian Navvies.—Lost in
darkness.—The Hotel at Suez.—The "American System."—
Picturesque dirtiness.—Arab Crafts and their crews.—Exhausting heat.

IF the bazaar of Cairo is still one of the most "Oriental-looking" covered ways in which commerce and trade ever slumbered and crept, the new town is most distressingly European in spite of donkey-boys, palms, and cypresses, and groups of women with the yachmak. Tall gaunt French and Italian looking houses, seem staring at each other over partitions and garden walls, as if in surprise at finding themselves in such a place. The junction between the two is as ill assorted as a Paisley fringe to a Cashmere shawl. It is just what one sees where the adjuncts of civilization are forced upon semibarbarous countries and societies. Once, I saw, in Russia, a man flogging a serf, who was fastened by cords to an electric telegraph post. In India, the wild beasts and monkeys destroy or play upon the wires, which are perhaps recording at the time a minute on education, or conveying an order to Calcutta for some new music. Thus, in Egypt to-day, I beheld the "old ship of the desert," stalking by the side of the locomotive, till the track diverged from the railway to some remote oasis across the desert. The rail is a great, but by no means a rapid civilizer. Just hear what happened last night. The Indian homeward mail had arrived at Cairo. With the felicity of arrangement, on which I have already complimented the administration, the passengers were at once hurried on to Cairo, where there were no places for any one to sleep. They were turned adrift in the streets of Cairo, at four o'clock in the morning. Some poor ladies made their way to the railway station, and there they laid down to stretch their weary limbs. A " gentleman," who spoke English, saw them—the man in authority. He, according to my informant, at once gave orders that these ladies—poor Indian refugees—should be put out on the stone steps of the station; or at least turned out of their poor shelter. This gentleman rejoices in the name of Ramseen Effendi. Although these people are on the highway between India and England, they either were very ignorant of events, or had made up their minds not to believe our intelligence, for a grinning Nubian, who attended at breakfast, asked if we were all going to Delhi. " Ah ! you may go dere and be killed — all killed, but you never get Delhi once more." He laughed incredulously, when we told him it had fallen months ago. " All you Inglis say dat. Why your soldiers beg leave to go by desert—Why your little army all come dis way?" And be it noted, that in the room where this occurred, there were gaudy French prints of the events of the last expedition against the tribes in Algeria, and French newspapers lay on the table. Whatever may be the reason, such civilization as the East may receive promises to be French. The children of the gentry are sent to France for instruction—their polite communications and their diplomatic communications are French—their European literature is French—their railway engineers were French, and if they could, they would get French ships, engines, carriages, and drivers. I speak this in no envious national spirit, but I regret the apathy and indifference, or whatever else it is, which deprives England of her just share of moral influence in the East. Nelson fought and Abercrombie died on the shores of Egypt, and yet they have left no trace behind them but the great cut and overflow near Damietta, whilst all the bazaars are full of portraits of Bonaparte and Kleber; the Battle of the Pyramids, and other bad copies of the pictures at Versailles. The insufferably rude and insolent behaviour of some of our fellow countrymen, which here I witnessed for the first time, does, in my mind, go far to create dislike to us. We are the only Europeans these people see *en masse*. We are generally in an excited state crossing the desert, going to and fro, rushing hither and thither, to make the most of a few hours, full of practical jokes, and rejoicing in the high animal spirits, which seem to be quite crushed out of a French boy at school or the Lycée! We ride at full gallop through the streets; laugh in the face of every long-bearded, odd-looking old Mussulman we see; despise all foreign dignity; scream with delight at the sight of an Egyptian officer, with spurs to his slippers and his pipe under his arm, and are the terror of quiet thoroughfares — that is, the lively young men are; and it was seriously propounded by one of my fellow-passengers, a man of great position and influence and intelligence in India, who shared my views as to our conduct, that whenever there is a large exportation of young cadets, medical officers, and hospital apprentices, it would be advisable to place an officer in charge of them till they arrived in India. The Oriental, under his quiet, dignified demeanour, may conceal hideous vices; but they are concealed, and to him our boisterous jokes and redundant spirits seem the very excess of vulgarity. To the credit of the great bulk of the soldiers, who were sent across the desert, be it declared, that their general conduct was exemplary. I was told by Major Collingwood, that 2500 had been sent from Alexandria to Suez without a single accident, and almost without a grave complaint. Mr. Holton, the Peninsular and Oriental agent at Alexandria, had been most zealous in perfecting the arrangements for their conveyance; and the Messrs. Betts, transit agents at Suez, had also exerted themselves greatly in expediting the transfer of the troops, and in arranging for their comforts. The men generally left Alexandria by 4 P.M., and got to Cairo by midnight, where they changed carriages, and were carried on to the twelfth station in the desert, which they reached by daylight. There, troops of donkeys were in readiness; the men, to their great delight, were converted into cavalry, and capered and paced, not without loss of seats and leather, to Suez, which they reached at 4 P.M. in the day.

The desert on which we debouched from the rich oasis of Cairo, even now a glorious mass of green, resembles the bed of some deep sea; not level and smooth, but corrugated; tossed into mountains and reefs of sand, seamed with shallow ravines, and enclosing in the sweep of the sand-hills immense plains, covered with a glistening, even coat of circular and oval stones, varying in size, from a nine-pound shot to a grape. How they shine in the sun! flashing back its rays from their polished sides, so that, at times, where the plain stretches far away to the tumuli on the horizon, it is scarce possible to believe that it is not a dancing, sparkling sea, which is bounding by the side of the railway. This effect is increased by the waving lines of the rarefied air, which gives to the verge of the great circle of desolation all the appearance of a rough and rapid tideway. No pen can describe, no pencil convey the real sentiment of "the desert." We watch, with the profoundest interest, a string of camels, mere specks in the distance, which, under the charge of two Arabs, are ploughing their way over the sandhills towards the horizon, on which stands a solitary date-tree. With some such feelings might the men of the early world have beheld the first barque bearing the *robur et æs triplex* of its framers towards the ocean wall, which would hide it from their sight. The sense of indefinite space is first impressed on one by that which is, we know, definite enough in actuality. But, somehow or other, the sea is bounded, in our notions.—We see it marked out in maps, and rounded off in terrestrial globes, so that its vastness is destroyed; but none of us can tell where this great desert ends, where are its bounds, how far it pushes its sandy waves into the heart of the continent. Sir Roderick Murchison may know; Burton may be able to tell us all about it: but it is not profitable to remove the feeling of immensity, of vagueness, and of barren grandeur and primæval antiquity, which is produced by the sight of the desert whereon the Israelites wandered, and where the legions of Cambyses found nameless cemeteries. To me, there is no sense of barrenness produced by the sea :—the desert's first effect is productive of the sensation of a world destroyed—of barrenness, waste, and lifelessness. Blanched bones of camels lie in dull whiteness on the sands. Not a bird fans the hot, silent air. Stones and sand, and sand and stones are all and everything and everywhere, stretched out dead and hard under the blue sky and the relentless sun. The rail which conveys us through this desolation is single, and the line is said by English engineers to be very badly made, as the French engineers, who laid it out, took it over a ridge 1100 feet high, instead of following a low level near the river, which would have greatly diminished expense and cost of working. The water and coal for the engines has to be carried by the trains out to the various stations. So they are like commissariat animals in a barren country, which have to carry their own fodder and diminish their public burthens. These stations are helpless, hot, ovenlike erections generally eked out by old Crimean wooden huts, within the shade of which may be seen an undoubted Englishman, smoking his pipe.

At the twelfth station we coaled—the train ended in the desert here; but at long intervals, for miles in advance, we could see encampments of Arabs who, for the time, had become navvies, and were engaged in picking and burrowing and blasting through the rocks a way for the iron horse. In a long wooden shed—the centre of a group of tents—were laid out long tables, covered with hot joints of recondite animals, papier maché chickens, and lignite vegetables. This was our dinner—it had come all the way from Cairo—so had the wine, and beer, and spirits. If manna and quails were at all eatable, we had envied the food of the Israelites. By a pompous fiction we were induced to draw lots, which were to determine our places in the vans, the passengers being divided into batches, one for each van. We looked out on the desert, and lo! there were seven or eight small vans, resembling Brighton bathing-boxes laid longitudinally on wheels, to which were attached creatures of an uncertain number of legs, resembling very much Scarborough ponies at the end of the season. There were passengers enough to fill them all five times over, but we were told not to be uneasy, and we quietly settled down to await the miracle which our senses told us was necessary to effect our departure. Miracle! Lord bless you, nothing of the kind, except one of that sort which does work wonders at times—a strong arm and resolute will; for whilst those who relied on their tickets were fighting the flies, or lying prostrate in the shade, and thinking, as one of my neighbours did, aloud, "whether the desert would ever be cultivated," to which his friend replied, "that he would not like mutton reared on its present grazing capacities," the strong-armed ones were spoiling the Egyptians, and were forcing their way into the vehicles over feeble Fellahs and imbecile Copts, and when once in, were poking the drivers with shouts—"Now then! we're all full here, none of your jabbering, but get off at once." Need it be said that all the strong men took the hint, and had the *premières places* at once, in spite of appeals on behalf of women and children, who fared very much as they did of Jenny Lind nights long ago at the pit entrance. It was indeed enough to nerve one's right arm to think of being left among the boxes and the flies in that desert station till the vans could return from Suez. After all, being rather late in my appreciation of the attitude of affairs, and having foolishly given way to several prize children and their anxious mothers, I did not get off till the last van was starting, but I stormed it in the teeth of *chevaux de frise* of umbrellas, and established myself in the bosom of a Bengal civilian. I hope he forgives me now—I did not ask him to do so then, for to a natural horror of interlopers he must have had superadded the sense of irritation caused by my pocket, which abutted upon him, being full of specimens of desert paving stones. In sooth, at one of the stations a madness had seized upon us. We all got out, and began dashing the stones to pieces, because there was just a chance that the process would reveal in the centre of the stone, when split, a hollow filled with shining crystals. Some vagabond Arabs helped us with effusion, and we were soon in a high state of Murchisonian affluence. The drawback to a seat in the last van is, that it gets all the dust from the wheels of its predecessors—the objection to a place in the first, is that the horses have a decided dislike to any ambitious attempt to "lead the van," and require infinite flogging, vituperation, and persuasiveness to start them and to keep them on their course. Nevertheless, we moved onwards, and anon the setting sun threw lengthening shadows of the terrible vans and their wild drivers and shaggy, bony, ragged, locomotive powers across the sands, till at length, in one great bath of purple cloud, he plunged out of sight, and left us to struggle onwards in the sudden darkness. It was a bad business for us. In half an hour more our van began to strike heavily, and to toss and pitch exactly like a ship amid shoals in a strong tide way. Our heads were knocked literally with violence against the roof of the vehicle, against the sides, and (what I found hardest of all) against our neighbours'. The solitary paper lantern, which we had purchased for large sums, and hung from the roof inside, danced up and down and backwards and forwards like a galvanized *ignis fatuus*. By a kind young moon, just got up, we saw our course lay amid giant boulders. After a few moments we halted—we had lost our way. The driver confessed as much, but, assuring us it would be all right, vanished into the darkness, in order to take an observation from the heavenly bodies. The occasion was improved by one of the passengers, who assured us that the whole affair, in his eyes, looked very like a concerted plan to rob us; and when in effect flambeaux and torches appeared in the distance, and, gradually approaching, revealed the faces of twenty or thirty Arabs running towards us in great excitement, some of us thought that passenger a very wise man, but his reputation was short-lived. These Arabs had been merely sent from their little camp, which the driver had stumbled upon, to assist us over the stones, and all the plunder they got was a few piasters as backsheesh when they had lighted us and hauled us to the nearest station. There we changed horses, and at 11·30 o'clock at night our van rumbled out of the desert into a sandy street, bordered by miserable houses, at the end of which it came to a full stop, in a large courtyard, surrounded by stone walls and corridors, which was in effect the court of the Suez hotel. We actually had supper in a dreary *salle-à-manger*, but it was of a sort that need not be particularized—it was only one remove from dining with Duke Humphrey. And then as to beds—why, there were some somewhere upstairs, but madame, the hostess, had evidently supped and would only deign to tell us that we might go to bed where we pleased,—and so we went along the corridors, popping our heads into rooms, and receiving abrupt challenges from agitated musquito curtains in morose tones and language, till at last we came to an eligible apartment in which some five or six of us "shook down" for the night, and resigned ourselves to the musquitoes and to slumber.

The first thing that woke me in the morning was the hands of a native barber who, having made himself master of my nose, was about availing himself of that *point d'appui* to remove my beard. Now, since with incipient moustache and hirsute undergrowth on chin I used to "dodge" Sir George Brown in the streets of Gallipoli, no razor had ever touched my face, and I had eschewed even scissors till my return to England, so that I resented this insidious attempt with proper spirit. I have since learned that it is the *chef d'œuvre* of Asiatic tonsorial art to shave one whilst he is asleep and without awakening him. The whole of the hotel was like a huge barrack, the inmates dressing in the lobbies, on the stairs, in the courts and corridors, and in the open rooms, where the air was conscious of the power of the morning sun. In the centre of the large corridor an American passenger and philanthropist was holding forth in a steady, well-sustained oration on the evils of the transit administration, on the badness of the "cars," on the wickedness of the horses, on the superiority of the "American system" generally, and on the inherent depravity of human nature; from which he passed by an easy digression to British rule in India, for the restoration and support of which he said there was nothing left but republican institutions and the introduction of African labour in the army and in agriculture—and there was interrupted (only, I regret to say, for the time,) by a descent to the breakfast table.

It was still early, for the time of year, in the morning, and yet the sun was shining fiercely from the east, just above the mountain tops, which seem to rise perpendicularly from the wide plains of sand that border the narrow strip of sea opposite the hotel. Although Suez is but a miserable aggregate of hovels and native houses, built on a small spot of sea sand, it is interesting on account of its vicinity to sacred localities, as well as because of its peculiar scenery and the novelty of the sights it affords. The Red Sea here runs into a point and melts away on extensive sands, which are, however, bounded on the west by the arid crags of the desert, and on the east by the mountains of Arabia, which, running southwards, embrace in their chain Horeb and Sinai. On a sandbank, only a few hundred yards long, which projects into the narrow end of this sea, and is only raised six or eight feet, I should think, above the level of high water, there are built of the stone (a soft, ragged kind of oolite, according to the best of my knowledge) of the desert, the hotel, the consul's house, and some three or four other residences with reminiscences of

Europe about them. These face the beach, the hotel being at the point of the Spit. Behind them are the wonderful structures of the native bazaar, which, for dirt, bad smells, darkness, flies, and intricacy, bears the palm easily from all the bazaars I have ever seen. The houses are composed of little stones, kept together in frames of little pieces of wood, and those tottering fabrics are poised higher than consists with safety in a breeze of wind, and pierced with lattice-covered, glassless window-frames. The streets are "paved" with the desert sand, trodden into a state of great fineness, so that each native as he shuffles along with his gondola-formed slippers kicks up a dust which almost smothers one. The pencils of light which pierce through the coarse matting cover of the bazaar, stretched across from one house to another, reveal something more palpable and substantial than motes in the thick, fog-like air which is filled with a turmoiling vapour of fine sand, dust, and flies. Beneath, in the usual *insouciance* of their race, sit cross-legged the bleareyed merchants, with their *entourage* of shop boys and gossips. Oranges, Swiss and Manchester and Mulhouse calicoes, Latakia and mountain tobacco, pipestems and heads, dates, a horrid compost of sugar, coffee berries, tin ware, and beads, seemed the principal articles of commerce. Of course all the dirtiness and nastiness of the place made it picturesque. Huge Nubians lounged through the narrow street; Egyptian soldiers, sadly out at elbows, affected the neighbourhood of the Kibob and sheeps'-head shop, and wild Arabs walked cautiously from street to street pricing the brightest pieces of calico, or inquiring after ropes and sackcloth. Let us get out of the heat and horrid atmosphere, and walk down to the hotel, from which (in the shade now) we can see far away of a clear day across into the Arabian desert, and mark the various hues of the desert mountains which bound it. In the foreground, only half afloat in the ebb tide, are some eighteen or twenty of those graceful Arab craft which in their lines are nearly the prototypes of the once famous and now rotten "America." They go to all parts of the Red Sea, of the Persian Gulf, down the coast of Africa, and up to Muscat, —make splendid weather even in hard gales of wind. Their crews, great bronzed fellows, with a sprinkling of Æthiops, far more than half naked, are splashing about in the shallow water under the hotel windows, or bathing listlessly in the tepid sea. As our countrywomen know they will have to become used to such sights in India, they begin their initiation here, and I am bound to say undergo the ordeal very gallantly. A crowd of boys running about in the front of the hotel, or diving for imaginary coins off the little quay, is kept in order by a morose policeman with a long whip. Some of them, however, are already bankers, and call up to the people in the balcony, "I say, I give change for sovren—nineteen bob and a tizzy." Wonderful proof of the spread of the English language, and of a just appreciation of the principles of commerce! Our passengers are engaged in exploring the mysteries of the bazaar, in philandering in the balcony of the hotel, or in watching with a lazy interest the interminable file of camels which comes in like an endless cable, link after link, laden with our luggage, and deposits it at the wharf, where there gradually rises a pyramid of overland trunks, portmanteaus, gun cases, ladies' boxes, of such magnitude that one turns to the steamer which is lying about two miles away down the gulf, with a sentiment of utter incredulity as to the possibility of stowing them all on board. The resources of Aden do not last long; after staring at the sea, and examining the mountains, having looked at the Arabs, observed that there was a tide at Suez, discussed de Lesseps, and made some remarks on the differences of races, and of the Egyptian and Turkish Yachmaks,—time hangs heavily on our hands, though the medical gents and the youngsters still found great amusement in oranges. The agents had promised that the small steamer should be at the pier to take us off at twelve o'clock, but though it was now two o'clock, very hot and very hazy weather, the little steamer could be seen smoking laboriously near the Calcutta and Bombay steamers, but not moving a yard. The tide was ebbing, for, be it observed, that there is a tide which rises six or seven feet at Suez on occasions. We listened to the blandishments of an Arab boatman, who represented his boat as only inferior in speed to a locomotive, and stepped on board. Ah! that sun! how it flashed down and struck us on the back, and flashed up from the water and smote us in the face! But the Arab and his crew of two lanky, muscular lads had stripped all but a very narrow substitute for a fig leaf. Carefully selecting the shoals which border the deep channel, they took out long poles, such as those used for rocking off the Richmond steamers when they run aground on those dangerous flats near Kew, and poled the boat along to the sound of a low guttural chant, at the rate of two miles an hour. There was not a breath of air. The steamers in the distance seemed suspended in the clear blue sky, and the white awnings spread over the decks gave us warning of the sufferings to come. Our Arabs revelled in the rays which were exhausting us, and as the boat shot off the long bank into deep water, they took to their oars and pulled away vigorously, as if the sun had given them life and vigour. Shall I describe the petty miseries?—presumptuous man! Shall I seek then to give a faint notion of the wretchedness of the seven days' passage down the Red Sea in a steamer which contained the passengers destined for two boats of the same size as that which carried the double burthen? Alas! to what good should the attempt be made? If the wars of the Almas and the Nubias are to be written, it must be by some of those accomplished civilians who took such interest in the daily changes of the combat that ever rose in excitement as the weather waxed hottest.

CHAPTER IV.

A vow.—An appeal on behalf of the ladies.—The surgeons' and officers' cabins.—Learned pundits.—The walnut-stage of argument.—La race blanche.—Why are we in India?—The hottest place in the world.—Flying fish.—The French at Pondicherry.—Mistake imputed to the English.—Is our French friend right?—A novel resting-place.—Astronomical contemplations.—Washing decks.

I FIND I have been going on in the career which at the outset I promised not to enter upon at all; and here, on the deck of the good ship Nubia, I must abandon it, or cut it short, or I shall never get to India. This deck aforesaid is an excellent place whereon to abjure any work of any sort without the smallest danger of being tempted to break one's vows. There is a heat such as one never experiences at home, even in Roman August, or in London July on the sunny side of the Strand. It is aggravated by a stifling crowd of moderately cross and indignant people. Every one is disgusted with every body else. Every one looks at his (it is oftener her) neighbour with an expression of extreme wonder that any one should venture to be a neighbour under the circumstances.

"I knew it, sir; I knew it. They never dared to ask such a thing round the Cape," shouted a very, very excitable old officer in my ears, pointing at the same time to a quiet, middle-aged gentleman who was going round the deck in a very demure way, followed by the purser with the air of a man who was collecting for a charity sermon. "Hang me if *I* do, tho'!" added the major. I watched our friend sidling along from passenger to passenger, stopping a few minutes with each male, and making memorandums with a little bow, as if he were putting down the amount of the subscription, whilst those whom he left looked very much like men who felt they had been too generous. At last he approached me and fastened me with his eye—"I am sorry, sorry indeed, sir, to trespass on your generosity," ('It's for a church at Suez,' said I, mentally, 'and I wont subscribe, for there will be no congregation,') "but," with a wave of the hand and a genial smile, "when I tell you that I make an appeal on behalf of the ladies on board," ('It's for a girls' charity-school at Alexandria, certainly,') "I am sure I shall not ask you in vain—You have berth No. 16, sir?" "I have." "It has probably struck you that this ship is very much crowded? The fact is, sir, that we are obliged to put the passengers who should have gone by the Alma into this ship, in consequence of the Alma being disabled, by no fault of ours, sir, but by a mishap to her shaft, and I am obliged to ask you to give up your cabin to two ladies, in whose name I already thank you. All the gentlemen have been good enough to grant this request—and you shall have a very comfortable cabin indeed—in fact, the best in the ship," ('why on earth doesn't he put the ladies there,' thought I), "which the surgeon will kindly make over to you." Of course I consented. To this day I consider those ladies owe me a year of my life. The surgeon's cabin might have been the best in the Arctic Seas, but in the Red Sea it was exposed to a few drawbacks. In the first place, it had a commanding view of the steam-engine, which worked pleasantly opposite the door, so that one could mark the details of the mechanism when in bed on the sofa. In the next place, there was an important portion of the steam-engine running down by the head of the bed in the shape of an immense waste-pipe, through which, at every throb of the engine, rushed and hissed a great column of water to the sea. Thirdly, the port, in consequence of the great exaltation of the waters at the junction of the ever-flowing stream, could scarcely be kept open if there was a breath of wind. And fourthly, there was an important cabinet at the end of the sofa called the ship's library, which the public frequented from morn till sultry eve in defiance of a notice to the effect that it was only open from 11 till 1 o'clock. Then it was a long time before the public could be persuaded that I was not bound to give them medical advice because I lived in the surgeon's cabin, and they evidently thought that I was in some sort connected with a system intended to deprive them of their lawful allowance of tonics and fluid magnesia. Where my poor friend the doctor, Mr. Williams, to whose agreeable society I owe most of the few pleasant hours I passed on board, was domiciled, I cannot say, but I have a suspicion that he slept somewhere in the rigging. The officers of the Peninsular and Oriental ships, who, *au reste*, are not always placed in the very best of cabins, always excepting the captain, are subject to those expulsions, for which they receive a pecuniary consideration; but, if I am to judge from their expressions, they would much sooner be permitted to retain the berths which are allotted to them, and they regard the treatment of the Company in this respect in a very unfavourable light.

Already my Indian difficulties commence. There are pundits on board, and learned ones. They have spent their lives in Hindostan among the people. They have mastered their languages — they have administered justice from the day when, very babes in the Company's swaddling-clothes, they began their lives in India. Do they agree upon any one point connected with the mutinies, or with the character of the people? Not one. There is one man who has been the annual historian of the Punjab, who believes that the only salvation for India is the application of the system of the Punjab and John Lawrenceism to all India. There is another who has passed a long career of active governmental life in Bengal, who declares that the attempt to introduce such a Lawrencratic, irresponsible, and arbitrary rule, would convulse his beloved province to the very centre. One man " hates the rascally Mahomedans," and says, there will be no safety for us till they are " put down," but whether into the earth, or by what process, he does not indicate. Another thinks that, after all, the Mahomedan can be made something of if a career is opened to him; but that those slimy, treacherous Hindoos, with their caste, and superstition, and horrid customs, constitute the real difficulty of Government. Our American friend, "tho' opposed to slavery in general terms," thinks the system of slave labour could be introduced with advantage into your British possessions in the East, and quotes a few passages in support of his views from the Old Testament. Meantime, sitting almost apart from the rest of the passengers, a few Englishmen, whom no one noticed, shook their heads as they listened, but the civilians took no thought of them. They had the brand of wicked, interloping, jealous Cain upon them. They were traders, merchants, indigo-planters, and such like, who viewed with as much prejudice and antipathy the servants of the Government under which they lived, as the latter exhibited in their demeanour for men who were undoubtedly developing the resources of the country in which they were passing the best part of their lives, and making their fortunes. All the evils which afflict India were and are, according to those gentlemen, the direct results of the rule of the Company. Why should they not be permitted to bring in their capital and purchase the soil of India? Why should they not be magistrates, and sit on the bench, and adjudge disputes between themselves, or their representatives, and the native landholders, or labourers? Why should they, as Englishmen, not be exempted from the operation of the ordinary tribunals of the land in which they lived, and have special courts of their own, as being peers and nobles of a natural aristocracy placed among serfs and ignobles? As you listen to this chaos of opinions, you see a row of animated machines sitting crouched down on the floor of the cabin, swaying listlessly to and fro, as they pull the punkahs. Their slender, well-knit frames, bright eyes, and glistening teeth, give those poor "niggers" some claims to be thought, as Mr. Carlyle would say, not quite unlovely, but they have a dark hide—they are low Mahomedans, and, to the intelligent Briton, they are as the beasts of the field. " By Jove! sir," exclaims the major, who has by this time got to the walnut stage of argument, to which he has arrived by gradations of sherry, port, ale, and Madeira,—" By Jove!" he exclaims, thickly and fiercely, with every vein in his forehead swoln like whipcord, " those niggers are such a confounded sensual lazy set, cramming themselves with ghee and sweetmeats, and smoking their cursed chillumjees all day. and all night, that you might as well think to train pigs. Ho, you! punkah chordo, or I'll knock—Suppose we go up and have a cigar!"

The fact is, I fear that the favourites of heaven—the civilizers of the world—*la race blanche* of my friend the doctor, are naturally the most intolerant in the world. They will forgive no man who has a coloured stratum under the *rete mucosum*. They have trodden under foot the last germs of the coloured races wherever they could do; in other instances, they have hunted them out of their own land into miserable exile—as they advance, the barbarian recedes. It is the will of Providence; it is the destiny of the white man, to whom God has given greater energy, intelligence, and physical resources, that he should spoil the dusky Egyptian. So far let it be; but what are we to do when we come into a land which we cannot enjoy, which is peopled by powerful, haughty, prolific races whom we could not destroy if we would? What course should we pursue when we find ourselves in a great empire, lords and masters indeed, but dependent every moment of our lives on the people we found at our coming, and unable to raise from the soil the feeblest stem of our own race? When our numbers depend exactly on the influx of the temporary immigrants and on the reflux of those who have departed from among the people and left no trace behind them? There are portions of the earth which seem to be specially reserved for the possession of the coloured races, and in which our residence and existence can only be accidental and abnormal. It is just in those regions ruled by the scorching sun, to which even profits, places, emoluments, the acquisition of wealth, and the use of artificial contrivances, cannot permanently attach us, that our antipathies and " natural " dislikes produce the most deplorable results in alienating from us the affections of the people among whom our lot is cast for the time. It is hard to bear the rule of an alien at any time; but when that alien is haughty, imperious, and sometimes insolent and offensive, his authority is only endured till the moment has arrived to destroy it, or at least to rise in rebellion, hopeless or successful, against a Government which has violated all the conditions of possibility. Our statesmen in India have seen those truths all along. The men who founded the Company and stabilitated that extraordinary and anomalous empire, which has no parallel, were deeply impressed by the necessity of maintaining the policy by which those results were obtained. The great and good men—for there are great men in India and elsewhere who are not good men, and many who call themselves and let themselves be called good who are by no means great men — in India to the present hour, anxiously seek to obviate the evils which are becoming aggrandized in proportion as we pour into India the surplus of our unemployed population to works which are now about to receive a large and necessary development. Do what we may or can, our race can neither destroy the inhabitants of India as the Americans destroyed the Red men, nor can it dispossess them and drive them out to other regions as the Spaniards drove out the Mexicans. And were it possible for us to succeed, Hindostan would at once become a desert in which our race would miserably perish in the first generation. It would seem, then, if those views are right, that the Anglo-Saxon and his congeners in India, must either abate their strong *natural* feelings against the coloured race, restrain the expression of their antipathies, or look forward to the day, not far distant, when the indulgence of their passions will render the government of India too costly a luxury for the English people. If we, who are the governors of the people, do not govern ourselves and protect the people, what redress have they, and what have we to expect? These were the sentiments which gradually grew upon me as, day after day, I heard the same expressions used with respect to the natives of Hindostan. Let every word that is uttered of that sort be granted in its entirety, and we come at once to the question, how can those who entertain such feelings govern a people in justice and in mercy? Why are we in India at all? "Because Heaven wishes it," says some gentleman, who meantime thinks that Heaven's sole design with regard to himself is, that he shall make as many rupees as he can, get his pension or his debentures, and at once leave the "confounded country" for ever. But before we came there were many races whose coming and whose going was the work of the same hand. The Macedonian passed away in a blast of mutiny on the banks of the river which Mr. Temple regards as the Rubicon that rebellion dared not pass.

The Mogul went out in a convict ship to some semi-Chinese prison; the Portugese crept away under a monk's cowl; the Frenchman holds Chandernagore and Pondicherry as material guarantees that history does not lie when she says that Englishmen met him in fair fight on the plains of India and crushed him. And who are we that we should deem ourselves exempt from the fate that has hitherto fallen on all the conquerors of India? We cannot say that we shall be exempt from it inasmuch as we carry the ark of the covenant, because in India we have sedulously concealed our trust, and ignored what we are now told is our mission. And now here is young Stammers, who never goes to church because "it's so far off," and who is said not to be a cleanly liver, declaring, as he makes up his hand in the rubber "we must do as the Mahomedans did—we must convert them, if needs be, by force. They must become ke-ke-ke-Christians!" I must get upon deck, where the major and a few of his disciples are playing at ship-billiards, and drinking brandy-and-water.

There were a good many young fellows going out for the first time to India—genial, gallant boys, but I am bound to say that they seemed to think they knew all that could be learned about the country and the people in which their lot was to be cast, and amused themselves with the light railway literature, French and English, which abounded on board the vessel. The ladies who were going out to be married were unconsciously studying their parts, and many little innocent flirtations, sorely harassed by the heat, commenced the first day of our voyage. Happy was the man who could distinctly indicate Sinai and Horeb. One lady asked, "Why

Moses went up so high," and was informed that it was probably on account of the heat. The French doctor who heard the little dialogue declared "*le vieux Moise était bien sage;*" but looking on both sides of the sea so blue and bright, bounded by red tumulary cliffs, which rise out of coasts of white sand, and swell into mountain ridges, he expressed his wonder that the leader of the Israelites could have found anything on the east side which induced him to go to it from the west, "*Selon moi c'est tout égal.*" "And now," said he, philosophizing after the manner of his countrymen, "it is the Mussulmans who make their hadj to Mecca, and kill themselves in passing this sea and desert at the hottest time of the year." But were there not Israelites on board, some flying from the Egyptians, others seeking the Canaan of rupees?

This blue strip of sea, hemmed in by sands and lined by mountains, which have wasted under the sun since they ceased to bubble with primeval fires, is I hear the hottest place in the world—that is, the mean temperature is higher than in any known spot, but I presume the Fellows of the Geographical Society know better, and after all it was only ninety degrees in my cabin to-day (January 6th). As our sharp bow sliced the blue depths there rose, right and left, flickering little wedges of silver out of the wave, gliding from the top of one lazy swell to the next, and at last dropping in circlets like the reflection of broken moonbeams into the sea—these were flying-fish. There was some anxiety to make a nearer acquaintance with them, principally caused by the averment of a long-legged midshipman that "they were deuced good to eat," but the flying-fish preferred being devoured raw, and dropped in among the porpoises and grampuses, who took them *au naturel*. Ah, this round, hot, glistening sea! If a fly were condemned to travel day after day across the shield of Achilles its reflections might be like our own, though we had the *délassemens* of many meals, and music, and whist, and songs at night, till angry captains dashed out of their tents and asked was Thersites mad that he kept the whole camp astir—and so to bed.

January 7th.—More flying-fish, less land, equal heat. There is an island called Shadvan on our left, where it is said there were most curious geological formations. It certainly requires something to attract people to it; and yet how many worthy Britons would at this moment set out hammer in hand from Pall Mall and chip away for a month, if they only had a chance of "benefiting" that remorseless, avaricious, all-absorbing ogress called "science," who (in England) gives nothing to her Owens, and Murchisons, and Faradays: lets Priestley be mobbed, (and Harvey's bones be rattled for twopence by the casual visitor!) Further on there are more islands, which attract pilgrims in search of guano, but their profits are doubtful, and their labours and trouble certain. My French friend gives me to-day some very interesting details of himself, or rather of his colony, at Pondicherry. The French number 450 or 500; they are one in seven as compared with the natives. But French is the language of the State, of the *employés* of the Courts, of the public schools, and of the Government factories, and any natives who desire the service of Government must speak the language of the governors. "And so," said he, "reasoning from a part to a whole,

ould you do in all India. But look what you do.
have been all my life actively employed in the navy.
receive as a reward for my services, from the
Minister of the Marine, a post, with which I am well
satisfied. I live in it for years. I use all my energies
in it, and for me there is no future except *en retraite*.
What do I get? 12,000 francs a year. To a Frenchman it is much. To an Englishman it is but 480
pounds sterling a year. I keep my little chaise and
my horses. I have servants as much as I want; a
good *petite maison*; a good cave with good wines of
Bordeaux and an odd flask of Sillery for a fête day.
I have and do all this on 6000 francs a year, and I
send home the rest to my family, who invest the
superfluity. But look now. I drive out of Pondicherry. I transgress the French limits on a visit to
my good English neighbour. He changes often;
sometimes he may be a young man just come a year
or two from England. He is alone in a district ten
times as big as Pondicherry without a countryman
near him. He administers law, or tries to do it, where
we would have twenty-five or thirty French and
native officers at least. But then he touches *son
argent*. He has twice as great a salary as our
governor; he has three times as much as I shall ever
have; and he will have five or six times as much very
soon. Here is your mistake. Till you govern all India
as we govern our little nothing of Pondicherry you
will not be safe, and you will do no good to the people.
Give my young friend fifteen or twenty assistants and
you will have your laws respected, your Government
liked and feared, you may establish your Christian
schools, and you may impose your language on the

people without fear of results." And is our French friend right? "*Je n'en sçais rien.*" "Yes, I know I am, and it can all be done for the same money, *voilà la bonne chose!* When I laid alongside the Spartan, in observation during the Texan and Mexican war, I saw" (this remarkable gentleman averred, but I do not think the surgeons or lieutenants of Her Majesty's navy ever made the same observation) "that your English officers have all too much money to spend." "That confounded Frenchman has been jabbering away at such a rate I can't tell what cards are played!" "Yes, I wonder at your encouraging him. He came with his jaw to me this morning, but I soon shut him up." These are boys, but they are going out to govern India, to be wigless judges, ædiles and proconsuls.

A strong south-east breeze raised a head sea last night, shut up the ports, and rendered the berths untenable. The animosity of the Nubians and Almaites was aggravated greatly by the difficulties of finding resting-places on deck. Each man went staggering and dodging about with coat and pillow on his arm to deposit it in a snug corner, which turned out generally to be a portion of some other "party's" dormitory. Having been driven in succession from a hen-coop, the boom, and the mizen hatch, I got under a seat on which a large man lay sleeping with a stolidity which gave me no apprehensions with respect to sea-sickness. Looking out from beneath my solid canopy, I watched the stars in the dense blue of the sky, much with the ignorant wonder of those who, thousands of years ago in many a long vigil, as they tended their flocks on Chaldæan plains, saw the same heavenly host move in solemn march through the yards of the night. How small, infinitesimally minute, seem, in such moments, the discussions, the questions, and the arguments which but a few moments before had engaged all the powers of the mind and moved the very soul in their contentions! Seers of Ur and Chaldea, who gazed on those glittering constellations till you thought each ray precipitate with knowledge, did you, even in your wildest dreams of prophetic inspiration, see a foreshadowing of the time when the Mede and the Persian should write their immutable laws in the sand of the desert, and when time itself should be beaten by the lightning in the race across those lifeless plains! 'Twixt the main and mizen shrouds now glistening over the main yard-arm, then diving under the mizen cross-trees, in a quivering, erratic, zig-zag path, danced stars, and planets, and constellations. The wind piped for them, and the sea rose and danced to the music. Long, seething, hissing lines of foam ran like armies to the battle, as the lank Nubia with her iron prow cleft the waves just like the salmon who rushes through the fiercest leap of the fiord-fall. My canopy got up in consternation, and scuffled away to leeward, and I reigned on the seat in his stead. "Pane! Sahib, Pane!" Alas! it is but four o'clock A.M. The sun is barely struggling yet for the mastery of the vapours over the holy mountains where the Law was given by the Almighty to His people, and where the grey prophets of the young world walked in His presence. How one would seek at such a time for the feeblest link to bind his existence to that sacred past! But in these latter days the search is vain. Here stood the half-naked, grinning, Mahomedan sailor, with his hose and his bucket of water, and if you wish to escape an instant ablution you will at once seek a retreat below in the cabin.

"Yes," said the major in the morning, "that's the way, sir; those" (here an adjective used by the British non-religious to signify dislike, and by ecclesiastics to indicate the result of wickedness on the part of Christians) "those rascally niggers delight to persecute you. I have been drenched by them repeatedly, though I knocked them down like nine-pins." "But," quoth I, "it must be the fault of their officer who orders them to wash decks, and who would punish them if they didn't." "Don't talk that way, sir! just look at the grin in the fellow's villanous mug when he holds the bucket over you!" I did look afterwards. I avow the major is right as to the grin. Is it such a terrible revenge after all?

CHAPTER V.

Music.—Pirates or pilgrims?—Miss Telle and Mr. Quel.—Flying-fish or sandlarks?—A doctrine both new and old.—Traditional nabobs.—Eagles and eaglets.—The Isle of Perinun.—Aden.—Simawlees and Arabs.—The "Prince of Wales" hotel.—Cowasjee's shop.—Athletic sports.—A souvenir of the Crimea.—The Nubians and the Almaites.—A Calvinistic sermon.—Sea-serpents and sea-snakes.—The harbour of Galle.

January 8th.—The sea very dull, though somewhat rough; no gulls; no flying-fish. There are some young gentlemen on deck though, playing backgammon with old ones; odd law of nature, each young one plays with an old one, but still there are no gulls. The *poissons volants* have been frightened off by the gale, but we have music now instead; there is Alma music and Nubia music, quite distinct the one from the other, and much vexed if those who make one are even listened to, unless in rapt silence, by those who make the other. Suddenly there is in sight an object which can attract Almaites and Nubians without any loss of dignity. A large Arab dow is flying, close-hauled as she can stick, right across us half a league off; she is full of people, "pirates" say some, "pilgrims" say those who are inclined to take a charitable view of everything suspicious (they were in the minority). "Turkish soldiers," reports a man with a spy-glass. He was right. In effect, though there have been pirates here, they keep now-a-days on land; it was not the pilgrim season, but there are Turkish soldiers in garrison at Jeddah, Mocha, and all the towns on the east coast of the sea, and we heard of course dreadful stories of poor " Bono Johnny" on his marches through the desert to relieve the Sultan's garrisons, and to take part in the pilgrimage, which they do very much as the Irish police " assist" at a " pattern."

The day passed principally in making ill-natured remarks about one's neighbours. It was all bile. What mischief that curious fluid has worked since the days of the " Iliad," and probably before the Vates Sacer recorded its effects! It was, I am bound to say, generally remarked that Miss Telle, who was going out to India engaged to Mr. Quel, had got up too strong a flirtation with Mr. Chose, who was known to be engaged to the daughter of a director then at a finishing school. But of course we have no marriages of that sort of *convenance* in England. The major who set the remark going before it was generally received was finally thought to be ill-natured, and had to redeem his character by singing a dreadful song about twining " Venus's Myrtle with Bacchus's Vine."

January 9th.—Flying-fishes, very lively. A griff (I am or intend to be one, and so speak respectfully of the class) offered to bet any money, which eventually resolved itself into one pound to five shillings, that they were " sandlarks." (Q. E. D. was difficult, and I believe he claims the money up to this day.) The awning to-day increases our sufferings. The wind has whisked aft, and so there is no head breeze, and the breath, and steam, and vapour, and hot air are all blown with us and hang after us. At breakfast the butter is fluid, at lunch the beer is boiling, at dinner

he stewards are deliquescent. Poor men! these
latter are perpetual motion for hours together, and bear
their wrongs wonderfully. I believe when hard
pressed the punkah coolies suffer—just as Sir Anthony
Absolute's kick descended to the footmen. To-day
a very clever and very charming woman propounded
a new doctrine to me—new to me, but very old in
India—namely, that there was an untitled Indian aristocracy which had as much right to cut all the bread
and consume all the fish produced in and by our
Indian possessions, as the Duke of Bedford has to use
the wheat of Woburn, or the Duke of Devonshire to
refresh himself with the trout of Chatsworth, selling if
they liked their corn and salmonidæ to others. These
natural aristocrats are many — Grants, Plowdens,
Elphinstones, Lushingtons, Beechers, and others, whose
names generally remind one of the sign-boards to be
seen in the lowlands of Scotland and in the north of
Ireland. And verily they were Anakim in the face
of the people amongst whom they came. I cannot
think that any romance was ever written which should
equal in real interest the lives of one of those early
adventurers, of which we have some faint domestic
traditions in the novel and stage portraitures of our
nabobs. The raw gaunt lad, fresh from the contests
of the village school, or the petty struggles of some
small college or academy, saw himself in a month after
he landed with a career before him in India, which to
him was Alexander's "other world." The pagoda-tree
tossed its branches to every breeze. Magic temples
offered their treasures to the strong hand and bold
heart that could fight and plot to take them. The
genii stood waiting till in broad Scotch, or good

Saxon, or feebler Irish—for Paddy came late to the gold-field—the magic " open sesame " of the resolute stranger threw open the gates of their hoarded wealth. For him ages of plunder, of bloodshed, of violence, and usurpation, and wrong, had ripened the harvest, and filled the garners which he was to gather and enjoy. He saw the daughters of the land and that they were fair to look upon. Thousands of miles divided him from his home. He was lord; self-made, and self-willed, and self-reliant in his own right, and he did as he listed. And the boy grew into the stern, resolute, tremendous despot, into *the man* with iron will and fearless soul, across whose track no shade of the unknown evil called public opinion ever cast its blight, and in whose way stood no trembling shade to warn that "the evil of his path should find him out." Sated with wealth, worn with the toils of that terrible career, gorged with plunder, the old man returned to his home. His shrivelled begums were left with attenuated competence to rear the children who bore indeed their father's name, but knew nought of him except that he had founded a race doomed from its birth to misery and contempt. And he—he bought estates, enriched universities, founded families, " wondered at his own moderation," and died in peace. But there is the aristocracy he founded also. The eaglets cried early in the nest. They looked out, and saw how fair were the wide plains over which their fathers had soared and preyed for many a year. With angry cries and claws and beak they claimed their inheritance, and chased the hawks and kites that dared to intrude on their domains. I see one of the young birds now; he is only a half-fledged little thing, n assistant on 1800*l.* a year, but he is very angry t the notion of certain steady young haggards called 'competition wallahs" getting on in his presence, and eclares the whole service is going (perhaps whence it ame) to the place paved with good intentions. And he mother eagle screams angrily, and says it is all Lord Metcalfe and his wicked liberty of the press. 'Law lords become peers of England." When you ave their equals from the uncovenanted ranks in ndia, then let them fatten on the folds which belong o Grants, Plowdens, Elphinstones, Beechers—*genus t proavos quæ fecimus ipsi.*

January 10*th.*—Service read by the Rev. Mr. Waterhouse. Congregation rather unsteady, as the sea rose towards noon. Then back to novels. The wind does not diminish the heat. A savage little thermometer in my cabin will not condescend to go below 90°. The spray renders the deck uncomfortable, and one must sleep. We were all roused out of our slumbers by the horrid Sepoy of the deck with "Sahib, Sahib!—Tow, Tow!" or some such adjuration, and staggered about in the moonlight with our beds like so many ghosts under a press of blankets. At night the sea gave us a taste of its quality, and drove right against our bows in short, hardy blows. Our Arab pilots, muffled from head to foot in long camel-hair robes, peered out silent and motionless from the bridge into the storm. The moon cast showers of light at long intervals through the driving clouds, and lighted up the heaving deck and its black groups of passengers and the two white figures of the Arabs. I went up on the bridge and looked out too. The captain was there straining his eyes, but nothing could I see, except the crests of the running seas and the shadows of the clouds in the waters. At last one of the Arabs pointed with his finger into the darkness; the other made a noise like the hiss of a snake, which rapidly ended in a rough "cluck" in the throat. The captain levelled his glass through the night—"Ah, yes! I guess you'll get into trouble, you Britishers, about that yet," exclaimed a voice beside me. "What on earth is it?" "What is it? Why, sir, it's the Isle of Pea-rimm that your Government has annexed, and ——" "Yes, I see it," said the captain; "sharp-eyed fellows, those Arabs!" And soon by the line of surf, and by a defined sharp ridge against the sky, we could make out the solitary isle. No lighthouse yet; but lighthouses cannot be built in a day. We passed to the east of this island. The port is at the west side. "They have hard times of it there, I should think—the engineer, officer, and sappers, and a few foot soldiers that are there," said the captain; "they get all their provisions from Aden by steamboat, and sometimes in bad weather it's not so easy to make the island as to go into the Straits." As it stands, the island commands the entrance into the Red Sea. It is situated towards the east side of the Straits of Babelmandeb; on that side the Straits are not quite two miles wide. On the west side the Straits are about three miles or a little more in breadth.

January 11*th*.—Early this morning saw in the distance a line of crags, like sharks' teeth, rising out of the water. These resolved themselves into sharp saw-backed ridges of rock, cliffs, and peaked mountains, of rich rufous and Vandyck brown, streaked with reds and blacks as we approached. Surely here are Vulcan's workshops! Here Brontes, Steropes, and Pyracmon have cleared out their cinders since the days of Saturn: here are the dust and ash-heaps of the Cyclopean forges. Not one little tree!—not one blade of grass!—not one patch of verdure the size of a man's hand! The eye seeks the summits of those tumuli in expectation of the smoke of the subterranean fires in which those rocks were melted and cast out in beds of scoriæ and ashes. The blue sea seems actually to fizz at the base of those tremendous hills of slag, and to boil and splutter as it heaves against them. High in the air, on the top of the highest peak, a flag is flying from a lofty staff. The old Union Jack is flaunting a welcome to us! A house which looks like a child's Noah's Ark, can be detected near the staff by the curious. Round by bluff and sloping sheets of ashes we glide swiftly; here and there white straight lines run across the ravines, which seem to topple over us. These resolve themselves into walls of solid masonry. Tunnels and archways are seen high up amid the crags. A round building of stonework, with black specks on the flat roof, looks very like a fort; and see! as we round the point, and run into the shallow bay before us, there is another house, from which the dull black eyes of the cannon are staring right at you. The bay holds some half-dozen merchantmen, most of which show French colours—a flotilla of Arab dows, an odd-looking steam sloop, and a small armed schooner. The cinders seem to have been shovelled away to form this bay. Before us there is a row of three or four white houses, one story high, thatched with reeds, rising out of ashes and backed by mountains of cinders. Here and there the cinders rise into cones over the bay, and on the top of those cones are perched some half-dozen isolated houses; one or two huts on the beach complete the public and private buildings of the port, but the military station is perched in an extinct crater about three miles away, where it is nearly as hot as if the volcano were in full activity.

Travellers have sought in vain to convey to their readers their impressions of the extreme aridity and desolation of Aden; because there are no words which can give an idea of a settlement of human beings fixed among a series of extinct volcanoes. I thought, as I looked at it, that I felt very much as a thirsty fly would feel, who had suddenly dropped down on the coking establishment of some great railway company, with this difference, that I could not fly away. The prophetic and hypothetical resemblance to the Inferno, with its fires extinguished, which is generally suggested to you by one of the ship's officers, or an old Indian, is falsified by the blue sky overhead, though the hideous Simaulees and demoniac shrieks of the creatures, who dance and whirl around one, would give fair grounds for believing that if it were indeed a deserted compartment of the Eastern Orcus, some of the spirits had been forgotten, and were rejoicing in their liberty.

The natives are putting off! "Now, then, who's for shore?"

In frailest canoes and lumbering boats—the castaways of the merchantmen of all nations—swarm the predacious Charons, and cling to the ship's sides like apes. Here are lank, lean, knock-kneed, hollow-thighed, calfless, lark-heeled, flat-footed, undersized, bullet-headed, narrow-chested, Simaulees — genuine children of the African littoral. The savages paint their faces, and wear huge wigs, of hair dyed a dull scarlet, which, contrasting with their black physiognomy renders their aspect more frightful than pantomimic masks. There is one feature inside their faces, if teeth can be called so, of exceeding beauty—close-set, snow-white, glistening dentistry, which must be quite lost on bad food and accidental cooking. Some boats are pulled by tawny Arabs—a race of men as superior to the Simaulee as the thorough-bred horse is superior to the donkey. Nervous, sinewy, quick-eyed, mad with passion and lust of gain, the thin nostrils swelling at every gesture and with every utterance of the mouth, broad-chested, narrow-flanked, full-thighed, well-limbed, these Arabs, whom one sees in a degenerate state at Aden, Suez, and all Eastern seaports on this side of China, are like the horses of their own deserts; with something of the gentility of blood about them, and an air ineffable which speaks of the times when there were distinct races and tribes of men as of animals, ere commerce had bundled them together in her universal cosmopolitan operations. A brisk little naval engagement alongside terminated in the capture of myself and two or three companions, who were at once carried off to shore in a canoe, paddled by red-wigged savages. Who would not go on shore to escape from a steamer coaling, with thermometer at 92° in the shade, even though the shore was that of Aden? Besides, a sea which had come in at the open port had wet all my clothes, and I wanted to dry them. And where could we dry clothes better than at Aden?

A paddle of ten minutes brought us to a rude pier, which led to a bank of rough shingle, and hot sand, whereon at some distance was placed the row of three or four white houses, which looked so white and nice from the sea. The centre bore over the door the legend "Prince of Wales Hotel." (His Royal Highness will never be able to appreciate the rare comforts of that establishment, for it is now—but I am anticipating.) The walk, short as it was, made us dreadfully hot, for we were out in the open sun. And more, we were surrounded and baited by a yelling, dancing, maddening pack of young savages, Africans, and Islanders, with naked figures, plaited hair, huge wigs, who presented us with ostrich feathers, muffs, and boas, and wigs of ostrich feathers, porcupine-quills, sea-shells, and leopard skins, and whirled around us in a feverish dance. Ah! Parsee Cowasjee, where did you get that soda-water? Anyone who remembers those early days when his nurse would put the soap-suds into his mouth, will know what we who drank of that Aden soda-water experienced. But who can describe the horrors of the brandy, except the man who can do justice to the strange qualities of the bottled ale? I asked for a glass of water. A thievish-looking, half-naked Mussulman waiter took up a long-necked pitcher of water, and handed me a glass, into which he proceeded to pour a whitish fluid; in the midst of the stream something black wriggled, and after a plunge to the bottom came up to the top of the tumbler and looked at me. It was a dreadful thing, about four inches long, the size of a full-bodied earthworm, with two sharp black eyes, and a large mouth, and palpitating sides, which were perforated with a row of mouths or gills, that worked incessantly, whilst with an easy motion the interesting thing swam about in my tumbler. The waiter admitted the creature was objectionable, but, said he, "there will come some more water by-and-by." I can merely add, that the hideous larva, or whatever it was, on being poured out on the sand, wriggled about for some time, and was lively when last I saw him. Our only resource, as it was too hot to visit the station till sun-set, was to inspect the stock in Cowasjee's shop next door, and to look at a very poor match of billiards between a blear-eyed little midshipman and a nautical gentleman who was suffering from delirium tremens. Cowasjee's shop consists of the whole of the house minus the roof, and it contains everything that a man does not want. I suppose that passengers going out to India anticipate here their Indian purchases, as passengers bound for Europe may here invest in Paris gloves made at Malta, or in Windsor soap. There are some people to whom a shop is an abstract necessity for disbursement. Here, then, in Cowasjee's you see men and boys buying Chinese slippers they will never wear, and all sorts of garments and articles they don't want. And Cowasjee, a Parsee, with large olive-coloured, oval, smooth face, quick-eyed, and intelligent, places his hands on his portly person, and smiles placidly, whilst his sleek Parsee assistants glide round the curious shelves, and recommend things they never tried, Yarmouth bloaters, pâte de diable, pith hats, pocket-handkerchiefs, eau de Cologne, Whitechapel cigars, Piver's perfumery (a wonderful man, Piver! I got one of his bottles in the casemates of the Redan, and yet it is *so* bad). When we had gone through those amusements, our party, now largely increased by fugitives from coaling, went into the verandahs, and therefrom gazed out upon the sea, the cliffs, the beach, and on the wild crowd of Simaulee boys and Arabs, who waved their wares before us, or descanted on the merits of donkeys, mules, and camels, all caparisoned, and ready to start for the station. A few of the old "die-hards" (H. M. 57th Regt.) came down from their bungalows to look at us, and from them we learned that the remarkable steam-sloop, which rejoiced in the name of Adjadah, or something approximate, was supposed to have a tendency to bathos, which would not render it desirable to send our detachment of sappers on board of her. Poor Lambert! I had really forgotten to mention that gallant, fine-hearted soldier, who—as I heard to my infinite regret, shared by every one who knew his kindly, honest, genial nature—fell a victim to the maliferous climate of China!

We had an odd kind of dinner at the Prince of Wales, which was chiefly remarkable for its extreme unfitness to support life and the good humour of those who tried to eat it. Then we organised races among the Simaulees, who ran on the strand, and among the camels and mules, which displayed remarkable speed over the shingle, whilst the runners and the riders never stopped shouting, "I say, saar, you give me five shillin'. I say, you promise me one pound." Amid these sports the noble art of self-defence was not forgotten. The Simaulees, aware of the Briton's love for athletic sports, paired off, and in a style which would have delighted the shades of Cribb and

Belcher—hit each other on the face and chest—got each other "into chancery," although they had no particular suits to speak of; and knocked their curly heads together with an astounding clatter, looking deceitfully in earnest, and claiming the reward of victory at every round. "You give me one pound, saar—me beat big fellow!" The sun began to set at last. We paid 6s. a head for dinner, and 6s. a head for *wine*, and set off for the station, up a steep road, which led us by cliffs overhanging the sea, to the wonderful basin in the mountain tops, where the English troops are stationed. I can say nothing of it now, for as I write remembrances full of melancholy steal over me. One of my companions in that pleasant excursion rests far away from friends and country, in a lonely grave.

January 12*th.*—As coaling was still going on when we returned to Lower Aden, the passengers who could get beds slept at the hotel, which offered to them a certain number of monks' cells, opening to a wide passage, which was screened by cocoa-nut matting from the outside yard. Stewart, who slept next me in the corridor, would insist on having two boys to fan him all night. Is it to be wondered at, then, that the two rings which I had placed on the table beside my head were gone in the morning? One was a souvenir of the Crimea, bought from a wounded Zouave, who had taken it *on* the finger of a Russian officer—and had taken *off* the finger to get the ring. I had found out the family of the officer by an extraordinary accident long afterwards, and the ring, which they begged me to retain, had a special value in my eyes. I wrote to all the authorities in the ill-regulated little dependency—to my comfort I heard that robberies were common at the hotel, and recovery quite unheard of. The police—for there are police at Aden—made a charge on a group of little boys and led one into captivity; but I shall never see my rings again. The hotel people look guilty.—But the Nubia's gun fires. At three o'clock we are steaming out of the harbour of Aden, leaving behind us fattened mosquitoes and enriched Parsees. Memo. for travellers—never touch one of the Simaulees; one of our passengers, provoked by the persecutions of a crowd of urchins, gave one of them a tap on the head with a cane, down fell the young rascal as if dead, and in an instant a stream of blood was flowing from his head upon the sand. He had taken up a sharp shell and cut open his scalp with it! The passenger was horrified. The crowd raised a dismal lamentation. The police came up, and the result was that the Simaulee received two pounds as hush-money and marched off rejoicing. Our American friend is rather indignant about Aden. "Why should we have such fortifications to keep out the Arabs? No, sir; it's a sham! But Aden will fall whenever it's invested, and in these days of progress no nation will be allowed no how to shut up seas and straits like the Turks."

January 13*th.*—A cloud on the sea; is said to be Socotra. The heat diminishes, but so does our patience, and if the sea be the great highway of nations, certainly those who traffic on it pay toll in the shape of patience. We have now double sets of meals. Alma people breakfast at 8.30, Nubians at 9.30; Almas dine at 2.30, Nubians at 4.30, not to speak of lunches, teas, and grogs. Then there is

Nubian music and Almaite music. Whilst we are at dinner the Almaites sing glees and choruses down the hatchways at us, and when we sing in our turn they play backgammon. The astute old American favoured us with some sensible strictures, as they appeared to me, ignoramus, respecting our conduct in China and Siam.—What right had Sir John Bowring to force the King of Siam to reduce his import duties to three per cent., when he must know that those duties are the main, almost the sole, source of the revenues of his kingdom? Thence he enlarged upon Brunel's mode of launching the "great Levy-a-than," and censured him sharply because he had substituted iron for wood on the ways. "Sir, if he had come to America and seen our yards, he would have learned something about the launching of big ships, and of iron ships too." And most of us who listened thought there was a great deal in what the American said. I almost forgot to say adieu to those who left us at Aden—some of the 57th, who have since passed, I hope, a pleasant time of it, and Campbell and Jex Blake, of the 18th, old Crimeans, bound for Bombay, to whom I wave my hand, and send my good wishes and remembrances.

January 14*th.*—Now we are settling down to India. The south-west monsoon brings it upon us. Cust talks wisely and well about the necessity of introducing a gold currency and a paper system into the empire; but, if it be wise and well, why is it not done? Then B—— brings arguments against him, and the dispute becomes technical. Shall I ever get at the truth? If I do, and tell it, will it be palatable?

January 15*th.*—A day at sea.
January 16*th.*—A day at sea.
January 17*th.* — Prayers on deck; a sermon; novel reading. Before divine service the heathen were paraded. The Mussulman crew, and the Chinese boatmen and steersmen all in holiday dress and fine robes. We have missionaries on board, but they do not seem to think their mission has commenced yet. One of the reverend gentlemen on board roused us this evening by a sermon remarkable for its bold, vigorous, uncompromising Calvinism. "Many, very many of those who pass through the world as good —whom you call good men—will, I fear, be damned eternally. If at this moment the ship in which we are on board of were to strike upon a rock and you were all to perish, I tell you, as it is my duty to do, that you would at once proceed to an eternity of bliss or to an eternity of torture. Let each judge which it would be." Whereupon we discussed and disputed gravely. One thesis was maintained with approbation. It assumed that "eternal" meant "equal" also. Is there to be no difference in the eternal fate of the "good" man, who was just a little too bad for heaven, and the punishment of Palmer of Rugeley? "But," said Mr. Jenkins, "who can tell what was Palmer's guilt, or who shall decide how bad was your 'good' man?" The ladies are very angry with Mr. Jenkins, and the wife of our chaplain is especially irritated against him for presuming to have such distinct information respecting the other world.
January 18*th.*—At sea,—"round as my shield," with this little palpitating, impetuous speck struggling in the midst of it. Discussed sea-serpents.—As

to sea-snakes there can be no discussion, for every seaman in those seas, and especially in the gulf nearer to the coast off Bombay, has seen them in myriads. Sometimes men have died from their bites. The tract is called the snake-ground. Now, if there be sea-snakes twelve and fourteen feet long, why may there not be sea-serpents eighty or a hundred feet long? Professor Owen says there can't. Peter McQuhae, Esq., Captain, Royal Navy, *magna comitante caterva*, says there is—at least one—for he saw it. Professor Owen shakes his head, but he cannot shake away the sea-snakes. In the Isle of Lewis there is a most respectable lady, whose assurance that she herself saw the sea-serpent swimming about in the Bay of Greiss, and scratching his head against the rocks on an island in the centre of it, can be corroborated by dozens of living people. But science, incredulous, evidently will never be satisfied till it has a body to dissect. Shoals of skipjacks are tumbling and leaping out of the water in great spirits near us, and more than twice to-day a shark showed his fin like a black cocked hat moving rapidly above the surface of the oily roll of the sea. The skipjacks are great, fine fellows, seven or eight feet long, as well as I can guess, rising like blocks of silver twice their length into the air, and falling with a thundering splash back again. Look out eagerly for a native boat of the Laccadive or Maldive people, but see none. Our captain says these curious and interesting groups of islands are constructed of coral raised round the edge of submarine mountains. The inhabitants are mild, amiable, and industrious, civil to strangers, but obstinate in refusing to allow them to settle. They make their own boats, ships, and compasses, and seem to enjoy a very happy civilisation, which "destiny" will compel some one to disturb some fine day.

January 19*th.*—A hot day at sea—nearing the tropics. The punkahs only fan oven-like puffs of air to and fro.

January 20*th.*—Early this morning high blue peaks appeared rising out of the sea on our port bow. Extraordinary boats with huge lateen sails skimmed over the sea with wonderful speed. By degrees the blue peaks grow higher, and grander, and more distinct; the island swells out of the water, till, as we advance, it spreads right across the horizon, and shows us a fringing grove of cocoa-trees, against whose stems the waves break, shutting up a wild sea of exotic vegetation.

A strip of bright yellow sand, on which the sea breaks among the cocoa-trees, is dotted here and there with boats. Inside the belt of trees there are, we are told, snakes and elephants beyond computation. Galle is in the distance, the entrance marked by a solitary cocoa-tree on an island. It was dusk when we anchored in the harbour.

CHAPTER VI.

Point de Galle.—Lorette's Hotel.—O'Dwyer, the waiter.—A slice of old Europe.—Old friends and old times.—Cricket, with thermometer at 98°.—Real tropical vegetation.—Departure from Ceylon.—Native habit of hoarding.—Our ignorance of Indian social life.—Approaching the land.—The pilot, and his letter-bag.—Startling news.—Corporal Brown.—India safer than Ireland.

January 21st.—Last night we went on shore—a lot of us. I can only recollect a pier shooting out from under an old wall crested with trees, a baronial gateway, a walk up a dark avenue fringed with trees, and the appearance of a dim little street, very clean and quiet, and lighted principally by fire-flies, in which was the Mansion House Hotel. But, alas! it was full of people for and from China, Malacca, Australia, the Spice Islands, and such strange places, that we could not think of intruding upon them. And so we went to Lorette's Hotel, and there we were permitted to lie on sofas in the verandah, as an *auto da fé* on the part of Lorette to the mosquitoes. I woke up this morning from horrid slumbers, in which I dreamed I was Regulus, and Curtius, and Saint—who is it that is pierced by arrows?—and found my face and hands like portions of ill-baked plum-pudding. Lorette declared it was wholesome—" Sine of the gude blode." I yielded with reluctance to the evidences of my excellent circulating medium, and sat down to breakfast, which was only remarkable for its marked contrasts to most good meals of that sort. Are there not coffee-planters in Ceylon, and is not Mocha round the next corner? Yes! Try to get an oyster at Colchester, or a lobster at Dalkey, and you will find that there is no such place to meet with poverty as at the edge of a gold-mine. But if we had no coffee worth drinking, and if the eggs showed a great deficiency in the powers of the active *gallinæ* which gave the place its name, we had abundance of physical exertions on the part of the inhabitants to show they were worthy of our support. Tall men, endued in large bed-curtains from neck to heel, with raven tresses fastened on the back of the head by large tortoiseshell combs, offered—nay, pressed upon us—every variety of article for which we could have no use. Umbrellas from China, made of paper and bamboo, price one shilling; slippers of very cutting hard fibre, ebony sticks, canes of cinnamon, jasmin, and orange, boxes of porcupine quills, Bombay inlaid cases for cigars and ladies' work, and cards made of carved sandal wood, elephants of ebony for paper weights, ornaments of elephants' tusks, collections of diamonds, sapphires, rubies, emeralds, cats' eyes, opals, which you might buy cheaply, and yet find not worth the money. In effect, Galle is the metropolis of false stones. The trade of deception is carried to perfection. One man had a cat's eye for which he would not take less, he said, than 500*l*. He had another for which he wanted 20 rupees, or 2*l*. He changed his hands and I could not tell the difference. After a hard bargain one of my comrades abated the price of a gorgeous ring from 15*l*. to 35*s*. A neighbouring *jeweller* offered him the counterpart for 1*2s*. "This real stone, other real glass." But let us get out into the clear air—into the town, which is an odd little reminiscence of Leyden mixed with Bröck. The mad waiter at Lorette's, whose name was O'Dwyer, and who boasted that "he had been in wid a grey dele of fitcin' all over the world, and had seen a grey dele of fun," came down to show us the antiquities, but we thought his antecedents might induce him to introduce us to old drinks and new squabbles, and declined his assistance, whereupon Mr. O'D. observed, "Now, mind! If yez come to harrum, don't blame me. Knock any of 'em down that torments yez," and retired. Admirable philosopher! Had your advice been followed, we should have formed a temporary pavement in Galle of the bodies of prostrate Cingalese. No! we walked down clean, sandy streets, which bore marks of Mynheer even yet, between rows of large one-storied, high-roofed, spacious houses, with a continuous line of porticoes in front, the doorways and windows open, but fenced from the gaze of the public by nice mantlets of fine horizontal matting. Vendors of curios marked us for their own, but invincible silence and hard umbrella points at last mastered the *auri sacra fames*. Galle, I should have said, is the oddest place in the world. Here is a slice of old Europe, 200 years old, thrust in among cocoa-nut trees, palms, coral reefs, a blue tropical sky and sea—men who dress like women and women who look like men,—with its queer gables, high roofs, abstruse ramparts, odd gateways and houses, which England has appropriated without in any way affecting the aspect of either the old or the new inhabitants. Jan Wyck sells groceries and spices to Frouw Winkel, and Bruggems acts as *notarius*, and old Jonghmans, the *opticus et mechanicus*, repairs umbrellas and obsolete old spying glasses in the open air, just as if they were waiting for the great Batavia fleet, under Admiral Vander Cappelen, to cast anchor in the Roads, with the flag of the Seven Provinces at the peak and truck. The Cingalese walks about pretty much as he did when the Portuguese and Dutch landed here. But he has been, to some extent, christianized and papalized, and he has also been turned into a lanky, lean, unhappy-looking rifle regiment. The old Porto Batavo walls still surround the town, with moat and escarpments, but he would be a poor commander that could not knock the whole place to pieces with the smallest gunboat that ever sailed down channel. Perhaps he would not get much by doing so, but he would certainly secure the magazines of coal, a good deal of false jewellery, and fine work in sandal-wood, ebony, and ivory. In fact, Point de Galle is virtually undefended. But are we not at peace with all the world?

We remained at Galle all day. An awful morning—shouting for towels, struggling for basons, fighting for water, and every man scratch scratching like mad. O'Dwyer, in great force, introduced to us an old Cingalese hair-cutter, who washed our heads in lime-juice and cocoa-nut oil, and delivered this remarkable opinion:—"Gentlemen want heads cut muss Ceylon come—Inglis barber kill gentleman's hair! French barber do murder hairs!" There was a fine touch of flattery in the distinction which cost me one shilling extra. As it was known the Nubia would not sail to-day, the jewellers made fresh demands, and all the other operators produced their choicest

stores. Several of the weaker vessels fell away into
ebony canes, and Chinese slippers, and umbrellas,
and elephants' tusks. Others played cricket (thermometer in the shade 98°)—but there is no lunatic
asylum at Galle. I am sure I was wise in starting
to see some old friends of the 50th, with whom I
talked over old times at Varna, Balaklava, and the
front of the Third Division. Times were changed,
for Purcell gave us the best meal in Galle that we
have had since leaving England,—our last together
was at the *Restaurant de l'Armée Alliée* at Gallipoli.
There was a certain Russian Count Medem here
whom I met for a short time—a traveller in India
and China, full of intelligence and observation, who,
for the first time, gave me, in a few suggestive sentences, a notion of what is the strangers' notion of
our rule and existence in India. But much more
pleasant was it to meet a kindly, hearty countryman,
whom I hope I shall not offend by naming here, as
one who made that day at Galle seem flooded with
home lights—Harrison, the engineer charged with
the difficult task of constructing the pier which is
intended, and much required, to render Galle a safe
harbour in bad weather. And had we not a great and
grand dinner? All the availables of her Majesty's
50th, and Engineers, and congenials of the passengers.
My notes relate to "richness of vegetation extraordinary." The pilgrim plant and its reservoir of water
—the bread fruit—the jack fruit, disagreeable odour
—prickly pear, &c. Birds very pretty: "Ceylon
Robin" size of thrush, black, with white bars on wing
covers—motacilla—honey-birds, apiasters. Excellent
punch and cigars—Harrison's diverting monkey, and

his friends, the mongoose, cockatoo, and parrot. Poigndestere—the engineer of the great work, the lighthouse on the Basses rocks, capital fellow! Row in the bay before dinner; story of sharks and diving-bell; *Hic est farrago libelli;* I can now remember nothing distinctly about it, except that the story of the shark and the diving-bell was very good. So far I feel like M. de Medem, who spent 50,000 livres in a year— he could not tell how, but he knew it was very pleasant.

January 22*nd.*—Purcell's gauze ramparts defended us from mosquitoes. Just at sunrise the boom of the morning gun—the concerted signal—roused us all for an excursion. Purcell on horseback, Harrison, Rendel, and I on Ceylon car (the driver *ran* by the horse's head all the time), set off for the country-seat of a clergyman six miles away. Road through most striking tropical scenery, all cocoa-nut and creepers— houses of cocoa-nut wood, walls, sides, roof. Every one of those apparently innumerable cocoa trees is marked, and has a master and owner; and if the cocoa is a good one it almost feed its man. Here is real tropical vegetation—the earth seems swallowed up by immense plants, grasses, wild flowers, heavy crops of rice, trees, and shrubs, so that one cannot see the rich bosom that nourishes such a profusion of vegetable life. Along a good level road, walled in by masses of trees and forests of cocoas, which are intersected by narrow paths leading to the bamboo, mud, and mat wigwams of the natives, we went on pleasantly till the car reached an ascent beyond the horse's power to draw us up. A short walk, ever upwards, led us to a pretty house perched on a small high plateau surrounded by trees: here our host was waiting to receive us. The reverend gentleman was in trouble, for he had incurred the censure of his bishop; and, not content with the result of the proceedings, had gone on battling and pamphleting till he had arrived at the condition of suspension, in which we found him. Placed at a table in the shade of the portico, we revelled in fruit and scenery. The blue mountains struck up towards heaven from a sea of vegetation. Adam's Peak looked some volcanic island rising from a fairy ocean. But amid this beauty the snake literally lay hid in the grass: one of our host's attendants produced a handful of scorpions from his sash, and played with the pretty things as they marched about the table brandishing their stings.—But I shall never get to India at this rate.

We left Ceylon with many pleasant memories, only regretting that we could not see more of such a magnificent island. I may add, that every person I met expressed the highest opinion of the remarkable ability, untiring vigour, zeal, and immense administrative ability of Sir H. Ward, the governor of the island. Already it has vanished in a golden haze amid the sunset; and we are running straight for Madras, avoiding those wicked Basses rocks, on which it will be weary work to build a lighthouse. The sea breaks roughly upon them, and there are very few days in the year when the workmen can land; even then they are secured with ropes. Few men can be found to undergo the risk and hardships of the task; and Government, or somebody, holds in a very miserly grasp the purse of supplies, and is very slow in deliberation on all matters connected with those important works. I am here up to the eyes in an *olla podrida* of notes. I must deny myself the pleasure of saying one word about Madras, Masulipatam boats—naked savages of boatmen, with cotton fig-leaves—the Club, and its luxuries and comforts. C., who landed here, declared he would never laugh again in India after what had occurred—his confidences shattered, his experience rendered worthless, his theories erroneous. Alas! that vow was soon forgotten; though once the memory of it returned upon him as, going down one of the by-streets of Madras, he heard himself abused by a native in language such as in all his life he had never heard applied to a European. The population of Madras blacker, more naked, and more ugly than I expected. But I am told one must not judge natives from appearances. I have a right, at all events, to form an opinion as to *what* they *look* like. Their habits of hoarding are remarkable. Mr. Grant, an old and valuable servant of the Company, who was a fellow-passenger, told me, that when the old rupees were called in some time back, the authorities at the mint knowing that between forty and fifty crores had been struck off, were alarmed lest the establishment should be overwhelmed in the first rush. However, only four and a half crores came in during the early days of the recall—the whole return never exceeded six crores—so that at least thirty-eight crores of rupees were absorbed among the people, hoarded, or used in ornaments and plate. Again, in one district which he named, there are 80,000 tons' weight of rice grown, the export value of which, paid for in cash, is 500,000*l.* per annum. The district only takes back about 50,000*l.* worth of manufactures and goods, so that there is a metallic balance in its favour of 450,000*l.* a year. It appears to be admitted by all those clever gentlemen on board that they know little or nothing of the inner social life of the people. One of them, indeed, said, "We know nothing of the natives as they appear to each other: their aspect to us is as different as possible from that which they present to their families, friends, and native rulers." Indeed it begins to grow upon me that we are in India rather on sufferance and by force, than by affection. Our friends on board bow their heads with resignation to the doom which they think must befall the Company very speedily; but they have little love for their masters, and they feel secure in their present posts, "because India can't be governed without us, let England do as she likes." There is only one apprehension in their minds with respect to the change—*surgit amari aliquid*—they fear a reduction of their salaries. They argue that reduced salaries and admission by competition will degrade the civil service, injure its efficiency, and drive "gentlemen" out of the ranks. Again: they say, one must be paid highly to live in such a country as India at all; and that every Indian officer has a right to a good retiring allowance, as he is almost certain to close his career in a very debilitated state of health. How is it that able men and gentlemen are easily had to discharge high functions in Ceylon at much lower salaries than in India?

January 27*th.*—The sea, by its colour, warned us that we were approaching land. The noon observation gave us a splendid run of 370 miles. The water rapidly became more turbid as we advanced, and speedily assumed the pea-soup hue which distinguishes the streams of great rivers. No land was visible in the morning; but soon after twelve o'clock a faint shadowy outline was seen on the horizon. Many ships and barks were edging along under full sail, for which there was but little wind; but the captain was more particularly interested in a fine handy brig, which lay, with her topsails aback, right in our course. Three similar brigs were anchored, or lying to, almost in a line with her. This was our "pilot" vessel; and at the word, all the old Indians, men and women, crowded to the forecastle. The quarter-boat was lowered from the brig, and made towards our ship. Long ago, before steam was, it was the great event of the voyage to receive the pilot on board, and to hear the news he brought, and read the letters which he had on board for the Calcutta-bound passengers. Some not very old men who were with us spoke of the intense excitement which prevailed the moment the pilot came in view, as productive of very strange effects. And, indeed, how could it be otherwise, when one thinks that life passed as rapidly then as it does now, and that some four or five long months had intervened since the outward-bound had received letters from India, which were, at the time of their receipt, probably three or four months old? What great events in the smallest household can be marshalled in the space of a few weeks! Even with all the acceleration of our present route there are few who have not felt, in India, that half the earth's circumference divides them from those they love, and that "distance" is as yet a perceptible ingredient in the cup of sorrow, and doubt, and anxiety, which separation fills so copiously. The wife heard, perhaps, that the husband she expected to have folded in her arms had been for months lying in his grave. In the district to which the old civilian was about to repair, in the hope of giving a last strong shake to the pagoda tree, all trace of British rule might have been swept away in a flood of Mahrattas or Pindarees for the time. There was scarcely a letter opened which did not contain a shock, a surprise, or a wonder, influencing, perhaps, the whole life of the recipient. But here is our pilot coming over the side. A portly gentleman, by our faith, not destitute of gilt buttons, and anchors, and gold bands. After him, his assistant, and then enter letter-bags. It is astonishing how affable the big civilians are with Mr. Pilot; and how very cool, and grand, and civil Mr. Pilot is with every one. Whilst we gaze from the outer edge of the great circle of which he is the imposing centre, he is suddenly wheeled away by the captain, under the pretence, probably, of the state of the tides, or of Cassiopeia being rather queer, and so we lose him for the moment—but not his news. The little drops of intellectual ointment which had run down his beard had been previously carried off by those near him, and they were now retailing it, with such additions of baser matter as fancy, imagination, and taste suggested. One gentleman reported to his own little circle, " The pilot says Sir Colin Campbell is surrounded at Cawnpore!" In a minute afterwards up came one to me, with consternation on his face, " God bless me! Have you heard this dreadful story?" "No: what is it?" " Why, that poor Sir Colin Campbell has been drowned at Cawnpore!" The outsider, who was listening intently for the second-hand news, rushed off immediately with the alarming intelligence, "Sir Colin Campbell has been drowned at Cawnpore!" However, we arrived at the positive fact, that the Commander-in-chief, having sent Windham up to Lahore after the overthrow of the Gwalior Contingent, who fled in great alarm before him, had established his head-quarters at Cawnpore, after his return from Futtehguhr, and was waiting there for the accomplishment of an object not known to the Indo-British public.

What a silence about Havelock! As we approach the soil to which he and his soldiers had given a European interest, the splendour of his reputation diminishes. It forcibly reminded me of "Corporal Brown."

On the occasion of the first review of the British army in the valley of Balaklava—an occasion made memorable by the extraordinary but unsuccessful exertions of the officer in command to get the men out of the valley, which lasted long after the evolutions had ceased, so that some of the regiments did not arrive at their camps till past seven o'clock at night—a group of the humbler class of T. G's., who haunted the army at the end of the campaign, was stationed close to the point at which the regiments of the Highland Division were marching past towards the ground; as each company wheeled round by this point, a long-legged, lean, elderly man, with a Glengarry bonnet on his head, a huge pair of horn spectacles on his nose, dressed in a suit of shepherd's plaid, addressing himself generally to officers and men, exclaimed with great eagerness, "Where's Corporal Broon—is Corporal Broon amang this lot? I wad be vara much obleeged ti ye if you'd point me oot Corporal Broon!" The poor man was in despair; for strangely enough, no Corporal Brown replied. It appeared that he had read, in some north-countrry paper, an account of "Corporal Brown of our's, having gone into a Russian battery in the night, killed the officer in command, driven out the men at the point of his bayonet, and then having returned with a number of trophies, among which were shameful books, which the corporal threw into the watchfire." The anecdote struck deep roots into his mind, particularly as the corporal was in a Scotch regiment (which had no Russian batteries opposed to it, but the British public never could understand those matters); and as it was insinuated in the newspaper that the corporal came from the same part of the country, the worthy man came out to the Crimea with the firmest conviction that Corporal Brown was the man of the day, and that the deed was the event of the siege. "And wull ye tell me, surs," he said, in piteous entreaty, "wull ye tell me, ye have nae heard of Corporal Broon, or of any corporal havin' jest cleared a Roosian battery, killed the captain, and made sax-and-therty of the Roosians to flee?" The fame of Brown and his exploit burned as a shining light, which warmed up the whole country side; but on the field they had never heard of him.

Of course there is no parallel between the extreme greatness and the infinitesimal smallness of the two men, or of the two things; but it has certainly struck me all along that the Indians on board do not, as a general rule, exhibit much enthusiasm about Havelock. It is about this time twelvemonths, that dining at the house of a friend, I happened to meet there a gentleman who had had a long and varied experience in Indian, or probably it would be more correct to say, in Calcutta, Serampore, and Lower Bengal affairs—a man of great sagacity, the friend of the most remarkable Governor-General since the days of Wellesley, and one who formed his judgments with care, and expressed them with deliberation. He, then and there, speaking of Indian subjects—in which I was little interested, but into which we were drawn by talking of the Persian difficulty—declared his conviction that India was as well-disposed and as safe as any part of the Queen's dominions—*safer* than Ireland, certainly; and that there was one soldier in India who, in the event of any occurrence giving him the opportunity of showing what he was made of, would astonish us all in Europe—Colonel Havelock. The success of one prediction may be balanced against the failure of the other. The ladies who had survived the miseries and the fire of Lucknow, are now on their way to Calcutta, or have reached it. At Aden, I asked one of the Peninsular and Oriental Company's officers how many mutilated ladies he had seen. "Seen!" he said, "why no one has seen any of them here. They all go round the Cape, I suppose." But I still believed.

CHAPTER VII.

The Hooghly.—Hindoo Temples.—Garden Reach.—Floating Hindoo corpses.—The Bengal Club.—The city of palaces.—The fort.—Simon, once Allagapah.—The Esplanade.—A drive in the dark.—Europeans and Indians.—The Auckland hotel.—Proposed objects for investigation.—Musquitoes and jackals.

January 28th. — Last evening's sun set over a wide waste of yellow waters, the bounds of which, low and desolate-looking, could just be made out on both sides of the ship. As the river contracts, the commercial greatness of the mighty stream and the port it feeds developes itself in hundreds of ships of the first class, magnificent clippers, weight-carrying Indiamen of the old school, fleets of country boats which, working up and down through the many tortuous channels, gave an appearance of life and activity to the scene which could not be surpassed by the Downs. The native shipping, in rigging, masts, sails, and hull, are odd-looking and dilapidated, and the only craft which they at all resemble, as far as I can remember, are the boats of the Turkish Black Sea ports with the high sterns. The crews of those we approach are thin slight men, nearly black, and very poorly attired. On our starboard quarter, towards evening, we have Saugor Island, much haunted of tigers, who feast on the deer abounding in the jungle, and keep the lighthouse people in a state of constant alarm; for there *is* a lighthouse on the island, the attendants on which are sustained by various artificial devices to supply the absence of water, and to compensate for the presence of wild beasts. *Non meus sermo, sed quæ præcepit O'Fellius—abnormis sapiens.* A grand idea of the Midasian magnitude of our Indian appointments was given to me this morning early, when, in order to account for all the buttons, and bands, and aureate trappings of the pilot, O'Fellius further informed me that the pilots *retire* on pensions of 700*l.* sterling per annum. Why don't Lincoln's, Gray's, and all the Temples emigrate, and force their way into the Indian pilot service? The only drawback O'Fellius could suggest was, that few of them lived to enjoy these pensions. They put in many hard nights, and the climate is unfavourable, and their duties are arduous; "therefore," quoth O'F., "in order to induce some of them to live, the high pension is put forth."

This morning the noble river—for all rivers are noble which are big, dirty, and have plenty of ships, though this stream is as full of danger as the Mississippi is of snags—has narrowed considerably. We lay-to during the night to suit some phase of tide or bank, and now we are screwing up against the very muddy boiling current, increased in force by an ebb tide. Here we are amid "The Silas E. Burrowes, of Boston, U.S.," "The Marquis of Tweeddale, of Glasgow," "Rustamjee Puckerjie, of Calcutta," "Les Trois Frères, Bordeaux," and several native vessels of large tonnage, which are trying, by the aid of a light wind, to beat up against the tideway, and the hands at our wheel must be strong and quick. And there, in effect, with real straw hats, under which are curled long tails which would enrapture Marsh or Truefitt, in neat clean toggery, bull-necked, square-shouldered, and stronglegged, stand the four Chinese helmsmen, conned by the English quartermasters, upping with the helm and downing with it, and—letting her go about or round, or keeping her just within a few yards of the Parsee's quarter—we scrape through and screw on, and by-andby, the banks on each side strike out bodily to meet us, and the faint verge of green, which refreshed the eye last night, turns into a belt of cocoa-nuts worthy of Ceylon. Villages there are also of muddy creeks, which put one in mind of tide-deserted eyots at Chiswick suddenly tenanted by quaint boats, and people who had just bathed in the Thames and had not scraped the black mud off them. There is one building, certainly, near to most of those villages, we should not see near the Thames. Heavy-domed, squat, and, to my mind, ungraceful, the Hindoo temple, surrounded by a clump of trees, raises its white cupola amid their tops, but has no beauty of elevation, and is utterly deficient in the simply beauty of the Mussulman mosque. They, however, presented the usual contrast observable in poor and ignorant countries, in the fineness of the temples to the poverty of the people. The great manufacturing town of Peddlington is content with a red brick temple, surmounted by a weathercock, which altogether looks like the workhouse built "*tempore Eliz., anno reg.* 10." In Ireland we have cut stone or elaborately-cemented cathedrals and parish churches. In Bengal, the heathen, who live in mud huts propped up by bamboo canes, worship in temples of marble or in finely-worked chunamfaced pagodas. Men and women were working in the fields naked to the waist, and reflecting the rays o.

the sun from their dark glistening bodies. The high banks of the river, which seem of artificial make, permit only the farther portions of the wide-spread plains, which melt into dense groves in the distance, to be seen. There are apparently no roads, and no traffic between the villages, but innumerable watercourses and cuts winding between muddy banks, and, no doubt, with internal communications. The Sonderbunds, which we passed on our right, the wide-spreading islands and deltas of the rivers which here join the sea, afford the greatest possible facility for canalization, but up to the present moment, in spring, when the rivers are low, a steamer coming down from Patna or Allahabad is obliged to double the length of her voyage at least, owing to the want of a channel of sufficient depth, amid islands and streams which want but little comparatively to be done to render them available as the banks and watercourses of a permanent and unvarying navigation. All this is "interloper" and anti-company assertion, and even hypothesis. The river itself is not interesting; the tropical vegetation and hues which give such a charm and novelty to Ceylon have disappeared, and the cocoanut trees which fringe the banks are wearisome to the eye, owing to their uniformity of size, foliage, and colour. The muddy river, churned into yellowish, buttery foam where it chafes against the sandbanks, is of the colour and breadth of the Mersey at New Brighton. There is immense noise on board, and great anxiety, for the luggage and baggage is coming out of the hold, swayed up by reckless arms on the running tackle, and the fine overland trunks, hat-boxes, gun-cases, and ladies' boxes arrive on deck in various stages of ruin. Indeed, one gentleman suggests that the Company must be in league with the overland trunk and portmanteau makers, and permit several of the *employés* of the latter to live down in the hold and break up the luggage at their leisure. Meanwhile, the river narrows, and the navigation becomes more dangerous. The masts of a full-rigged ship, which rise above the surface close to us, at an obtuse angle, point out the place where one fine vessel was lost a few days ago. The tides and currents are so very strong and rapid, that if a ship touches the bank they capsize her the moment her keel strikes, and the suddenness of the exploit is in proportion to the fineness of her lines and the depth of the keel.

About noon we have advanced to a more civilized country; the villages are larger, the fields better cultivated. After a time detached houses, with high sloping roofs like those of the older Swiss farm-houses on the Bernese overland, come into view, mostly on the right bank of the river. A few of them are two-storied, and the sides are protected by deep verandahs and porticoes. They are painted white and buff, or lightbluish grey, and stand in detached gardens, fenced in by trees, plantations, and shrubberies. I make my first bow to a "pucka" house. In the balconies, sheltered from the sun, are groups of Europeans—mostly women, for the bread-winners have gone up to Calcutta—who salute imaginary friends and wave their handkerchiefs as the vessel surges upwards. Then the houses become more dense and continuous, and appear on both sides of the stream. Plantations and fences grow down to the water's edge; the throng of drifting vessels, the number of stalwart little steam-tugs, carrying off their big ships as ants run off with a grain of corn, impede our progress. A bend of the river shows us the stream, higher up, interlaced with hulls, and masts, and rigging, which, in the distance, blacken and harden, as it were, into impassable *chevaux-de-frise*. White houses, as close set as the villas at Richmond, run into lines of streets on the upper banks, which are fringed with trees, and with a broad walk covered with natives and carriages. Out of a green bank dotted with black teeth, a flag-staff carries aloft the union-jack. Close at hand, on the right, is a long wharf, whereat lie many ships. Inside the wharf, gardens, hedge-rows, and fine houses, mostly two stories in height, and behind them a few spires, which do not, however, appear very distinct, owing to the haze caused by the heat. * * * *

"And about the dead Hindoos in the river?" said I to my friend, as we were going off in our boat towards the ghaut, a landing-place in a strong muddy tideway, gurgling through cables and hawsers of many ships. "The dead Hindoos in the river? I declare to you," quoth he, with much gravity, "it's all stuff. I have been for years in Calcutta, and never saw half-a-dozen in my—" "Whew!" interrupted I, "what a dreadful smell! God bless me! Look at that thing!" And down with the swirling tide came towards us, bloated face downwards, with arms outstretched, a human body, bleached white where it was exposed to the air, and serving at once as a banquet and a perch to half-a-dozen crows and buzzards. Our rowers lazily lifted their oars to let "it" float past, without a word. As we neared the landing-place we saw two more, dreadfully decomposed, churned about in an eddy. My friend was disconcerted a little. See how oddly the laws of evidence and observation often run. Had I come ashore at a few minutes earlier or later, I might have said "the gentleman who accompanied me, and who has lived for a long time at Calcutta, assured me he had never seen half-a-dozen bodies in the Hooghly in ten years' time; and I am bound to say that I saw none in my voyage up the river."

We drove to the Bengal Club, where I had been kindly put up and elected as an honorary member. The benefit and advantage of the courtesy were all the greater that, in the Indian clubs, members can have bedrooms if they are vacant; and one had been secured for me. Although it was January the heat was very great on board the steamer and along the road, which had not been watered. The delights of that club bedroom were great; for attached to it was a dark latticed room, in which stood many large red earthen pitchers of water, and a glorious tub. It is the one constant luxurious necessity that one repeats in India—that universal bath-room!

"And what do I think of Calcutta?" Well, I am fairly puzzled to say whether it most resembles Moscow or Nicholaeff; but assuredly it does make a Muscovite impression upon me. Parts of it remind one of the Neva banks at St. Petersburg. Then, again, the white houses, surrounded with walls, provided with green verandahs and small porticoes, the *porte-cochère*, the courts and enclosures, and the low elevation of the dwellings, and the width of the streets, and great open spaces suggest Moscow; whilst the trans-Hooghly district, seen through a mass of spars and shipping, looks like the view of Nicholaeff (Nikolaev, if you like it better), as seen from the right bank of the Boug. Garden Reach, and the fine broad causeway by the wide river, lined with trees, look well; so do the green parapets of the Fort, with its bastions and curtains rising sharply above the verdure of the glacis. On the land side of the Fort is a beautiful lawn-like sheet of grass, intersected by roads studded with trees, and fenced in by a line of shining white houses, elaborately porticoed and colonnaded, which sweep round from Government House on the left to the regions of Allipore on the right of the Fort, as we look from the buggy. And pray, what is a buggy? It is a gig with a hood. The European drives, the Syce runs by the horse's head with a fly whisk in his hand, or perches up behind, at the back of the hood. Seen thus, with the light falling on the houses of Chowringhee—not too near, pray—whilst the grass of the glacis and plain is still green, and the trees are clothed in leaves, the first aspect of Calcutta is agreeable. But "the City of Palaces?" Well, well! As to palaces, we really must see! The Fort to me is the most interesting edifice of all. It was impossible to survey without emotion the spot of ground where, a century and a half ago, a doubtful little colony took possession of the *pied-à-terre* presented to them by the pet son of the great Aurungzebe, and in fear and trembling at the boldness of their step across the Hooghly, where they were flourishing well enough, made their first settlement amid the native villages assigned to them. Here was the work commenced by Clive, after Plassey, and which, but a few short months ago, was the refuge of the Europeans of Calcutta from what they feared would be a fate worse than that which befell the victims of the

Black Hole. The fort looks stout and solid, and is constructed after the best principles of fortification of the last century, on which, as far as I know, there has been no improvement, except Ferguson's untested system be one. The embrasures are too much crowded, I think: and the armament, though numerous, is light, as opposed to modern siege guns. The defences against vertical fire are by no means perfect. But I am getting far beyond my notes. * * * *

Let us return to that cool club, with its open court, shaded passages, and well-blinded windows, where not a sound is heard but the twittering whistle of the kite, or the thirsty caw of the Indian crows. Inside there is equal silence, broken now and then by "the rustle of a newspaper," the pop of a cork, the click of billiard balls, or a feeble "qui-hye" from a distant sofa. It is January; but no one goes out in the sun. As I doze away in the cool shade of the darkened room, a shadow in white glides before me—a small, bright-eyed, slight-limbed man, with a curl of grey hair escaping from under his enormous turban. He salaams to the Sahib, and says, "My name Simon! me master's servant." Then, standing with his arms folded across his breast, he waits till I have read the certificates to his character and attainments, which are placed in a little pile before me. He has been engaged for me before my arrival; and though his wages are very high for India—25 rupees a month—as he speaks English, and has travelled over most of India several times, I am glad to get one who is well recommended. Among his papers is one to the effect that he was once a heathen, named Allagapah, but that he was baptised by a missionary of St. Francis d'Assisis, and is now a Christian, Simon by name. Installed, he at once set to work to open all my boxes, to take possession of all my keys and effects, and to make an inventory of the same—for his own satisfaction, I presume. When it was getting dark D— came round for me in his buggy, to perform the great ceremony of Calcutta life—to take the evening turn on the Esplanade, or on the Course. The Esplanade lies in front of Chowringhee, and it is therefore in front of the Club. In the midst, on the right of us, is a bad imitation of the Nelson monument, in Trafalgar Square, with Nelson removed from the top. Before us is the Fort.

* * * * *

Is this a limbo in which all races, black and white, are doing penance on the outside of strange quadrupeds and in the interior of impossible vehicles? The ride in Rotten Row, the dreary promenade by the banks of the unsavoury Serpentine, the weary gaiety of the Champs Elysées, the Bois de Boulogne, and the Avenue de St. Cloud, the profound austerity of the Prater, are haunts of frivolous, reckless, indecorous, loud-laughing Momus and all his nymphs— Euphrosyne, and Phryne, and others—compared with his deadly *promenade à cheval et à pied*, where you expect every moment to hear the Dead March in Saul, or to see the waving black ostrich plumes sprout out of a carriage top; not that there is not frivolity, recklessness, indecorum, and laughter here, too, but Momus wears a white hat and has lunched at the club; Euphrosyne's husband is weary, and she is obliged to be quiet, as the Melpomenes are in town; and Phryne is going to be married to old Rhadamanthus next week, after the heavy case is disposed of. These are, indeed, solemn processions, which not even youth and beauty, or their simulants, can make gay. The ground is well watered—no dust rises beneath the tramp of the many horses. But darkness has set in on the faces of the multitude. The moment the sun made a decided bow to the horizon, out came carriages, phaetons, and horses; but scarcely have they revolved twice in their course, ere that sun has vanished into darkness. Phœbus and Nox have here a sterile union; and the sturdy long-lived Crepuscule of our southern climes is unborn and unknown here.

It really was little more than ten minutes from the time we got on the course, ere the darkness to me destroyed all the attractions of what, for a brief period, was a very interesting and novel scene. But imagine a drive in the dark—not twilight—but darkness so profound, that lamps must be lighted to prevent collision. For the ten minutes or so it was a very gay, a very curious, but not a very satisfactory or assuring sight. I think the most stern and patrician of Roman consuls must have something of an uneasy feeling when he saw the plebeians in the Via Sacra, presuming to walk forth in purple and fine linen among the offspring and relatives of the Conscript Fathers. But here on this esplanade, or race-course, or corso—whatever it is—there is something more than such pretentious equality. It is, that there is such insult offered as the arrogance of the most offensive aristocracy—that of complexion—can invent to those who by no means admit themselves to be the plebeians of the race. See: there is a feeble young man dressed in white, with a gilded velvet cap in his hand, trying to drive a vehicle, which looks like a beehive, from the cluster of his attendants on all points of it. That is Chuck-el-head Doss, the great little young Bengal merchant, the inheritor of old Head Doss' money, and the acceptor of the less doubtful gain of a Germano-Hindoo-Christianic philosophy, which teaches him that, after all, whatever is is best, and that the use of the senses is the best development of the inner man. Is he a bit nearer to us because he abjures Vishnu, accepts providence, and thinks our avatar very beautiful? Ask "Who he is." "He's one of those nigger merchants—a cheeky set of fellows, and d—d blackguards, all of them." Then there is a morose old man in a chariot drawn by four horses, with two well-dressed fellows with their backs to the horses, outriders, and runners, and a crowd of servants. He is a handsome, worn-out-looking man, with a keen eye, lemon-coloured face and gloves, dressed in rich shawls and curious silks. Who is he? A few Europeans bow to him. "He is the Rajah of Chose—a great rascal. None of us know him; and they say the Company were jockeyed in giving him such an allowance." You feel some historic interest when you are shown Tippoo Sultan's son and grandson; but your friend is too busy, looking at Mrs. Jones, to give much information on these points, or to direct your attention to anything so common-place (to him) as the appearance of some natives on the course. And indeed, to tell the truth, the pretty fair face of Mrs. Jones is, perhaps, better worth looking at, in the abstract, than those bedizened natives. Still it is striking, for the first time at all events—but I suppose the impression soon dies away—to see the metaphysical Mahratta ditch which separates the white people, not only from the natives, but from the Eurasians. They drive and ride in the same throng, apparently quite unconscious of each others' presence.

The only spectators by the sides of the drives are Europeans. Perhaps a few sleek fat young baboos, with uncovered head, white robes which allow the brown calf and leg to be seen, and the foot thrust sockless into a patent-leather shoe, are walking about with umbrellas under their arms; but it is evidently for the walk, and not to look at the Sahibs. The high-capped Parsees, who are driving about in handsome carriages, are on better terms with the Europeans, as far as the interchange of salutations go; but the general effect of one's impressions, derived from a drive in the Calcutta Course, is, that not only is there no *rapprochement* between the Indian and the Englishman, but that there is an actual barrier which neither desires to cross. There are some few good horses and many very good carriages on the esplanade. A turn-out, worthy of the best days of Long Acre, with adjuncts of turbaned coachmen, and crowds of black footmen, looks rather odd at first; but the liveries are very picturesque, and sometimes in very charming taste as to colour and combination.

Just as night falls, and the lamps are lighted, the scene resembles a little bit cut out of the Champs Elysées avenue at the height of the season: lights gleaming and moving in all directions, carriages and horses passing indistinctly in the dusk, and gay dresses, feathers, and plumes caught at intervals as the lamps flash upon them, and then vanishing into darkness. Round and round they drive till dinner-hour comes.

The variety and splendour and number of the equipages would give one a great idea of the immense wealth of the European community at Calcutta: but it must be remembered, that the high functionaries of Government, of the law, and of many branches of the Administration, are here; that there are professional men who make large incomes in law and physic; that the Church has its representatives; that there are wealthy merchants of all nations settled here, bankers and traders. But it is not considered quite proper for shopkeepers to drive on the Esplanade. "Whose is this magnificent carriage, with the gold liveries?" "That? Oh, that's Bunkum; he's a merchant who has broken several times—but they don't think much of breaking in Calcutta. It's very easy to pass the court, and they come out as strong and as bright as ever." It is, indeed, a fact, that Calcutta commerce has been subjected to many crises and panics; but a certain proportion of the houses has always passed through the ordeal with credit,—which is as much as can be said for London or Liverpool. There is an impression, however, that the relief given by the bankruptcy and insolvency courts is administered too largely and too carelessly, where every clerk keeps a buggy, every merchant has a carriage, and lives in a style which speaks of enormous profits, or little conscience. It's lucky the weather is too hot for an Italian opera and a French company, or the increment to expenditure would be considerable in the matter of boxes, millinery, &c. The habits of the city life are traditionally expensive; the whole scale of living is large; and the merchants of Calcutta are celebrated for a frank and liberal hospitality, which dates from the time when every European hung up his hat in his banker's or his agent's house on his arriving in the country. The greater influx of Europeans rendered this a heavy item in the expenses of the mercantile class, which was rapidly augmented by steam; and hotels then sprung up, which took the pressure off private resources.

One of these hotels, the Auckland, is a wonder in its way; at least, I have never seen anything like it. In one large house there is an attempt to combine a tailor's, a milliner's and dressmaker's, a haberdasher's, a confectioner's, a hardwareman's, a woollen merchant's, a perfumer's, a restaurateur's, a spirit and wine merchant's, a provision dealer's, a grocer's, a coffee-house keeper's establishment, with a hotel, and with a variety of other trades and callings. I should say, from my own experience, the hotel suffers in the amalgamation; but it is a great advantage to have at your feet all you want, although, I must confess, I could not manage to get a chop one morning for breakfast below stairs. Mr. D. Wilson, who created this establishment by his energy, ability, and industry, has made a large fortune; and judging from the zeal with which he advertises all over India, is bent on making it larger.

Dinner at the club—a kind of *table d'hôte*, very well served. A battalion of native domestics in the club livery in attendance, almost one behind each man's chair. After dinner, a very abrupt, good-natured, and energetic attempt was made to carry me off, there and then, or at dawn next morning, by a Calcutta barrister, whose practice is not confined to the courts, with the object, as far as I could ascertain, of showing me " the worst road in the world, that I might judge of the way the scoundrelly Company developed the resources of India." But I successfully pleaded the nature of my mission, the importance of my getting up to the front immediately, and the utter unfitness of my unworthy self for the duty the gentleman proposed to me. Indeed, upon that evening it was proposed to me to examine the working of our legal system, with which object I was to go and live with the proposer somewhere up country for as long as I liked—to expose the ruinous land system, as affecting the introduction of British capital, for which task the same means and facilities were afforded to me; to go through all the missionary schools, ditto, ditto; to "show up" the iniquities of the government of the Company generally: to investigate the system of non-canalization, non-irrigation, non-road-making, non-railway constructing: to hold up to public obloquy the partial and defective administration of various courts, by which the Europeans were harassed, and natives unduly protected. Such were a few of the objects proposed to me; *my* object, in the present state of my knowledge of India, being merely to give an account of the military operations, and to describe the impressions made on my senses by the externals of things, without pretending to say whether I was right or wrong. There are few men in the world qualified to execute any one of those tasks—perhaps scarcely one, unassisted by the labours and counsels of competent men.

I was glad to go up to bed after such a fatiguing day. Opening my door, I fell across a soft roll, which lay on the floor. It was Simon, who was asleep across the doorway. The room contained a few articles of furniture; a bed, shrouded in musquito curtains. Ere I sat down, Simon had commenced to undress me, pulled off boots and socks, made a desperate attempt to rub the soles of my feet with a rough towel which I rejoicingly defeated, and at last salaamed, and left me to the musquitoes. Three or four of the blood-thirsty little beasts managed to get into bed with me, and punished me greatly. Just as I was going to sleep, there sounded in the night air, a scream, as of a dying woman close at hand, which chilled the marrow in my bones. It was repeated, mingled with cries and barks, which swept past the club-house. It turned out to be only a pack of jackals running over the Esplanade in the moonlight.

CHAPTER VIII.

A delightful rush at clear, clean cold water.—Black Washerman.—The Ochterlony monument.—Government House.—Absence of English domestics.—Interview with Lord Canning.—Hospital for sick and wounded officers.—Kindness of the ladies of Calcutta.—The "upper ten" at Lucknow.—The Southwark of Calcutta.—Paucity of white faces.—A row by moonlight.—Burning Ghauts.—Indian official papers.—General Dupuis.—A ball at Fort William.

January 29*th.*—Woke up about six, by a storm of "qui-hyes," from the windows. The club is getting up. All the shaded jalousies are thrown open. Simon glides into my room with a cup of tea, and a cheroot; opens the windows; pretends to kill the musquitoes, which, gorged to treble their usual size with my blood, are hanging on by the curtains, sleeping like aldermen. I take a prompt vengeance on them. "Master's bath ready!" After that fuzzy, stewy, muggy, clammy ship, how delightful it was to rush at all that clear, clean, cold water! Simon is mourning over my trunks. "Many things master got no use! Master not got things which much use." And so I believe, indeed, it was. The first washing shrivelled all my flannel shirts into jerseys, too small for wear; seams opened and buttons disappeared from all my garments; my canteen was pronounced to be no good at all, and my clothes were said to be "no use for wear, for not bear washee." To washee, however, the large ship's bag, containing the spoils of the voyage, was sent; for as Simon was speaking, "dhobyman" was waiting outside, and in a few moments made his appearance—a black washerman, dressed in cotton, which, as a proof of his skill, was decidedly unsatisfactory in colour. It is now seven o'clock only, but the horizontal rays of the sun are unpleasantly hot. Simon looks at my hat and cloth clothes with infinite earnestness and compassion. "Master must buy sola topee and loite jacket." He was rapidly making himself master of the situation. So I was obliged to check him in mid career, and to tell him that I knew better than he did what was necessary for India; a statement that made him open his eyes and shut his mouth.

There was just time ere breakfast to do one of the sights of Calcutta, and to climb to the top of the Ochterlony monument. Fortune did not favour me in the result, for the greater part of the city was shrouded in a grey mist; but the course of the broad river laden with ships, the Government House, the Fort, and the European part of Calcutta were distinctly visible, and formed rather an agreeable *ensemble*, in which there was, however, nothing altogether compensating the toil of the ascent. It is always the way with high places. I never knew one that I was not glad to get down from, not from any dizziness, for my head is not affected by height, but because I felt it was uncomfortable to be there, and to take so much pains for nothing. The Mont Blancists—now tolerably numerous—must confess that the view and their raptures are impostures. Whoever went twice into the ball of St. Paul's? or twice up to the top of Salisbury spire, or of Milan, or Antwerp steeples? So I returned sorrowing to breakfast.

As the Governor-General is going to Allahabad at dawn to-morrow, I drove over to present my letters early in the forenoon, to Government House, a residence not altogether unbecoming the Viceroy of India, but at the same time by no means overwhelming, splendid, or in faultless taste. The general effect is nearly spoiled by a huge dome, perfectly "bald," rising out of the centre of the roof like a struggling balloon. Once on a time, Britannia, I believe, with trident or spear, shield and helmet, sat on the apex of the dome and kept it in order, but the lightning frequently smote her, and the Snow Harris of Calcutta did not know how to get over the difficulty. The goddess— for is she not as good (much more real and practical certainly) as Juno or Athené?—was taken from her high estate and put away in some lumber room. Placed in the midst of a large open space, with green lawns, not very extensive, but covered with fine clean-shaven sward, and aqueducts around it, and almost within an arrow-shot of the Hooghly, the Government House should be as cool as any house can be in Calcutta; and the great number of windows on the side elevations, give it an appearance of airiness, which the "sunny side" by no means deserves. If that dome could be removed, or put straight, or got something to sit on it, taking it all and all, as seen from the exterior of the fine gateways which lead to the entrance, the Government House reflects great credit on the engineer officer who designed and built it, at the cost of (St. Stephen protect us!) just 150,000*l*. At the gateways, with nothing more formidable than canes in their hands, were real sepoys—each "in shape and hue" so like a

British soldier, when his back is turned, that at a sudden view he would beguile; tall, broad-backed, stiff-set, but with lighter legs than the Briton, and a greater curvature in the thigh. There he is, doing his regulation stride, saluting every white man who enters, civilian or soldier, dressed after the heart of army tailors, pipe-clayed, and cross-belted, and stocked, and winged, and facingsed, every button shining, every strap blazing, and each bit of leather white as snow—the sepoy, of whom his officers and those around him, contenting themselves with that fair outer show, know as little, if we are to believe what we hear, as they do of the Fejee Islanders. They cleaned the outside of the platter, and cared little for what was within. Having whitened their sepulchre, they were satisfied. But it was not the outer portals of Government House only that were trusted to sepoys. At the doorway, at the reception rooms, in the corridors, paced up and down the old troopers of the body-guard, dressed somewhat like our lancers; tall, white-mustachioed veterans, on whose hearts glittered many medals, clasps, and crosses won in action against Sikh and Affghan. I am not sure whether my own feeling of mild surprise, that at the Viceroy's palace, not a single English domestic was visible, would not be shared in by most of my countrymen. White-turbaned natives, with scarlet and gold ropes fastened round the waist, glided about in the halls; and some of the more important added to the dignity of their appearance by wearing large daggers in their cummerbunds.

At half-past six o'clock I waited upon Lord Canning, whom I found immersed in books and papers, and literally surrounded by boxes, "military," "political," "revenue," &c. I had never seen him before, to my knowledge; but the striking resemblance of the upper portion of his face to the portraits and busts of George Canning would, I think, have told me who he was. His Excellency was kind enough to explain to me at great length, and with remarkable clearness, the actual state of affairs at that time in India; to show me on the map what had been effected, and what yet remained to be done, in order to re-establish our power; and to indicate generally what the operations would be by which that object was to be effected. In doing so, it is true, Lord Canning took for granted I was in ignorance of what had happened; but, though a little time might have been lost, there was certainly no room left for misunderstanding upon my part. Looking at the map, the work seemed heavy. In Oude, Bundelcund, Goruckpore, Rohilcund, and portions of Central India, the British rule had ceased to exist for many months, and the rebel leaders almost fancied they were secure in their new possessions. He seemed proud—and, am I not bound to say, with justice?—of the exertions of his Government, to forward the troops up country with comfort and dispatch, and to provide for them when sick and wounded; but it struck me that he over-estimated the amount of work that can be effected by any one man, however zealous and self-sacrificing, unless indeed he be such an administrative giant as Cæsar or Napoleon. I was not astonished to find a Governor-General of India at such a time worn-looking, and anxious, and heavy with care; but when I learned incidentally, and not from his own lips, that he had been writing since early dawn that morning, and that he would not retire till twelve or one o'clock that night, and then had papers to prepare ere he started in the morning, I was not surprised to hear that the dispatch of public business was not so rapid as it might have been if Lord Canning had a little more regard to his own ease and health.

I told his Lordship that I was going to start for Cawnpore as soon as I possibly could; and he said he could and would facilitate that object by ordering a dâk to be laid for me, though he could not at all answer for what Sir Colin Campbell, as Commander-in-Chief, might do when I got to his camp. On that point I had but very small misgivings; for I could not but think that the excellent judgment and good sense of the Commander-in-Chief would lead him to the conclusion that there was no evil to be dreaded from my presence in his camp which he could not control, and which did not exist in greater force before my arrival; and that the advantages to be derived from a truthful narrative of what was done placed before the public, who would be scarcely satisfied with the short official reports that leisure and precedent prescribed to generals, in detailing the operations of war, would be considerable, whilst that narrative acted as an effectual antidote to the erroneous statements which were made in India out of ignorance or malice, and thence reached England, where they caused great anxiety and misapprehension. Lord Canning told me that whatever might be the views of Sir Colin Campbell—and on that point he could not speak, though he thought it probable I should find no difficulty there — he would let me have a letter which would show the General that there was no desire on the part of the Government to prevent my being in the British camp. In case of any difficulty, however, his Excellency assured me that I would find every facility in accompanying the head-quarters of Jung Bahadoor with the British commissioner. In this and subsequent conversation that evening on the subject of the mutinies, the causes of them, the extent of the atrocities perpetrated by the sepoys, the stories of mutilations and outrage, the Governor-General evinced a remarkable analytical power, an ability of investigation, a habit of appreciating and weighing evidence, a spirit of justice and moderation, and a judicial turn of mind which made a deep impression upon me. His opinions once formed seem "inébranlables;" and his mode of investigation, abhorrent from all intuitive impulses, and dreading, above all things, quick decision, is to pursue the forms of the strictest analysis, to pick up every little thorn on the path, to weigh it, to consider it, and then to cast it aside or to pile it with its fellows; to go from stone to stone, strike them and sound them, and at last on the highest point of the road, to fix a sort of granite pedestal declaring that the height is so and so, and the view is so and so—so firm and strong that all the storm and tempest of the world may beat against it and find it immovable. But man's life is not equal to the execution of many tasks like these; such obelisks so made and founded, though durable, cannot be numerous.

January 30th. — Went after breakfast with Hume (Dr.) formerly Principal Medical Officer of the Fourth Division in the Crimea, and visited the hospital for sick and wounded officers at No. 1, Little Russell Street; a large detached house, standing, as do all the houses of the British residents in this part of Calcutta, in an enclosure within high walls, with a bit of green and a few trees around it. The rooms were large, airy, and sweet, and I was glad to see so few wounded men there. Some were old friends, and their wounds and sickness gave them little concern now they were "going home." Pets there were plenty—mongoose, monkeys, and birds. There was a kind of reading-room supplied with books and papers; the meals were good and wholesome. Dr. Ligertwood took the greatest pleasure in showing all the means and appliances he had contrived for the comfort of his patients in this establishment, which is nearly self-supporting, owing to the payments received from the officers. The latter told me that nothing could exceed the kindness of the ladies of Calcutta, who sent them books and luxuries, and took them out to air in their carriages. Not one of them could tell me of a single mutilation of any woman to which they could depose of their personal knowledge. Delafosse, one of the two survivors of the Cawnpore massacre (at the boats), was, as well as I can recollect, in this hospital, but he was asleep, and I would not disturb him. I say as well as I recollect, for my Diary, which was sent to London for this month and part of February, was lost in the Ava, and I have only a few rough notes in some odd leaves of pocket-books here and there to remind me. From Russell Street, drove over by a very dusty road, which encircles the plain and fort glacis, to the Orphan School at Kidderpore, which has been converted into an hospital for soldiers, and is under the charge of my old friend Longmore of the 19th, with Chargneau of the Rifle Brigade in charge under him. The rooms are very large and lofty, and the men had plenty of room, but the heat, in some places, set at defiance all efforts to prevent close smells. The sick of the 54th, the regiment which had acted so nobly when their ship Sarah Sands took fire, are here, many suffering from diarrhœa and dysentery. There are here, also, a number of wounded men from recent fights at Lucknow, Cawnpore, &c.; several with legs and arms carried away by round shot. I passed one poor fellow with a stump outside the clothes. "Was that a round-shot, my man?" "No, Sir, indeed it was not! that was done by a sword!" On inquiry, I found that a great proportion of the wounds, many of them very serious and severe, were inflicted by the sabre or native tulwar. There were more sword-cuts in the two hospitals than I saw after Balaklava. The men were cheerful, and spoke highly of the attention paid to them. By each man's bedside, or charpoy, was a native attendant, who kept the flies away with a whisk, administered the patient's medicine, and looked after his comforts. There is something *almost* akin to pleasure in visiting well-ordered hospitals, and I renewed my old sensations with interest, but it is a feeling which I would fain combat and remove. There is a morbid and unwholesome excitement about it, after all.

Paid a visit to Sir Robert Garrett, whom I was glad to find looking just as well as in the old days when he used to trudge past my hut with his "trench-stick" in his hand. He is going to take his command at Umballah, but I think the old soldier would be better pleased if Sir Colin gave him a division in the field. There was in the room a lady who had been besieged in the Residency at Lucknow, and who had just arrived in Calcutta. From her I heard some strange tales respecting the internal condition of the garrison. Whilst some were starving, half fed on unwholesome food, and drinking the most unpleasant beverages, others were living on the good things of the land, and were drinking Champagne and Moselle, which were stored up in such profusion that there were cartloads remaining when the garrison marched out. There was a good deal of etiquette about visiting and speaking in the garrison! Strange, whilst cannon-shot and shell were rending the walls about their ears—whilst disease was knocking at the door of every room, that those artificial rules of life still exercised their force; that petty jealousy and "caste" reigned in the Residency; the "upper ten" with stoical grandeur would die the "upper ten," and as they fell composed their robes after the latest fashion. It is a pity that our admiration for the heroism of that glorious defence should be marred by such stories as these; but I felt the lady was speaking the truth.

There was a kind of grand dinner at the Club to-day, and a very good one. Among others there I met Fairholme, of the Navy, who did me a great kindness without knowing it once, for which I now thank him. He carried over to Kamiesh, one day that I was more dead than alive, my despatch for the mail, containing a description of the attack on the Redan. The mail had started from head-quarters, when after thirty-six hours of excitement and hard work and want of sleep, I rode across to the huts, but Lieutenant Fairholme had just started with his little escort and the despatches for the mail; •from the rising ground at the back of head-quarters I could see the cloud of dust which enveloped them, and digging spurs into poor old Bob, I managed to come up with him, and, thanks to his courtesy, to save myself a journey—a saving which I converted into the sweetest sleep I ever enjoyed.

These dinners at the Bengal Club are by no means so good as they are thought to be; that is, they are not equal to a dinner at Philippe's, or the Maison Dorée, or the Clarendon, or at a good club, but they are undoubtedly very cheerful contrasts to the meals on board ship, or to the banquets at the dâk bungalows, which latter are, on the whole, monotonous. The Bengal Club is cunning enough in its liquors. The wines are admirably iced—the Champagne dry and good, and the sherry wholesome. Curry of prawns, I will none of you! Away those pleasant fictions, that the giant prawns come from a salt-water lake into which the Hooghly or its horrors never flow! Soup—never so pleasant as when 'tis hot in hottest weather; soup almost gelatinous in its strength, and gram-fed mutton and a fowl-curry; there, one is enough for me, but the gentlemen around me eat everything. They had tiffin at two; hot lunch and ale and brandy-pawnee. *Hinc perfervidum jecur!* A very social and agreeable sort of men, but their conversation is of mint, and anise, and cummin of Calcutta, which is to me of interest limited by amount of knowledge. A rubber terminates the evening—*igneus est ollis robur*—and causes discussion, in which the aid of the deities Hoyle, Major A—, and Major B—, is angrily involved.

January 31*st.*—Had many visitors. Among them General Michell, who is going to his command at the Bombay side, General Dupuis, Colonel Adye, &c. Throwing myself on the kindness of my friends, and throwing two of them over, I went off with Mr. Meredith Townsend, of *The Friend* of India, to Serampore. Crossed the river by boat near the railway station, where a carriage awaited us, and thence drove through thick woods of cocoa-plantains, &c., lined with native huts and miserable villages—the Southwark of Calcutta—for some sixteen miles to the village or station of Serampore, which is on the right bank of the Hooghly, opposite the station of Barrackpore. The latter, with its pretty park, in which is the Governor-General's summer residence, and the snow-white houses of the station, makes a fair show from the opposite bank. Serampore—which still retains traces of its Danish origin in a certain neatness and rigidity of outline, and in substantial houses, one of which belonged to my host, and was decorated with portraits of honest-looking Holsteiners—is famous in the annals of missionary enterprise, and, let me add, of missionary devotion, if not of success, in India, and the records of the good men's lives who made it the scene of their labours possess an enduring interest for all Christians. When we arrived, my attention was directed to several matters of a controversial, or, at least, of a discussionable character. However, I had not got my eyesight sufficiently clear in this Indian sun to examine the objects set before me.

But what I was looking for, and had been seeking as we came along, as an antiquary would hunt for an inscription, or a botanist for a new plant, was a white face amid these leagues of black and brown fellow-creatures, with scant attire, who are swarming in and out of their miserable dwellings. I see not one, not one, till I enter Mr. Townsend's house. It was the first impression made on my mind as to our numerical nothingness amidst the people. All the splendour of Calcutta carriages could not efface it. When I crossed over to Barrackpore, instead of looking at the fine trees in the park, or admiring the outside of the Governor-General's country house, or the lawn and bungalow and officers' quarters, I was looking out for white faces, and here at last I found them. Under every shady clump of trees, at every lazy corner, were groups of great, well-made, six-foot soldiers, in red coatees (for the tunic cannot be enumerated among the causes of the sepoy mutiny), but their faces were black. I never set eyes on men who had more the look of soldiers when their backs were turned. These were the men of the disarmed regiments, two of which are stationed at Barrackpore, held in watch and ward by one English regiment. The men saluted us as we passed, but my companions made a point of *not* returning their salutes, or taking the least notice of the men. Several of them were doing a mockery of sentry's duty, with canes instead of firelocks. It is said they have recently become civil—almost abject in their demeanour. A few weeks ago they were insolent and haughty enough; even now the officer in command (the veteran Hearsay) is frequently alarmed by reports of plots and conspiracies, and the Europeans are ever on the alert. The guards on the governor's house were Europeans. They, and a few officers lounging about near their bungalows, owned the white faces to which I have adverted. I could only wish the owners were better employed, but there is doubtless great difficulty in the question. If these men were dismissed at once, no precautions in our power could prevent their joining the rebels if they were disposed to do so. And little else would have been left to them to do. Being mostly men of Oude, now occupied by the enemy, they would have been treated everywhere with suspicion and distrust. It seems an absurd way of paralyzing a portion of our much-needed Europeans, to keep them watching sepoys who cannot be trusted. The remedy is not so easy. One was suggested—that "the sepoys should be let break loose if they liked, and that then our men should dispose of them." But we in India, are a Christian people, and the Government adopted another course. It has cost money, and it has, to some extent, deprived the army of the services of soldiers much wanted. It has also created anxiety and alarm, but the question was full of difficulties, and I have not yet seen any solution of it proposed by those who grumble the most loudly, nor indeed any plan open to the Governor-General except that which he followed.

If I were to stop here and describe Serampore and Barrackpore, which, by the bye, I should be little competent to do, I shall never get up to camp, and the news is that Sir Colin will move immediately. It is the opinion of some people in Calcutta that he might have taken Lucknow the other day. What would have become of Windham, of Cawnpore, and of the women and children?

Late at night, and with some difficulty, we managed

to get a boat—the "we" being a gentleman who was, I think, Principal, or one of the professors of the Doveton College, and myself; and, I am bound to say, that we did not, in getting the conveyance, act quite like Israelites in whom there was no guile. Standing on the muddy and slippery shore of the river, now running with stream and ebb tide fast towards Calcutta, we hailed boat after boat of the many which were gliding down noiselessly in the moonlight; but as soon as the boatmen heard what we wanted, being bound most probably for some intermediate ghaut, they shot out from the bank and left us lamenting. At last craft prevailed. A boat ran in, in reply to a mild hail, and the moment her bow came to the bank, sliding and slipping through the mud, we boarded her. At the words "to Calcutta," delivered in the vernacular, a loud wail was raised by the boatmen, who declared they could not go; but we were now the masters, and evading an attempt to leave us in the boat by pushing her off from the bank before the boatmen could reach it, we pushed off into the stream, and there was nothing left for the grumbling natives but to take to their oars and talk of "backsheesh." This little act of piracy was avenged by many insects, which immediately came out of the cabin of the boat and the woodwork, or flew off from the shore, and devoured me, at least, with avidity. Under other circumstances, I should have much enjoyed that long moonlight slide down the great river, which ran along with a soft gurgling song, as though rejoicing in its coming liberty. In the indistinct light the wooded banks softened into a velvet forest, amid which shone out at intervals the white houses of merchants. The noise of tom-toming in the villages, the braying of innumerable dogs, and the wild choruses of the jackals as they swept along the shores, gave the scene its true character, and effaced the impressions of civilized life produced by white palaces and park-like woods. For more than two hours we glided on, the boatmen rowing to the sound of a wild and not quite unmusical strain, and guiding the boat as the current was strongest, from bank to bank or in mid stream; and at last we became aware that the villages on shore were running as it were into a continuous line; that big native boats, with uncouth rigging, were moored in clumps here and there off the banks; that the dogs barked louder, the jackals yelped less frequently, and the hum of voices and the noise of drums waxed stronger, and now and then great budgerows crossed our path, or lay anchored in the tideway. Some distance before us, as we swept close in shore, a red light streamed upwards into the air, through a cloud of smoke, which looked black and heavy in the moonlight. As we got nearer, I could make out some seven or eight fires, all together, some blazing fiercely, with sparks flying upwards, others in a dead red smoulder. The glare fell on the black faces and white turbans and dresses of a small crowd of natives, who were busied among the fires. Some threw in fresh logs, or moved the piles to make them burn quicker; others sat round the fires silently; others ran about in an excited way, tossing their arms as if in frantic joy, or grief. All around were the black walls of the houses, which set, as it were, the fires and their attendants in a framework, completed by the river, across which the flames cast long black shadows, as the figures passed to and fro, conquering the moonlight in their power. It was a most wonderful and striking picture—nothing I have ever seen came near to it for variety of effect. The black figures, streaked with white waistbands and turbans—the contrast between the repose of the groups seated near each fire with the energetic, active, and ceaseless movement of those who were running about —the fires slumbering out quietly, or glowing with the dull red of charcoal, or blazing, hissing, and splintering into sparks, which rose from the many tongues of flame that cleft the dark clouds of smoke rolling out heavily towards us in the night wind—the mighty river rushing by like a torrent of quicksilver, striving in vain to carry off the shadows which ever dinted it from the ghastly bank—those wild weird men dancing like demons.—"Pooh! what is this dreadful smell— like—like coarse roasting meat?" I glanced at my companion, who was holding his nose, and in reply to my look, he said, "It's one of the BURNING GHAUTS!" "Boatmen! boatmen! pull for your lives!" It wanted very little to make me sick to death. I remember such another horror in an old book of travels—"cannibals feasting by moonlight."

Not very long after we passed those incremations I was seated in the drawing-room of the Bengal Club, with mirrors and lights, and tables covered with books and papers all around me, while skilful cooks were preparing supper, and the wine was getting *frappé* artistically. In India, indeed, extremes meet. Heard dreadful stories of these ghauts, and of the deeds supposed to be done at them. How the last offices are sometimes complicated with parricide and murder, how the old are brought down to die, and are smothered with the filthy mud which is thrust into mouth and nostrils, the screams of the murdered being overwhelmed in the infernal din which is raised in mockery of grief, and such like tales that make one's blood run cold. And we are the legislators, the law executors, and the teachers of this people! If the vices attributed to the Hindoo by the English exist to their full extent as described—if youth is made inexpressibly corrupt, and age is a maximized villany—if infanticide and parricide are practices and customs of the people—how is it that the race itself maintains its vitality — that it increases whilst the Mussulman declines — that its numbers show no mark of diminution and no sign of physical deterioration?

February 1st.—This morning to Mr. Cecil Beadon, who gave me an order for a post dâk (or what in Russia would be called a *padarodjnic*), which I had to communicate to the postmaster, and which will entitle me to one of the dâks or relays of horses for Wednesday next. The Government has hired all the vehicles and horses of the private companies, and every sort of quadruped and carriage on the main trunk road, for the public service. Mr. Beadon, who is a man of great importance, as Secretary of Government in Lord Canning's absence—and otherwise—is said to be a man of ability, though his name is not much known out of India. I found him courteous. He is far above the middle height; has a good head; clear, intelligent eye; straight, vigorous figure; and, altogether, is as unlike the popular notion of an old Indian as man can well be. If you met him in England, you would say he lived a good deal by the cover side, and that his hunters cost him a great deal of money. What wonderful piles of papers Indian officials get about them! I have been in all the great public offices at home, and have seen the interior of minister's workshops, but never did I behold out of Calcutta such heaps of despatch boxes, such mounds of record boxes, such vast fabrics of pigeon-holes, such *abandon* of red tape!

Thence to lunch with my old acquaintaince, Major-General Dupuis, where I met Colonel Adye, a name well known in the Crimean camp, and in the corps to which he belongs, as that of a most excellent soldier and thorough good fellow. In the course of conversation I heard enough to make me believe that the officers of the Royal Artillery in India—and certainly those in the higher ranks—thought they had not been quite well treated by the Commander-in-Chief. General Dupuis, for instance, was sent out by the Commander-in-Chief to command the Royal Artillery in India. When he saw Sir Colin, he was told to remain some time at Calcutta to superintend the disembarkation and arrangements connected with the force at his command, Colonel Adye, as his brigade-major, of course being with him. As soon as a considerable force of artillery had landed, and gone up to Sir Colin, then preparing for his relief of the Residency garrison, the general went up to Cawnpore, and was by no means well received by the Commander-in-Chief. Whereupon Dupuis sent in his resignation, but he withdrew it on the understanding that he was to be permitted to accompany the field force. However, it would seem as if he did something which displeased the Commander-in-Chief, for in a day or two Sir Colin sent him orders to go to Calcutta, as the Governor-General had informed him the head-quarters of artillery was to be at Dum-Dum, or Barrackpore. Ere he could get down, however, the Gwalior Force attacked Windham, and both Dupuis and Adye rendered services which were warmly acknowledged by that officer on the day when our troops were obliged to retreat into the *tête-de-pont*, and lost their camp. In their opinion Windham was placed in the most difficult circumstances, and did the best he could—an opinion which is fortified by Sir Colin's last despatch in reference to the action. The whole truth of the affair cannot be made public yet; and, indeed, it would at any time come with bad grace from the lips of any officers of rank, who would find themselves in telling it obliged to make painful accusations.

Dined at the Advocate-General's (Mr. Ritchie), where there was a small and agreeable party, and went afterwards to a ball given in Fort William by Colonel Mundy and the officers of Her Majesty's 19th, at which I met many old friends and acquaintances. The arrangements were admirable. The rooms—curious, quaint, old barrack chambers — were well lighted, decorated with flags, flowers, and fire-arms; bowers and pleasant arcades were improvised in the open. Dancing vigorous, music good. The supper-rooms gave one an exalted notion of the resources of Calcutta, and one could not help asking himself, " Has there been a mutiny at all? Is this a delusion? Do the enemy still hold Oude, Rohilcund, Jhansi, Calpee, and vast tracts of Central India?"

CHAPTER IX.

Preparing for a start.—The king of Oude's menagerie.—Simon and Sally Bridget.—My fellow-traveller, Dr. Mouat.—The Rajah of Pachete.—Raneegunj.—A mess-dinner.—Camp of Government elephants.—Locomotion by gharry.—A shattered wheel and its consequences.—Fording a river.—Numerous tanks, birds and squirrels.—Bungalows.—Theory and practice.—" Serry Shrab."—Approach to Benares.—The Holy Ganges.

February 2nd.—Busy making preparations for my start. The postmaster cannot give me a dâk before the 4th. In India the disturbance caused by the movement of great bodies is widely felt. For instance, the Governor-General, in moving to Allahabad the other day, absorbed all the bullock-waggons on the road *for five days*. When Lord Dalhousie crossed the Ganges, he had *one hundred elephants* in his train. Sir Colin Campbell's baggage, &c., extended *for eighteen miles*, when he came down from Lucknow. The preparations to be made for going a journey up country in India are very troublesome and expensive, and at first a European thinks they are supererogatory, whilst his favoured and cherished campaigning utensils, such as a well-fitted canteen, are pronounced to be useless. It was just at this crisis that my man Simon deserted me. He was invisible all day—a great increment of trouble to my good friend D——.

Dined with Colonel Champneys, who certainly deserves his reputation as a Calcutta Lucullus, and who is more—a kindly, genial host. He has a dreadful *rôle* to fill, for as Auditor-General he has to clip and cut at pay and allowances—the latter of which, in India, are subjects of incessant contentions. At dinner met Colonel Lugard, Captain Mallison, a very intelligent officer, who seems to have paid great attention to Indian politics; another officer, whose name I forget; Captain D——, and one of the principal Calcutta merchants.

It is strange enough that the nation which is so chary of any appearance of meanness or unfair dealing in its acts, should be so indifferent to the most calumnious accusations against those to whom it delegates power in remote parts of the world. As far as I know, the people cared very little about the monster indictment against Warren Hastings. All the wondrous eloquence of his accusers failed to create any popular excitement against the man for acts done thousands of miles away. But suppose they had been committed, or said to be perpetrated, in Ireland, in Scotland, or the Channel Islands? So to-night I hear that the menagerie of the King of Oude, as much his private property as his watch or turban, were sold under discreditable circumstances, and his jewels seized and impounded, though we had no more claim on them than on the Crown diamonds of Russia. Do the English people care for those things? Do they know them? The hundred millions of Hindostan know them well, and care about them too.

February 3rd.—An awful night with mosquitoes. Got up in the morning with my eyes bunged up, which did not account, however, for my not seeing Simon, for he had not been in all day or all night, and the mosquitoes had taken advantage of his absence to carry the curtains by storm. As I was in my bath the little gentleman crept into my room, and demurely announced that "he look for dhobyman for master's clothes all night." Sit down and write all day, whilst Simon, who is whiter in the face, unsteadier in the legs, and redder in the eyes than usual, is busied with the final packing. A day of hard work, in which all Calcutta is tabooed to me. To bed and to mosquitoes at midnight, quite worn out with heat and labour.

February 4th.—Dawn saw me up, and busy. Finished my letters and sent them off.* Breakfasted at eight at the United Service Club, and received more last words of counsel from my good friend D——, who had done his best to fit me out in an old Indian style, even to pepper, salt, and candles. Simon, whose exertions in pursuit of the dhobyman were attended by a violent thirst, holds a levée of his relatives. His wife, Sally Bridget, richly attired in bangles and fine robes, and though not fair, by no means unpleasant to look upon, brings her little son to me, as much as to say, "take care of his father;" but, in fact, it is his father who must take care of me. The heat is so great in Calcutta, that I am anxious to be out of it in the field once more, though I hear it will be much hotter up country. Set pistols and rifle in order, as one travels armed now-a-days, and drove down to river, which we crossed to station in steamer. At 9·30, the train, of which the third-class carriages are filled with natives, penned in as close as sheep in a market van, moves off from the station. In my letter to *The Times*, which consisted of pages torn out of my note-book, I gave my impressions of the scenery

---

* They went down in the Ava, were recovered, but were late and illegible.

and the country. The whole looked like a flooded brick-field, amid which spring up groves of dates, plantains, and dirty villages, made of mud and bamboo matting; and, crouched under clumps of trees, the natives—men, women, and children—are making bricks, or paddling in the mud, hunting for the tiniest sticklebacks and minnows of an Indian sort, with much eagerness, by means of puerile little nets. They are burnt and black as the land itself; miserably clad; the children, up to six or seven, being in *impuris naturalibus*.

My fellow-traveller, Dr. Mouat, the able Inspector of Prisons, explains many things to me, and from him I derive much information as to external objects which strike me. He has just returned from an interesting excursion on the Andaman Islands, or, more properly speaking, to them, with a view of ascertaining their fitness for penal settlements. Like Sterne's starling, prisoners there may cry "I can't get out" for ever. But there is no food on those savage-haunted isles, and I think I remember water is scarce. One of the savages was captured, and Dr. Mouat gave me a photograph of the interesting creature, who must have been of a very low type of the human race. However, there is little proof that they are cannibals, as is popularly supposed, though they are unmitigated savages.

Dr. Mouat is on his way to Burdwan, which is at one of the stations on the line, to take a look at the Rajah of Pachete, who is confined in the gaol there, awaiting his trial on a charge of disaffection to Government. I got out with the worthy doctor, and paid a visit to the Rajah, whom we disturbed at his dinner. The gaol is a very discreditable establishment—a series of long stone sheds, one story high, situated in a court surrounded by a high wall. In the court were prisoners heavily shackled, picking oakum, and pounding a sort of red earth into powder by rude levers, all in the broiling sun. The warders wore their tulwars by their sides. Entering a room in one of the sheds, we saw a stern, rather ill-favoured young man, seated cross-legged on a mat on the ground, with some four or five natives standing before him, their hands crossed on their breasts. Silver dishes, clay pots, remains of curry and rice, showed the Rajah was just finishing his mid-day meal. Like the French prisoners, whose moroseness astonished our cockney friend in the play, the Rajah was by no means cheerful, and eyed us unpleasantly, and "wanted to know what he was there for?" The Government had received information that the people of his district, which is not far from Raneegunj, had threatened to deliver him by force, and Dr. Mouat was about to assist at his removal.* Before I left the prison I visited the women's ward, which was in a most disgraceful condition. There is no classification of prisoners. The young girl committed for a theft is thrust among old hags who are poisoners and child-murderers. This is not becoming to a civilized Government; but I was assured the prison would be improved. At 4 o'clock, after a hot and tedious journey of

---

* Several months afterwards he was tried, and, as well as I recollect, acquitted. But he was nevertheless detained in prison by the Government. The courts at Calcutta refused to liberate him, and when I left India, the Rajah was still, I believe, in custody.

120 miles, the train shot us out amid a heap of cinders, and a wooden station at its terminus—Raneegunj. A level arid country, a few trees, some faint outlines of hills in the distance, and smoke rising from a clump of tall chimneys. A white-washed, high-roofed, one-storied building in front, was indicated as the dâk bungalow and posting station. The baboo informed me all the gharrys were gone, and that I must wait till to-morrow evening. But was not the bungalow open? Fortunately, there is a little station here, consisting of a few huts, in which are the commissariat officers appointed to look after the troops starting hence up country, and a few troops are encamped at a little distance from the terminus. Captain Sadler is kind enough to ask D——, who has accompanied me in his good-natured solicitude so far, and myself, to their mess-dinner. It takes place in a shed of matting, and is very pleasant, Brigadier Horsford, of the Bengal Artillery, presiding, and some five or six officers forming the party. After dinner, a young bear and a beautiful tame little fawn introduced, and behave very properly. Break up early, and D—— returns to Calcutta by the night-train. I go to feed my mosquitoes in the bungalow. In the night, Sir Robert Garrett and Major Oxenden arrive, and Major Dallas, the General's Aide, drops in later. Much struck by the adroit manner in which my man Simon, as soon as he has tucked in the treacherous mosquito-curtains, rolls himself up adroitly in a napkin and goes to sleep, outside the door, apparently a huge snowball.

February 5th.—Breakfasted and lunched at the hospitable little mess. By the bye, " the authorities" here tell me they have not seen or heard of any mutilated women passing through this station, or going by rail to Calcutta. The day is intensely hot, as I feel when I take a short walk over to the camp of government elephants, only a few hundred yards away. There are seventy or eighty of these huge quadrupeds drawn up in double rows, heavily ironed by fore and hind legs, each with a large heap of leaves and branches before him, which he uses to eat, or to throw over his back, or to whisk the flies with. Their keepers live in wigwams of straw, reeds, and grass, about three feet high—the women sit at the entrances, the children creep about among the elephants' huge heels, a wild, squalid-looking race. The ground is covered, as is the neighbourhood of all road-sides and camps in India, with bones of cattle and animals, white as ivory, and with horns and teeth of cattle. At various distances outside the camp of elephants are picketed, sentry-wise, well secured to the trunks of trees, and stakes driven deep into the ground, evil disposed and unsafe members of the community, who are in love, or are mad, or are jealous, and wicked. One of these was covered with bullet marks, having been practised at by a body of soldiers, but he would neither be killed nor give in. He had covered his back with dust, straw, and leaves, not in humiliation, but to keep off sun and flies; and he was daintily sucking sugar-cane, when I saw him, as quiet as an alderman at turtle time. Another creature was pointed out to me as being far more than 100 years old—a warty, gnarled, grizzly, old elephant, which looked as if he was made out of old oak stumps, and has the most intensely knowing little shrewd grey eye I ever saw in my life. He looked as if he could tell us

all about the Rise and Progress of the British Rule in India, and it was something more than curious to look at a beast that might have seen Clive at the battle of Plassey—that was advanced in years when we were fighting Mahrattas and Pindarees, and were invading Rohilcund for our good ally the Newab Vizier of Oude. Bulky as the elephant is, there is no repose about him; some part or other of his great carcase is for ever in motion—an ear is flickered to and fro, or the tail is switched about, or there is one foot propped against a leg, and all the time the trunk is at work, like a huge snake, coiling itself up or stretching itself out, or turning up or down, or trumpeting with pleasure or pain.

I passed the afternoon among the elephants till 4 P.M., when it was announced that the gharrys were ready—and so indeed four or five bakers' carts, or penitentiary laundresses' vans—boxes of wood on wheels—were duly waiting for our accommodation. An inspection made it appear that there were slides which pushed aside, or opened out, and served as doors or windows. The traveller, when he has one to himself, gets his bed made, and stretches luxuriously at full length; for a spare cushion is made to fit the interval between the seats, and beneath it is stowed some of the luggage. There are shelves and lockers at the ends of the vehicle, and—when it is well slung on the springs, and the four wheels are properly consorted —it is not by any means, apart from the question of horses, an uncomfortable means of locomotion. Like the Russian boyard in his carriage, or tarantassee, the Indian traveller lives in his gharry, sleeps in it, and often eats in it. Ere we started, one of the party had a row with a driver; he took up his horn, which hung from the box, and blew it—and the fellow, who was a Mussulman, swore it was defiled—a question of rupees. There were only four gharrys available. General Garrett had one—Dallas and Oxenden another—Sladen, of the Madras Fusiliers, and Surgeon Beath the third—and the fourth fell to my lot. Simon got on the roof, the driver—of course a tall, heavy man—dressed in a tattered blue caftan with a red trimming, bore on his heart a brass badge with the words "mail driver." With him was a sprite, whose business I found was to flog and otherwise excite the horses to start and keep at it; and, after much reluctance cunningly overcome, the horses rushed off in a cloud of dust at a gallop, and away we went along the main trunk road, which lay like a great white riband straight before us. * * * *

I was awoke by a violent shock about three hours after we started—the carriage was nearly on its side—the driver was shouting furiously—and his poor sprite lay with a fractured leg by the road-side. The tire of the fore wheel had come off, and the spokes were shattered to pieces. We were nearly thirty miles from Raneegunj, where alone another wheel could be procured. This was an inauspicious commencement to our journey. The driver must ride back to Raneegunj—Simon must start for the nearest police-station, to get some Chowkeydars to watch the carriage—and I am left alone in the dark with the poor lad, who is moaning and crying with pain. It was a long, sad vigil. After a time the moon rose. Jackals and wolves howled in the field close at hand—a few natives crept past like ghosts—not one stayed to comfort the poor boy, whose language I did not understand, and who rejected the flask I offered him. In a couple of hours —they seemed long ones—Simon came back with half-a-dozen native policemen. They lighted a fire in the road, and sat round it talking till dawn. At last another gharry had arrived from Raneegunj—the luggage was transferred to it, and the boy with the broken leg was taken on one of the policemen's shoulders.

Soon after we started, at five o'clock or so, the carriage again halted. The door was opened by a wild-looking man, who, with signs, seemed to intimate that Simon had fallen off and broken his thigh. The more correct interpretation was given by Simon himself—who made his appearance at the other side, and explained to me that the ferryman wished me to get out, as the water at the ferry was as high as his thigh, and would come into the gharry and wet me. And so we forded the Burakur River, the carriage being pushed and dragged over a rude bed of sand by a band of coolies. The pace is good when the horses do start—the stages are only about five miles long, and the driver goes at full speed, but the quadrupeds are painful to look upon. At two o'clock arrived in Nemcaghaut, and found two officers in possession of the bungalow, who shared their rations with me.

The country is changing its character, and rises into broken hills and tumuli covered with brush and scrub, which seem to assume a mountainous character in front of us. Dark clouds rest on the range of hills which bound the western horizon. At seven o'clock, as we toil up the Parisnath hills, we enter the very heart of the thunder-storm—the darkness is profound

—the rain falls like the rush of a river—the lightning quivers, flashes, and darts about in balls of fire, and the thunder never ceases. Suddenly, my rifle, which is slung from the roof of the carriage, seems a blaze of light—the horse shies and stops, and a crash of thunder shakes the very earth. I get out, and find the driver and his help under the carriage—the water streams down the road like a brook. With the help of Simon, I roused the men to push the carriage through the storm. I was in my slippers, and as I shoved, my foot came on something soft and round, which moved from under it—a living thing. "It snake, sir;" said Simon, "that get out of hole not to be drown!" As the officers told me that a man had been carried off the road by a tiger a few nights before, and the driver said there were many about to-night, I began to comprehend that I was travelling in India. All night we toiled up hill through the tempest which abated after midnight, and I was glad to lie down in the gharry, soaked as I was with rain, where I soon fell into a sound sleep.

February 7th.—Passed Shergotty about nine. Here a baboo, who spoke English very well, came out of the post-office, professed a sudden attachment to me, and begged I would take him into my service as a writer, "for," quoth he, "I know it will be my fortune if the lord will grant this petition." He told me further, there were "plenty budmashes about," but they fear to come near the trunk road. A detachment is stationed here to watch them. I am so anxious to get on, I stop at no bungalows if I can help it, and travel day and night. It struck me the Shergotty people had an evil look about them, and scowled in the white face that passed them so carelessly. The country has resumed its dead level character about here, and is fertile and well cultivated. Tanks are numerous. The villages rarely adorn the road-sides, but seek the privacy of distant groves, but there are some long straggling bazaars, which put me in mind of the entrance into a country town in Connaught, stretching on each side of the way at intervals. About the tanks are many sorts of birds, and the trees by the road-sides give refuge to others, and to innumerable striped squirrels very pretty and playful. I have observed cranes, whimbrels, himantopi, avosets, sanderlings, hoopoes, jays (very common and very beautiful), king crows, crow pheasants, minas. Shrikes perch on the telegraph wires, which are also the favourite haunt of the jay and fly-catchers. Kites and buzzards fill the air near the villages, and now and then a withered tree presents a horrid crop of satiated vultures. Huge trains of bullock carts, with Government brands upon them, pass to and fro in clouds of dust, which with the heat after mid-day render the journey by no means agreeable.

At Muddenpore, 306 miles from Calcutta, came upon Sladen and Beath in the bungalow. "A cock is sacrificed," to furnish a very tough meal. The bungalows, though varying greatly in actual comfort, are all on the same plan. A quadrangular building of masonry, one story high, with a high-peaked roof of thatch or tiles, projecting so as to form porticoes and verandahs. The house divided into "suits" of two, three, or four rooms, provided more or less imperfectly with charpoys, deal tables, and a very deteriorated tripodic and bipedal establishment of chairs. Windows more or less damaged as to glass and frames. Doors with perverse views as to their original purposes. Off each room, however, is that universal bath-room, and the earthen jars of cool water. The interior accommodations of the bungalows depend a good deal on their position. None are exempt from the visits of travellers—all ought to be ready to receive them, but in point of fact some are naturally much more frequented than others, in consequence of their situations being better adapted for halting. In some, the whole of the apparatus consists of a broken glass or so; a common earthenware plate; a knife, of no particular use in cutting; and a fork of metal, from which one or more of the prongs has lapsed. There are no napkins or tablecloths; the table is a rude piece of deal. The khitmutgar is a dilapidated old man, who places his hands together in extreme deprecation the moment he sees you, and to every question, says, "Nae hai Kodawun." (There is none, my lord!) But your servant is placing your little private store on the table. Your salt and pepper-castors (which even go out into society with you under many circumstances) are brought forth, and the death-cry of Dame Poulet or Lord Gallus proclaims that you will feast on curry speedily. In other bungalows there is a full establishment of knives, forks, plates, dishes, table-covers, and napkins. Pale ale and soda-water are not unknown, and the khitmutgar is cunning in condiments, and has store of groceries. The bungalow generally stands at a distance of twenty or thirty yards from the road, in an enclosure, which contains the kitchen and sleepng-places of the khitmutgar and his servants. The former is generally a man of the sweeper caste, a circumstance which does not recommend his cookery to fastidious old Indians. The Government charges eight annas, or one shilling, to each traveller for the use of the bungalow whilst he halts; and a book is kept in which he enters his name, the time of his arrival and departure, the amount paid, and any remarks he pleases to insert respecting the attendance and state of the bungalow. Small as the charge is, there are frequent attempts to evade it. As to refreshments supplied by the khitmutgar there is no rule, and he charges as he pleases, or as you may bargain with him. These buildings, though in theory open to all, are in practice and reality reserved almost exclusively for Europeans. I never yet met a native gentleman stopping in one. I have looked over the registries of many, and found, perhaps in half-a-dozen instances in the space of a year, the name of an Anglicized baboo, or Parsee merchant, or native prince inscribed therein. No!—These and all such Government works are for the white man, and not for the black. The latter buries himself in the depths of some wretched bazaar, or in the squalid desolation of a tottering caravanserai. There would be as much indignation experienced at any attempt on the part of natives to use the stageing bungalows, as there is now expressed by some Europeans in Calcutta at their audacity in intruding upon "ladies and gentlemen" in first-class carriages.

Dined at Barroon bungalow, I think it is called, near the Soane, which was crossed by a fine bridge (my notes are very hazy, and I have no map). Sladen and the doctor were my *convives*, and we had a very remarkable old fluid brought to me by the khitmutgar, which he assured us was "serry shrab" (the wine of Xeres). The basis seemed to be a gooseberry ground up with ink and vinegar. It was only eight shillings, which, considering the extreme rarity of the drink, was by no means dear. To the gharry once more. Watched the sun, which looked like a sign-painter's moon, swoop into a dirty haze in the well-loved west. Where are the glories of the gorgeous east in scenery, clouds, skies, jewels, purple or fine linen or palaces? I see them not.

February 8th.—The same roll and rattle all night. I only wake up when there is a more violent row than usual on starting the horses. Look out and see the same poor sheds by the road-side, the same signal men with flambeaux, the same horses constantly reproduced as it were at each stage. Halted for a short time to breakfast at Nowbutpore bungalow, which is situated on the bank of a deep river called the Kurrummussa, crossed here by a fine stone bridge. *Si sic omnes!* The kit told us the bungalow had been destroyed by the Dinapore mutineers; the roof was new; the walls blackened with smoke. Wherever a bit of white could be found it was covered with the writing of men of the various detachments passing up towards Cawnpore. "Revenge your slaughtered countrywomen! To the —— with the bloody Sepoys!" Rough sketches of men hanging from trees and gallows, and various eulogiums of particular regiments, which if read by a foreigner would lead him to believe our soldiers were fond of blowing their own trumpets. Alas! some of these gallant fellows found their graves here; some were drowned in the shoals of the treacherous river in bathing; others died of disease, and their graves dot the enclosure, their names rudely carved on blocks of wood and trees fast vanishing.

* * * * * * * * * * *

As we approach the sacred city of Benares, the mass of people on the trunk road gives one the impression of a fair or procession. They are in small groups, or travel in large parties, men old and young, children and women. All shuffle up the fine dust with their toes, or pointed shoes, and the air is filled with a choking precipitate of the kunker, or carbonate of lime nodules, which form the metalling of the road. Long strings of creaking country-carts, heavily laden with bales of cotton, and drawn by mild-eyed humped oxen, followed each other continuously towards Calcutta. The human current headed the other way. It is worth observing the immense difference between the young and the old of the poorer classes of Hindoos. The former are broad-chested, straight, muscular men, albeit from sitting on their "hunkers," as the Irish say, the muscles of the thigh are drawn up flat from the knee to the hip, and give them rather hollow thighs and large knees. The old men are bowed, and feeble, and thin exceedingly; their skin hangs in loose folds crossed with innumerable wrinkles, and beneath it the lank muscles and sinews can be seen working distinctly on and over the bones of the skeleton; it is darker than when they are young, and the creases look white, so that they have a disagreeable animal look, and seem as if they were covered with a hide instead of a skin. Each man carries his bamboo latee shod with iron, with a bundle at one end, and the unfailing loto, a

VOL. I.　　　　　　　　　　　　　　L

polished brass pot, used for cooking, and drinking, and drawing water, for which purpose there is a string attached to it hung at the other. Poor is the wretch who carries one of earthenware, and poor as he is he must, like poverty, pay more dearly than wealth does ever, for his earthen pot is broken after every meal. The halting-places under the trees at each side of the road are full of broken earthenware and whitened bones of cattle. The women carry bundles animate and inanimate; the former seated cross-legs over one big hip, and clasping their bearers round the neck, the latter on their shoulders. Children of all ages, from five to twelve, toddle along the road, taking their share in the family troubles. In no instance is a friendly glance directed to the white man's carriage. Oh, that language of the eye! Who can doubt? who can misinterpret it? It is by it alone that I have learned our race is not even feared at times by many, and that by all it is disliked. Pray God I have read it falsely. These passers-by are wondrously squalid and poorly clad. But already I have been told I must not judge from appearances in India. The climate does not demand the use of clothes. The people, I am told, when they are *chez eux*, take off as much of their cotton covering as they can. But I see a native "swell" pass me in a tatterdemalion shigram, or a quaint little shed upon wheels, a kind of tray placed in a bamboo framework, and he is dressed in shawls, and wrapped in profuse clothes. That signifies nothing. "Those fellows like to show how rich they are by sporting fine cashmeres and gold embroidery." "Then when men are rich they dress well, and nakedness and rags are a sign of poverty?" "My dear sir, you are a griff; you don't understand those niggers yet." * * * * * * * * *

Before us there is a long line of roofs, temples, cupolas, pillars, minaret-like spires rising up on a high ridge, between which and the road as it melts away among the trees is a deep ravine. As we drive always amid dust, and trampling feet, and multitudes of people, the ridge seems to rise and the ravine to deepen. At last in the far side under the ridge, the eye catches a streak of water which becomes broader as we get nearer, and then we see that underneath the sacred city of Benares, washing the steps of its temples which stretch for miles along its bank, flows the Holy Ganges, spanned by a large bridge of boats. We had still a toilsome descent and struggle through deep sands left uncovered by the river, now at its lowest, ere the gharry arrived at the rude planks which form the causeway of the bridge. The city, seen from the right bank of the river, looks right glorious. If the Rhine flowed under the walls of the old city of Edinburgh, and swept along from the castle to Holyrood over the railway ravine, the scene would be *something* like that presented by Benares. But there are no lofty hills; no Calton; no Arthur's Seat in the distance. In lieu thereof, over the bridge towers the high mud walls and batteries of the Raj-ghaut fort, which was erected recently to secure the passage of the river. It was intensely hot when we got to the bridge, and the moment had just been selected to open it for the passage of some native boats downwards.

So General Garrett, his aide Dallas, Oxenden, and the whole party had to sit—and not cool their heels— till the process, which was directed by an extremely irritable and intoxicated European, was at an end. Then a drive through a long street of detached houses and gardens, along a road bordered by fine trees, in which screamed legions of green parroquets, brought us, after some two or three miles, to the English station, where we took refuge in Charles' Hotel. (N.B. A hotel in India, up country, is a place where you can get everything that you bring with you, and *nothing* else, except bed and soda-water.) Here we had dinner and much argument; in fact, whether it be the heat, or the curry, or the state of one's liver, it seems that the disposition of Englishmen alters in India, and they become very argumentative and theoretical. There is not one point or view we advance which is not sure to be contradicted. Even if one says, " This is a hot day," another is sure to observe, " I don't agree with you. There was a nice breeze about three o'clock this morning; and if you had ever been at Stuffcote you would not call this hot." " Stuffcote! why I have been there—was there for years—and *I* call it one of the coolest stations in India." " What! in August?" " Yes; especially and most particularly in August. I have felt chilly in August, sir," &c., &c.

CHAPTER X.

Outside of Benares.—Allahabad : the fort.—A canvas wall.—
The Governor-General's tent.—Lieut. P. Stewart.—A colonel
of sepoys.—Poor Clarke!—Question and answer.—Railway
terminus.—A short walk.—Gharrys for Cawnpore.—Sir Robert
Garrett's tongue.—Hall at Futtehpore.

February 9th.—Left Benares early, without seeing anything of it, except the long line of ghauts and temples, the outside of the college and of the church, the same of Dr. Ballantyne—whose name is identified with the former seat of learning, and whom I regretted I could not do more than shake for one moment by the hand—and the inside of Charles' Hotel. Our stout landlord, fertile-in-item-in-bill-compelling-resources, Saxonically and Bonifacically saw us off—a good easy man, who was happy in the belief that he kept rather a good hotel, and did good to all men thereby. The country outside the city is one great garden—fertile exceedingly; the road still thronged with cotton-carts, and pilgrims, and foot-passengers. On, on! all day, fast as we could go; but do what we could, daylight failed us ere the gharry reached the waste of sand which forms the uncovered bed of the Ganges, opposite Allahabad, and it was quite dark before we got on the bridge of boats which spans the now-diminished volume of the stream. Where to go, we knew not. The fort was closed at night-fall. The bungalow, when we reached it, was quite full; but we were told some tents were pitched on the esplanade in front of the fort, by an enterprising person, who called them a hotel; and there, in fact, after driving about for an hour, we found shelter. Not only were there sleeping-tents in this welcome little camp, but a mess-tent, in which supper was ready, and to which the travellers did full justice. Each had a tent to sleep in, and each slept well in it, spite of the sniffing and howling of the jackals.

February 10*th*.—Is it not hot this morning? But is not this tub, and the great generous jars of cold water—is not this glorious after the smother and heat of the long journey! And the khitmutgar tells us there is grilled morghie, and eggs, and bacon, and tea, and beer, and jam for breakfast, and plenty of hot chupatties. It is true the flies make a stand-up fight with us for our meal; but we beat them in the end. The quartermaster-general of this camp is a livery-stable keeper as well, and so I hire a buggy from him, and drive over to the fort, within which the Governor-General's camp is pitched. This fort is worthy of the best days of the great Mahomedan conquerors and rulers of India. It came upon me like the vision of some distant land—like Ehrenbreitstein, or Edinburgh, or some great middle-age fortress. A massive face of rich red solid masonry, garnished with Saracenic loopholes, and embrasures, and peepholes, towered up solemnly from the waters of the Jumna and Ganges, which here mingle at the point of the rectangle on which the fort is placed. This melts away into certain ravelins and bastions, garnished with guns *en barbette*, and with embrasures. Then there is a fine broad glacis with a deep ditch, revetted on scarp and counterscarp—drawbridges, portcullis, all the materia appearances of a great fortress are here. Strange, again, is it to think, that this city and those walls, which seem such essentials of our existence in India, were bestowed on us in times not beyond the memory of living man, by the ancestor of one who is now captive in our prisons. Excepting the rise of the United States, I know of nothing so rapid and so wonderful in the history of nations as the growth of our Indian empire. When Mandelslo, the attaché of the Duke of Schleswig-Holstein's envoy, whose travels, translated into English nearly 200 years ago, are well worth perusal now—when he, I say, visited India, he found the court of the Great Mogul in all its magnificence, and England was represented by a factory of merchants, at Ahmedabad, not remarkable for the purity of their lives or the cleanliness of their morals. How vast is now her empire in the East! how great her responsibilities! Had the gate through which I am now passing, been opened to the mutineers, who filled the station outside with murder and fire, it is not too much to say that, for the moment, the English empire in India was lost. All honour to the few who saved it! Had it been lost, there would have been scarce any one to blame. When Outram heard of our troubles, he wrote the most pressing and the most masterly state-paper respecting the paramount necessity of securing Allahabad. The necessity was admitted; the inability to meet it was deplored. Allahabad was saved by no act of Government, by no care of man; but by one of those extraordinary developments of accidental ability and energy in unlooked-for, and unexpected places, which are called interventions of Providence. Had such things taken place at Meerut, or Cawnpore, we might now be revelling in false security. Now, all we can say is, with Agag, "Surely the bitterness of death is past!"

In a large *place d'armes*, into which I debouched from archway and port, I found a square wall of canvas, stiff and perpendicular, glistening in the sun. The place itself was a large green lawn, with avenues of trees, and walks leading to square blocks of buildings, crowded with soldiers. This wall was the screen which protected the Governor-General's camp from intrusion. Passing inside, by one of the portals—a chink in the canvas—I found myself in a spacious square with two rows of tents, pitched with great regularity, inside. Those on the right were large double tents, and before one floated the Governor-General's flag from a lofty staff.

After a short delay, I was told his Excellency would receive me, and I was introduced to one of those grand tents which would be a palace in the eyes of any field-marshal in Europe. A few servants, in the red and gold of the Viceroy's livery, were sitting under one of the spacious canvas eaves, where, indeed, the shade, even now, was not ungrateful. There were purdahs of fine matting, and doors, and flaps to pass, ere one could get inside. There soft Persian carpets received the feet in beds of flowers; the partitions of the tent, which was as large as a London saloon, were fitted with glass doors; but I was told afterwards, that Lord Canning had by no means carried tent-luxury to its fullest extent, and that, in fact, as Governor-General, he had rather curtailed the usual establishment. After a moment's delay, the aide-de-camp in waiting told me his Excellency would see me, and I passed in through a partition into a tent where Lord Canning was sitting, surrounded by maps, and boxes, and papers, at a table covered with documents—just as I had first seen him. There was but little change in the situation. Just across the river, all Oude was in rebellion; and Lord Canning told me that the day before he distinctly heard the fire of the guns by which a petty rajah had announced his independence. Mr. Wingfield, at Goruckpore, was surrounded by enemies; but still he bravely held his own. (Remembering, now, the terms in which the Governor-General spoke of him, I am not surprised that, without favour, interest, or application, his Lordship appointed this gentleman, to his own surprise, Chief Commissioner of Oude.) He spoke to me of Maun-Sing, of the part he was playing, of the efforts he had made to save the lives of certain Englishmen; but as that chief is now high in favour, and is one of the props of our power in Oude, there would be no object in alluding to his Lordship's opinions of our ally. Again Lord Canning caused me to understand that he would in no way answer for Sir Colin Campbell's views in regard to my presence in his camp; but he was good enough to add, that, so far as he knew, there would be no objection to my being there, as it was of consequence that the operations which were about to take place should be made known to people at home. In order to facilitate my journey to Cawnpore, Lord Canning said he would introduce me to Lieutenant Patrick Stewart, the Deputy-Superintendent of the Indian Telegraphs, whose name I had heard more than once from friends in Calcutta and elsewhere; he was also good enough to say, that any telegraphic despatches relating to the operations which I might wish to forward, could be sent next in order after important service messages. Of course, those facilities were given to the representative of a great English journal, the only one that had sent a representative to the seat of war; and I believe, that had any gentleman presented himself in a similar capacity to mine, he would have received the same reception and the same facilities.

After a long conversation, of which I have said quite enough, I went into one of the tents to present a letter of introduction to one of his Lordship's suite. A young slight active officer was sitting in a chair at a table, covered of course with papers, when I entered. That cheery genial voice, that bright look, full of intelligence and life, struck me at once. "L—— is not in just now; but I am a friend of his," quoth he; "and if I can be of any service, pray command me." When he knew my name and errand, he at once proposed to show me over the fort. I could not have had a more intelligent guide, and so we sauntered about the old lines of Akbar's engineers, and observed where his work was dovetailed into ours, and censured defects, and praised good points as long as we could stand the sun. As Stewart —for it was he—heard he was to accompany me to Cawnpore, we made arrangements for starting ere we parted. The rail, which once more makes a spasmodic effort to establish itself in India, here goes about halfway to Cawnpore. One is weary of thinking how much blood, disgrace, misery, and horror had been saved to us if the rail had been but a little longer here, had been at all there, had been completed at another place. It has been a heavy mileage of neglect for which we have already paid dearly. But the bill is not yet settled in full.

Hereafter, and elsewhere, I will give some account of the mutiny at Allahabad. It was characterized by extreme blindness and want of foresight on our part; by the utmost cruelty and cowardice on the side of the mutineers. I was told, as a proof of the infatuated ignorance displayed by an officer, in reference to the feeling of their men, that the colonel of the sepoy regiment which committed the greatest excesses, having seen some statement in one of the Calcutta papers reflecting on the loyalty of his corps, wrote a very prompt denial, and further expressed the fullest reliance on the temper of his men, and their attachment to the service; that statement appeared in the same paper which contained in another column the announcement by telegraph of the mutiny of the regiment, and of the murder of the writer by his men! Had the mutineers attacked the few Europeans who, with a handful of Sikhs—themselves at times disorderly—composed the garrison of the fort, with vigour, they must have soon got possession of it; and with it in their hands, it would have been impossible for Havelock or Neill to have collected their columns, and to have proceeded to recover Cawnpore and secure the garrison of Lucknow. Every one felt that, if Allahabad had gone, it was scarcely possible to save India; that it did not fall was little short of a miracle, as we shall see hereafter. It was sad to see the walls of the roofless bungalows blackened by fire, the pillars of the gateways prostrate, the wrecks of flower-gardens, where roses contended in vain with choking weeds; but I had seen worse at Balaklava, on the Katcha, and at Kertch. The outward features of war, mutiny, and wholesale murder are pretty much the same all over the world. Allahabad is destined to be the finest city in India, if the money can be found to make it so. So far as its situation is concerned, it has every requisite for an inland capital; but many years must elapse, and many thousands of pounds be spent, ere the full advantages of its position are developed.

February 11*th.*—Up early, preparing for our start, though the train does not go till 9·30. Met Lord Mark Kerr, who is in command of Her Majesty's 13th Regiment here, at the railway side, for there is no station, and had a slight inspection of the regiment, which marched past, with band playing, as a little mark of attention, I conceive, towards Sir Robert Garrett. Lord Mark, faithful to his peculiar vestiary and sumptuary laws and customs, had his head uncovered and his hair cut short, the result of which was, that the sun had blistered his occiput severely. He wore his old Crimean blue stuff trowsers, and long untanned leather riding-boots. Like everyone else, Lord Mark was pining for active service; and having, as he says, as fine a regiment to march or fight as any Highlanders in the service, he is very anxious to be employed against Lucknow. In fact, if officers had their will, nobody would be in garrison at all; all would be in the front—a very fine feeling, but one which, without being unduly repressed, cannot be gratified to the detriment of the public service. Those who know Lord Mark will be amused, and I am certain he will not be offended, at the repetition of the little incident at the railway station this morning. Among the passengers were a number of soldiers going back to their duty at Cawnpore, one of whom had yellow crossbelts, and seemed altogether, little as uniform is regarded in India, very oddly dressed. Lord Mark saw him, dashed down the bank at him, and came back in a few minutes in a terrible rage. "There! what do you think, General, of the discipline these fine fellows are kept in—one of your Highlanders, too! I asked that fellow who he was, and what regiment he belonged to. And what do you think was his answer—his answer to me, sir? Hang me, sir, but the fellow turned round, stared at me, and said, 'What the —— is that to you?' Did you ever hear such a thing?"

"Well, what did you say?"

"Say? Why I told him who I was; that I was Colonel of the 13th Regiment, and officer in command of the station; and then the fellow saluted, begged my pardon, and said, 'He never would have thought it!'"

Lord Mark did not mark the irony of the soldier, which was certainly so far founded on fact, that it would have been difficult for any one to have divined that the person who stood before him, dressed as I have described, with the addition of a ragged tunic of red calico, wadded with cotton, was a colonel in the army.

At last the train was ready, filled with soldiers, officers and their servants, and no passengers; for the Government has monopolized the train: and only those who get tickets on service are permitted to go by it at present. The carriages were old second-class invalids of English lines: but they were luxurious enough after the long journey in dust and sun. Stewart was ready to his time, and duly superintended by Captain Maxwell, the quartermaster-general, who acted as station-master, we started not more than one hour behind our time, which was not of any consequence, as there was no fear of collisions. How many of my fellow-passengers are gone to their account, or are disfigured by wounds, or enfeebled by the fevers and sicknesses, which in India leave their mark on a man for his lifetime! There is one, I see, before me now—a tall deep-chested fine young fellow —blue-eyed, tawny-maned—the old Scandinavian type, full of energy, "dying to see service," hurrying up now to the front, with a wound, received in the first encounter he had with the enemy, not yet quite healed. Poor Clarke! The last time I saw him he was one of the most dreadful objects I ever beheld— burnt, black, and covered with blistered skin from head to foot, blown up by that horrid explosion of powder at Lucknow. But he was at peace, poor fellow! for ever; and great as his agony must have been, he carried none of it out of this world; for his face bore, at the moment of his death, as I was assured, a calm and peaceful expression. It is sad, indeed, to look back now in one's mind, and to remember the conversation and the plans of those fellow-passengers who have since then gone on their long journey.

For some distance outside the station we passed through deserted villages, through lines of bungalows devastated by fire; then we entered on a plain, burnt and dry, covered with bushes growing out of sand, the favourite resort of nylghy (blue cow), deer, and antelopes. Here and there were villages abandoned, and never very desirable. The stations, such as they were, seemed crude and incomplete. The bright hot sun lent no joyousness or pleasant life to those arboriferous wastes; and I was glad to arrive at the terminus of the line, which consisted of a cessation of the rails in the sand, at a place called Khaga, about sixty-five miles from Allahabad, at two o'clock. Under a grove of trees, filled with green parrots, and vultures, and buzzards, were pitched a few tents, which represented the station. The clerk and station-master was in one, sick with fever; the others were occupied by travellers waiting for dâks, all of them connected with the public service. Those who were going towards Calcutta were invalids, some of them with their families. In griffinhood I admired the proportions of their establishments; but I could safely say, "*Haud equidem invideo, miror magis.*" A luxurious little baby was carried forth for a walk under the shade of the trees; it was borne in the arms of a fat ayah, beside whom walked a man, whose sole business it was gently to whisk away the flies which might venture to disturb baby's slumbers. Another man wheeled a small carriage, in which lay another little lord of the Indian creation, asleep, likewise with his human flapper by his side, whilst two ayahs followed the procession in rear; through the open door of the tent could be seen the lady-mother reading for her husband; a native servant fanned her with a hand-punkah; two little terriers, chained to a tree, were under the care of a separate domestic. A cook was busy superintending several pots set upon fires in the open air, a second prepared the curry-paste, a third was busy with plates, knives, and forks. In the rear of the servants' tents, which were two in number—making, with the master's, four —were two small tents for the syces, grass-cutters, and camel-men, or doodwallahs, behind which were picketed three horses, three camels, and a pair of bullocks, and ere we left, another servant drove in a few goats, which were used for milking. I was curious to know who this millionnaire could be, and was astonished to learn that it was only Captain Smith, of the Mekawattee Irregulars, who was travelling down country, with the usual train of domestics and animals required under the circumstances. The whole of this little camp did not contain more than eight or nine tents; but there were at least 150 domestics and a menagerie of animals connected with them. The tope was exceeding rich; the trees swarming with the common noisy green parroquet, and with the ever-active squeaking squirrel.

As there were no gharrys ready for us, Stewart and I started off on a walk through the country—a short one—incited thereto by the possibility of putting up a deer, or slaying a jackal. The fields were covered with dall-crops—a tall pulse with deep green leaves, which grows to the height of seven or eight feet; narrow foot-paths led here and there through them, and appeared to form the boundaries of the fields. Whitish-grey mud walls, rising a foot or two above the level of the dall-fields, or visible through the topes, indicated the native villages, which seemed especially wretched, from the want of windows and the apparent absence of roofs to the houses. The natives we met avoided us, skulking off by side-paths; and one or two women drawing water at a well, fled at our approach, as if we were demons. Their antipathy was shared by a herd, or drove, or flock of apes, which we encountered in one of the topes; a wilderness of young and old and middle-aged ladies and gentlemen, who chatted and grinned at us, from stumps and branches in endless variety of grimace and contortion. How is it that one is influenced by their offensive resemblance to humanity to abstain from shooting them? I am sure that a young quadrumane is by no means bad eating; but all are agreed that the sufferings of one wounded by the hunter are expressed in a manner so terribly human, as to cause great repugnance among those who have once killed an ape or monkey to fire at one afterwards. And yet they were very impudent indeed—scolding and abusing us as hard as they could chatter, whilst the matrons, in evident distrust, carried off their family to the remotest branches.

On our return we found gharrys waiting for us, and the whole of the party which had started from Allahabad set out for Cawnpore at five o'clock at night. As there was no advantage to be gained by arriving at the Cawnpore cantonments in the middle of the night, we halted on the road after half-an-hour's drive, and in the shade proceeded to make our dinner. Sir Robert Garrett had a preserved tongue in a tin case, like a huge red sugar-loaf, and a strong wish was expressed to investigate the interior, which would, it was supposed, form an agreeable addition to the resources of our banquet; but we had no means of opening it. It turned all the edges of our knives, broke all their points, set forks and hunting-knives at defiance; at last, in a rage, we put it up on end against a tree, and I fired my revolver through the angle of the case, so as to make a hole in the tin. Having first made this lodgement in the salient, the rest of the work was easy, and the tongue almost answered our ardent expectations.

About seven we halted again at the bungalow, in a very decayed straggling old town, called Futtehpore. There were many sheds well-thatched, and substantial enough, in the court-yard, which had been erected for the soldiers on their march along the trunk-road; and again one read the old stereotyped inscriptions on the walls, which almost made me regret that writing was included in the branches of education taught to the soldier. Near us was encamped a small force—some infantry and guns. Sir Robert with Dallas set out to visit the camp, in order to see his old friend Colonel David Wood, who was in command, whilst Oxenden, Stewart, and myself managed to extricate a supper out of the Khansamah's very limited *repertoire*. At night the gharrys came round, and we rumbled along in peaceful sleep over the trunk-road by which Neill and Havelock had advanced to attack the Butcher of Cawnpore—a road, by the way, of which many of the trees had been hung with natives' bodies as the column under Neill and Renaud marched to open the way from Allahabad. I hear many stories, the truth of which I would doubt if I could. Our first spring was terrible; I fear our claws were indiscriminating.

CHAPTER XI.

Look at Cawnpore!—Its atrocities paralleled in History.—Azimoola Khan.—Strange curiosity in an Asiatic.—Barracks.—Miserable defensive position.—Camp of Sir Colin Campbell.—A compact.—The Highland bonnet.—Head-Quarters' staff-mess.—General Mansfield.—My tent and its attendants.—Dinner with the Commander-in-Chief.—The French General, Vinoy.

February 12th.—It was actually chilly last night! Dallas said he had never suffered so much from cold in all his life. It was 6·30 in the morning, when Stewart, who has the art of compressing himself into a very small compass, woke me up, "to look at Cawnpore." The scenes where great crimes have been perpetrated ever possess an interest, which I would not undertake to stigmatise as morbid; and surely among the sites rendered infamous for ever in the eyes of British posterity, Cawnpore will be pre-eminent as the magnitude of the atrocities with which it is connected. But, though pre-eminent among crimes, the massacre of Cawnpore is by no means alone in any of the circumstances which mark turpitude and profundity of guilt. We who suffered from it think that there never was such wickedness in the world, and the incessant efforts of a gang of forgers and utterers of base stories have surrounded it with horrors that have been vainly invented in the hope of adding to the indignation and burning desire for vengeance which the naked facts arouse. Helpless garrisons, surrendering under capitulation, have been massacred ere now; men, women, and children have been ruthlessly butchered by the enemies of their race ere now; risings, such as that of the people of Pontus under Mithridates, of the Irish Roman Catholics against the Protestant settlers in 1641, of the actors in the Sicilian vespers, of the assassins who smote and spared none on the eve of St. Bartholomew, have been over and over again attended by inhuman cruelty, violation, and torture. The history of mediæval Europe affords many instances of crimes as great as those of Cawnpore; the history of more civilized periods could afford some parallel to them in more modern times, and amid most civilized nations. In fact, the peculiar aggravation of the Cawnpore massacres was this, that the deed was done by a subject race—by black men who dared to shed the blood of their masters, and that of poor helpless ladies and children. Here we had not only a servile war and a sort of Jacquerie combined, but we had a war of religion, a war of race, and a war of revenge, of hope, of some national promptings to shake off the yoke of a stranger, and to re-establish the full power of native chiefs, and the full sway of native religions. There is a kind of God's revenge against murder in the unsuccessful issue of all enterprises commenced in massacre, and founded on cruelty and bloodshed. Whatever the causes of the mutiny and the revolt, it is clear enough that one of the modes by which the leaders, as if by common instinct, determined to effect their end was, the destruction of every white man, woman, or child who fell into their hands—a design which the kindliness of the people, or motives of policy, frustrated on many remarkable occasions. It must be remembered that the punishments of the Hindoo are cruel, and whether he be mild or not, he certainly is not, any more than the Mussulman, distinguished for clemency towards his enemies. But philosophize and theorize as we may, Cawnpore will be a name ever heard by English ears with horror long after the present generation has passed away.

Whilst I am writing about it, I may as well relate an incident in connection with one of the Nana's chief advisers, which I mentioned to the Governor-General, who appeared much struck with it. After the repulse of the allies in their assault on Sebastopol, 18th June, an event closely followed by the death of Lord Raglan and a cessation of any operations, except such as were connected with a renewed assault upon the place, I went down for a few days to Constantinople, and, whilst stopping at Missirie's Hotel, saw, on several occasions, a handsome slim young man, of dark-olive complexion, dressed in an Oriental costume which was new to me, and covered with rings and finery. He spoke French and English, dined at the *table d'hôte*, and, as far as I could make out, was an Indian prince, who was on his way back from the prosecution of an unsuccessful claim against the East India Company in London. He had made the acquaintance of Mr. Doyne, who was going out to the Crimea as the superintendent of Sir Joseph Paxton's Army Works Corps, and by that gentleman he was introduced to me one fine summer's evening, as we were smoking on the roof of the hotel. I did not remember his name, but I recollect that he expressed great anxiety about a passage to the Crimea, "as," said he, "I want to see this famous city, and those great Roostums, the Russians, who have beaten

French and English together." Indeed, he added that he was going to Calcutta, when the news of the defeat of June 18th reached him at Malta, and he was so excited by it that he resolved to go to Constantinople, and endeavour thence to get a passage to Balaklava. In the course of conversation he boasted a good deal of his success in London society, and used the names of people of rank very freely, which, combined with the tone of his remarks, induced me to regard him with suspicion, mingled, I confess, with dislike. He not only mentioned his *bonnes fortunes*, but expressed a very decided opinion that unless women were restrained, as they were in the East, "like moths in candlelight, they will fly and get burned." I never saw or heard anything more of him till some weeks afterwards, when a gentleman rode up to my hut at Cathcart's Hill, and sent me in a note from Mr. Doyne, asking me to assist his friend Azimoola Khan in visiting the trenches, and on going out I recognized the Indian prince. I had his horse put up, and walked to the General's hut to get a pass for him. The sun was within an hour of setting, and the Russian batteries had just opened, as was their custom, to welcome our reliefs and working-parties, so that shot came bounding up towards the hill where our friend was standing, and a shell burst in the air at apparently near proximity to his post. Some delay took place ere I could get the pass, and when I went with it I found Azimoola had retreated inside the cemetery, and was looking with marked interest at the fire of the Russian guns. I told him what he was to do, and regretted my inability to accompany him, as I was going out to dinner at a mess in the

Light Division. "Oh," said he, "this is a beautiful place to see from; I can see everything, and, as it is late, I will ask you to come some other day, and will watch here till it is time to go home." He said, laughingly, "I think you will never take that strong place;" and in reply to me, when I asked him to come to dine with me at my friend's, where I was sure he would be welcome, he said, with a kind of sneer, "Thank you, but recollect I am a good Mahomedan!" "But," said I, "you dined at Missirie's?" "Oh, yes: I was joking. I am not such a fool as to believe in these foolish things. I am of no religion." When I came home that night I found he was asleep in my camp-bed, and my servant told me he had enjoyed my stores very freely. In the morning he was up and off, ere I was awake. On my table I found a piece of paper—"Azimoola Khan presents his compliments to Russell, Esquire, and begs to thank him most truly for his kind attentions, for which I am most obliged."

This fellow, as we all know, was the Nana's secretary, and chief adviser in the massacres at Cawnpore. Now, is it not curious enough that he should have felt such an interest to see, with his own eyes, how matters were going on in the Crimea? It would not be strange in a European to evince such curiosity; but in an Asiatic, of the non-military caste, it certainly is. He saw the British army in a state of some depression, and he formed, as I have since heard, a very unfavourable opinion of its *morale* and *physique*, in comparison with that of the French. Let us remember, that soon after his arrival in India he accompanied Nana Sahib to Lucknow, where they remained for some time, and are thought by those who recollect their tone and demeanor, to have exhibited considerable insolence and *hauteur* towards the Europeans they met. Afterwards the worthy couple, on the pretence of a pilgrimage to the hills—a Hindoo and Mussulman joined in a holy excursion!—visited the military stations all along the main trunk-road, and went as far as Umballah. It has been suggested that their object in going to Simla was to tamper with the Goorkha regiment stationed in the hills; but that, finding on their arrival at Umballah, a portion of the regiment were in cantonments, they were able to effect their purpose with these men, and desisted from their proposed journey on the plea of the cold weather. That the Nana's demeanor towards us should have undergone a change at this time is not at all wonderful; for he had learned the irrevocable determination of the authorities to refuse what he—and, let me add, the majority of the millions of Hindoos who knew the circumstances—considered to be his just rights as adopted heir of the ex-Peishwa of the Mahrattas. When the great villany was planned is not now ascertainable; but it must be remarked, as a piece of evidence in some degree adverse to the supposition that Nana Sahib had successfully tampered with the troops at Cawnpore, that the latter did not evince any design of making him their leader, nor did they hold any communication with him on their revolt, and that they were all marching off for Delhi when he and his creatures went to their camp, and by his representations, promises, and actual disbursements, induced them to go back and assault Wheeler in his feeble entrenchments.

There, standing in the lightening morning, is their

melancholy outline in sharp relief against the sky! At the first glance I was struck by the resemblance of those white walls, pierced in every direction with black shot-holes, shattered and rent and blackened with smoke, to the white buildings of Sebastopol, in rear of the Redan. But then, these before me are roofless, and stand in a large sandy plain away from any houses, except an échelonned line of sloping mud-walls, which once formed the sides of some native barracks, and which nearly join a deserted suburb of the station. A more miserable defensive position could scarcely be selected. The walls of the barracks show, that, instead of cover, they brought danger to the garrison. The low earth-work, hastily thrown up round the quadrangles, barely covered the head, and from their size must have been liable to be searched out by reverse and enfilading fire. "I will show you all over it by-and-by," quoth Stewart; "and you will see what a place it was to select!" The dust and heat, for which Cawnpore is famous, made us rejoice to rush into the dilapidated building which served as an hotel—windows broken, and frames sometimes gone altogether, doors broken and unhinged, shot-holes through the walls, the only furniture a long table, some rickety chairs, and charpoys in the bed-rooms. But at least there was plenty of water, and there was something to stretch one's legs upon.

After breakfast, Stewart, who is charged to put the end of a telegraph wire into Sir Colin's hand wherever he goes, sets off to the camp, which is at some distance from the hotel, on a sandy elevated plain near the *tête-de-pont* which defends the bridge across the Ganges. The camp consists of the tents of the Head-Quarters'

Staff only, and is drawn in stiff precise lines, such as Indian quartermaster-generals delight in. Outside each tent hangs a little black board with the rank and title of the occupier described in white letters, thus: "Military Secretary," "Deputy Adjutant-General, Queen's Troops," "Deputy Adjutant-General of the Army," "Commissariat Office Head-Quarters," "Chief of the Staff," &c. The Commander-in-Chief's tent, undistinguished by aught else except its position, is marked by a union-jack pitched close to the adjacent mess-tent; and at the end of the street, a little in the rear, is the large tent of the Head-Quarters' Staff mess.

Whilst Stewart went off on his business, and to see his old friends, I made out Sir David Baird, senior Aide-de-Camp to the Commander-in-Chief, and sent in my card. The flap of the little tent was raised immediately, and I made my bow to Sir Colin. He was "frank" and cordial. After a few remarks about the Crimea, his Excellency said, "Now, Mr. Russell, I'll be candid with you. We shall make a compact. You shall know everything that is going on. You shall see all my reports, and get every information that I have myself, on the condition that you do not mention it in camp, or let it be known in any way, except in your letters to England."

"I accept the condition, sir; and I promise you it shall be faithfully observed."

"You see," Sir Colin continued, "you will be among a set of young fellows here, surrounded, as all of us are, by natives who understand all that is going on better than we think. They talk about what is happening, or what is going to take place; and all that gets to the ears of the enemy. So that our best plans may be frustrated. It is most essential for us to preserve secrecy in war, especially in a country like this." I could only assent to Sir Colin's remarks. As we were speaking, in came an officer with a number of despatches. "See," said Sir Colin, handing one to me, "we will begin our compact at once." (The despatch related to certain movements in the rebel force at Lucknow, and was of no great importance.) My interview was long and interesting—to me at least. Sir Colin seemed better, stronger, and more vigorous, than the last time I saw him, which was on his return to the Crimea. The first occasion that I can remember to have "laid eyes" on him was on the slope of the Alma, in rear of the Russian field-work, when he received Lord Raglan after the day was won, and when he made the request to be allowed to wear the Highland bonnet, of which so many absurd stories and versions were afloat at the time that are now precipitated into hard Scottish heads like pebbles fixed in concrete.

Three or four days afterwards, just as an odd little party were sitting in our much-relished room in Balaklava,—then fresh, vine-clad, grape-clustered,—in came Sir Colin, Highland bonnet on head, full of life and spirits. The "we" were Macdonald (93rd, the Provost Marshal); Romaine (Judge Advocate); Kingslake (Eöthen), who had come out to see the landing of the expedition; Layard (Nineveh), who had just come from on board the Agamemnon; Dr. Fowle Smith, and your humble servant. The reunion was broken up by a false alarm that the Russians were coming down to attack us!—Ere I left to-day, he gave me some information with regard to his plans, and showed me the necessity imposed on one in his position to act with such caution that success must be the certain concomitant of every step. The delay, at which some people were affecting ill-bestowed wonder, resulted, he said, from two causes: the one was the necessity of completing his arrangements and securing every gun and man that could be had ere he marched against Lucknow; the other, his desire to be assured of the safety of the women and children who were travelling down the main trunk-road from Agra, where they had been in a state of *quasi* siege, and of constant alarm in the fort. They were strongly escorted, but the relief of Lucknow would have met with a heavy counterpoise if any accident had happened to these ladies: and it must be remembered that, as they travel down the road, they have an enemy on their left flank across the Ganges, that Calpee is occupied by another enemy on their right, and that numerous bands of rebels, strong enough in numbers to be considered as separate corps, are scouring the country not yet held by our troops. Ere I left, Sir Colin was good enough to invite me to his table; but as he gave me the option of joining the Head-Quarters' Staff-mess, I preferred availing myself of the opportunity thus afforded me of subscribing to the expense of maintenance, at the same time that I felt very sensibly the kindness of his Excellency.

Those who have experienced the difficulty of living on one's private resources at this time in India, well know how great was the accommodation afforded to me in joining the Staff-mess, over which my excellent friend, Captain Goldsworthy, was now presiding as caterer. I was further enjoined by Sir Colin to make application to Captain Metcalfe for whatever I might require for the use of my tent, and I had at once to acknowledge the promptitude and courtesy of both the gentlemen I have named, in doing all they could to make me comfortable. I next paid my respects to General Mansfield, the Chief of the Staff, whom I had been acquainted with at Therapia. Like Sir Colin, he was surrounded by papers, plans, maps, and despatches; but the General is one remarkable for a *lucidus ordo* in head and in external matters. The faculties of observation, of deep thought, of self-command, of application, of firmness, and the possession of sagacity and penetration are chiselled on brow, forehead, and face, sharply and unmistakably. From over-work, perhaps — for the General is yet a very young man in regard to his rank, and does not look more than forty-two or forty-three years of age — his eyes, which are *per se* clear enough, have become impaired in vision, and he is obliged to wear glasses or spectacles, the use of which, combined with the cut of his lips, the *pose* of the head, which is thrown back with the chin forwards, gives General Mansfield an air of *hauteur* — some people say superciliousness — which is not found in him by those who are brought in contact with him, though it is unquestionably attributed to him by strangers who have merely judged by his looks. We had some conversation respecting what had been done and what was to be done; and, taking up a large map of India, the Chief of the Staff pointed out with clearness and sequence, the operations and their results, and the work before us : exhibiting, as he did so, very remarkable powers of memory in respect to the position and strength of regiments, and complete mastery of the combinations by which the reduction of Lucknow and of Oude, and the restoration of our power in Rohilcund and in Central India were to be effected. I learned to-day, for the first time, that Sir Colin, when he marched up from Cawnpore to Futtehghur, after routing the Gwalior people, intended to have crossed into Rohilcund and to have swept it clear of the enemy; but that Lord Canning conceived the political effect of leaving Lucknow in the hands of the rebels would be so mischievous that the city should be taken ere Rohilcund was invaded. Hence the delay at Futtehghur; because, in order to besiege Lucknow, it was necessary to get a siege-train from Agra and elsewhere; and all preparations were kept as secret as possible, and in order to deceive the enemy a bridge was prepared at Futtehghur, whilst our guns were being slowly massed together, and the material for the siege collected. There were dreadful cries of distress from Calcutta all this time; but Sir Colin could not afford to appease them by revealing his plans to all the world.

When I left the General, I found that my tent was already struggling into life at the corner of the street, opposite the Chief's. "Who is coming here now?" asked Colonel Pakenham, who was passing by at the time. "I have seen a great many distinguished people take up their abode here for a short time." In fact, the site was that given to *généraux passagers*, and others, and it had, as I learned from the adjutant-general's remark, witnessed many changes of fortune. But what a tent it was! True, only a simple single pole; but then it was on the Indian establishment. I thought of the miserable little shell of rotten calico, under which I braved the Bulgarian sun, or the ill-shaped tottering Turkish tent in which Collingwood, Dickson, and I had suffered from insects, robbers, and ghosts, not to mention hunger, in the onion bed at Gallipoli; of the poor fabric that went to the winds on the 14th November before Sebastopol; of the clumsy Danish extinguisher-shaped affair under which I once lived, and was so nearly "put out," and then I turned round and round in my new edifice in ever-renewed admiration. The pole is a veritable pillar, varnished or painted yellow, with a fine brass socket in the centre; from the top spreads out the sloping roof to the square side walls. The inside is curiously lined with buff calico with a dark pattern, and beneath one's feet a carpet of striped blue and buff laid over the soft sand is truly Persian in its yielding softness. There is no furniture. "We must send down to the bazaar," says Stewart, "and get tables, chairs, and charpoys (bedsteads), and whatever else we want, such as resais, or quilted cotton bedclothes, which serve as sheets, blankets, and mattresses, all in one." "But how on earth am I to carry all those things?" "Make your mind quite easy about that; you have only to make a requisition on the commissariat and they'll provide animals enough to carry all Cawnpore, with you, if you are ready to pay for it." Not unused to campaigning, I confess this fertility of resource was surprising to me; and there was still more novelty attached to my position when on going out of my tent I found myself the centre of a small levée, whilst Simon, acting as a general master of the ceremonies, introduced to my notice the two kelassies, or tent-pitchers, and a sprite in attendance, the bheesty, or water-carrier, the mehter, or sweeper, all attached to the tent; and then, a host of candidates for various imaginary employments whom I dismissed instantaneously. All these gentlemen salaamed and hit their foreheads in great subjection, and then retired under the projecting eaves of the tent, where they smoked, talked, ate, and slept. To each tent there is generally attached a small pall, or low ridge-pole tent, for the servants; and another little canvas structure placed in the rear; but as yet there were no palls issued, and the servants slept out in the open air, and under the eaves of the tent.

The camp is on a high sandy slab, which forms, in fact, the level of the plain above the river. Some forty tents, dispersed in one long street with an open square in the centre—a camp, all of officers, and no soldiers. I dined with the Commander-in-Chief in the evening. The head of the table was occupied by Captain Metcalfe, Commandant at Head-Quarters, and Interpreter to his Excellency. Opposite to him sat Colonel Sterling, the Military Secretary; Sir David Baird, Captain Alison, and Captain Forster, Aides-de-Camp, and one or two invited officers, completed the party. There can be no more genial host or pleasant company than Sir Colin. His anecdotes of the old war, of his French friends—made friends in the vicissitudes of field-service—are vigorous and racy; but when you think of the dates, you are rather puzzled to imagine how the gentleman who sits beside you, looking so hardy and active, can have participated in the scenes which occurred so many years before, and mingled with people who have so long ago departed from the world. He is no dull *laudator temporis acti*, but gives to the present all its due. There is no parade or display at his table, but everything is very comfortable and very good. I was able to tell Sir Colin some news of his old friend in the Crimea, General Vinoy, with whom I had travelled to Paris, and who was loud in his praise of "*Mon bon ami, Ser Colan,*" and of the famous revolver he had received of him as a *gage d'amitié*, that did good service on the memorable day of the capture of the Malakhoff. Their friendship is not interrupted; for his Excellency told me he had received a long interesting letter from General Vinoy, in which he exhibited great interest in the progress of our arms in India, and expressed a strong opinion against the infliction of indiscriminate punishment; adding, that in his experience of war, *les représailles sont toujours inutiles*. As I had not been able to get horses, Sir Colin was kind enough to say that I might have the use of his stud till I had succeeded in procuring some sort of quadruped—a favour which the difficulty of walking about the station made me appreciate all the more.

CHAPTER XII.

Wheeler's intrenchment.—Windham's position.—The two parts of an Indian station.—An imaginary review.—The Cutchery.—A Bedouin of the Press.—Generals cannot "do the graphic."—Bottled beer.—Members of our mess.—School of dialectics.—Improved life of Europeans.—Want of sympathy for natives.—Up-country life and Calcutta life.—Sir Hugh Wheeler's ayah.—Sir Archdale Wilson.—Captain Peel and his blue jackets.—Cawnpore dust.—"A shave of old Smith's."—Cawnpore in its palmy days.—Beggars and wigwam villages.

February 13*th*.—The tent-equipage not being quite complete, went down to the hotel after dinner last night. Early this morning, drove over in a hired buggy, with Stewart, to Wheeler's intrenchment. To describe it would be to repeat my letter written at the time. The difficulty, in my mind, was to believe that it could ever have been defended at all. Make every allowance for the effects of weather, for circumstances, it is still the most wretched defensive position that could be imagined. Honour to those who defended it! Pity for their fate! Above all, pity for the lot of those whom those strong arms and brave hearts had failed to save from the unknown dangers of foul treachery! It was a horrible spot! Inside the shattered rooms, which had been the scene of such devotion and suffering, are heaps of rubbish and filth. The intrenchment is used as a *cloaca maxima* by the natives, camp-followers, coolies, and others who bivouac in the sandy plains around it. The smells are revolting. Rows of gorged vultures sit with outspread wings on the mouldering parapets, or perch in clusters on the two or three leafless trees at the angle of the works by which we enter. I shot one with my revolver; and as the revolting creature disgorged its meal, twisting its bare black snake-like neck to and fro, I made a vow I would never incur such a disgusting sight again.

From this spot we made our way over to Windham's position, on the second day of his engagement with the Gwalior force, swelled by many thousands of armed natives and by fugitives from Oude. In the Appendix, will be found all I have to say on this matter. Thence we returned through part of the native city, which is like the worst part of Gallipoli; narrow tortuous streets of tumble-down houses, which must have been built of the materials of some city that perished from rottenness. Still it teems with life, and there is far more noise, bustle, and business in those crowded thoroughfares than in our Turkish town. Again I am struck by the scowling, hostile look of the people. The bunniahs bow with their necks, and salaam with their hands, but not with their eyes. There is not a European to be seen, for there are few soldiers near Cawnpore. They are away over beyond that sandy shore at the other side of the Ganges. You see the green trees rising above that belt of sand, and the level strip of cultivated land? Our soldiers are massed there, along the road which leads in a straight line from Cawnpore to Lucknow by this bridge of boats just below us. The line of earthworks from which the bridge springs constitutes the *tête-de-pont* left in Windham's charge, now greatly strengthened. Hundreds of coolies, men, women, and children are working, as you see, at it now. Clouds of dust are shovelled up by their feet as they move backwards and forwards with little baskets full of earth to deepen the parapet.

You find by degrees, that an Indian station consists of two parts: the cantonments of the Europeans, the native city and bazaar. The west and the east end are far apart, separated by a waste common, or by fields, or gardens. Belgravia is not so much removed from Houndsditch in *feeling*, modes of life, and thought, as our western station from our eastern bazaar. There is no bond of union between the two, in language, or faith, or nationality. The west rules, collects taxes, gives balls, drives carriages, attends races, goes to church, improves its roads, builds its theatres, forms its masonic lodges, holds cutchery, and drinks its pale ale. The east pays taxes in the shape of what it eats grown on taxed land, grumbles, propagates, squabbles, sits in its decaying temples, haunts its rotting shrines, washes in its failing tanks, and drinks its semi-putrid water. Between the two there is a great gulf fixed: to bridge it over is the work reserved for him who shall come to stabilitate our empire in the East, if ever he comes at all. The European station is laid out in large rectangles formed by wide roads. The native city is an aggregate of houses perforated by tortuous paths, so that a plan of it would resemble a section of worm-eaten wood. The Europeans live in detached houses, each surrounded by walls enclosing large gardens, lawns, out-offices. The natives live packed in squeezed-up tenements, kept from falling to pieces by mutual pressure. The handful of Europeans occupy four times the space of the city which contains tens of thousands of Hindoos and Mussulmen. The sole mark of the rule of the former which exists in the latter, is apparently a large native house, from the top of which floats a flag, and in front of which is a group of natives in blue cotton tunics, with red piping and tulwars by their sides. They are the police, and the house is the kotwalee, or residence and office of the native mayor, or kotwal. The Russianized air of our stations particularly strikes me; and from what I can hear of the Muscovite cantonments in Georgia, they must in actual form, and in their social relations, be very like our own in India. But there is this great dissimilarity in the latter and in the former case, that the Georgians are Christianized and Russianized this many a long year.

"Whose buggy is that, preceded by two native troopers, and followed by five or six armed natives running on foot?" "That is the magistrate and collector." "What does he do?" "He sits in cutchery to settle civil cases, and collects the revenue, and adjusts matters connected with the civil administration of the province—for it is one—confided to his control. He is the burra sahib, or big man, of the station."

"Who is that in the smart gharry, with servants in livery?" "That is the chaplain of the station, who marries, and baptizes, and performs service for the Europeans." "Does he go among the natives?" "Not he; he leaves that to the missionaries, of whom there are lots here; but he has a school, which children may attend or not, as they please; and he is a very good chaplain, and very much liked and respected."

"Well: and who comes next along the drive, in that very smart buggy, with the bay mare?" "That is the doctor of the station. He attends the sick Europeans. He also gets, under certain circumstances, head-money for every native soldier in garrison." "Does he attend them?" "*I* should think not! Why, how on earth could he attend a lot of niggers?" "But why is he paid for them?" "Ah, that is another matter. You must understand our system a little better before you can comprehend things of this sort."

"Who is this jolly-looking fellow on the grey arab?" "That is the judge of the station: a very good fellow; all judges are rather slow coaches, you know. They do the criminal business, and it is not much matter if they make mistakes, as they don't meddle with Europeans. When they can do nothing else with a fellow, in the civil service, they make him a judge." And so, in review, there passed before us the chiefs of an imaginary station, deputy collectors, assistants, *et hoc genus omne*—a wonderful genus! a race of prætors, ædiles, proconsuls, and consuls, more than worthy of Rome, and fully worthy of England, or of the civilization she inherits. Some I had met that day; for, in the course of our drive, we came upon a bungalow surrounded with natives in array, with brass badges on their breasts and swords by their sides, and some with shouldered firelocks. "This is the cutchery, and nearly all the civilians live together and have a little mess." So we called; nearly every one was out, as we have seen, but there was a wounded officer in one room, and a sick one in another, and the servants looked as if they expected we were coming to live there, as a matter of course, and suggested to us several drinks as an initiatory process. When we returned to the hotel, we found that General Garrett was still there with his aides, as it had been communicated to him that the trunk-road was not safe, and there was not an escort ready for him. At the hotel were many officers waiting for an opportunity to join their regiments.

February 14th.—Sunday. All is ready in my tent, and I move up to the camp and begin once more this life under canvas, which makes us all feel that there is a Bedouin drop in our blood that only requires a little play to make it dangerous to civilised life. We are waiting here for some days, and there is little use in transcribing the daily details of an imperfect diary. I do not know whether a Bedouin of the press, being a sort of pariah, is not a wilder creature than the more orthodox members of the Rechabite order. Our life was, however, a simple one. Just as the sun began to throw up a light lemon-coloured semicircle into the broad shield of the blue night, a stifled sort of life woke up with it in camp. The servants came with tea to their masters; the syces brought round horses to the front, and out went the early Indians for a gallop or canter before breakfast. I confess that the dust at Cawnpore always repelled me from those morning rides. One got hot, stuffy, and powdered all over with impalpable, but visible leg-bones, and skulls, and mud, and nastiness, which the bath could scarcely clear away. And so I waited in general till seven o'clock; then had a bath, and at nine walked over to the mess-tent, where breakfast was ready as we entered. Each man's servant brought over from the tent his chair, knives and forks, plates, salt and pepper castors, and placed them properly at the mess-table. The breakfasts were not to be despised. Tea or coffee, goats' milk, butter, bread, chuppaties, fish, mutton-chops, or grills, and curries. Then came a long slice of the day devoted to business. I hunted about for news from tent to tent, or heard what was doing from Sir Colin, who came over to me with papers, and explained the daily position of affairs; and I learned—not to the detriment of the public service; not to the diminution of my self-respect; not to the deterioration of the relations between the Commander-in-Chief and the person whom he thus permitted to know his councils —that which it was of advantage for the people of England to know.

Generals cannot write long despatches; they cannot "do the graphic;" they cannot always tell all the truth. Without saying that long despatches are always instructive; that the graphic is always agreeable or desirable in the horrors of war, or that the truth is always pleasant, it cannot be denied that the people of England like them all and all together. And here let me say, that I do sincerely believe, if gentlemen in the capacity in which I presented myself, had come out to Sir Colin Campbell, properly accredited, they would have received the same courtesies, facilities, and kindnesses which I shall ever acknowledge, though I quite dissociate them from my person, and attach them unreservedly to the mission on which I was sent, and which to the best of my ability I endeavoured to fulfil. I received no instructions or suggestions, as I had no prejudices to justify or destroy, or views to upport or demolish; so, if in the end I had no violent theories to defend, I hope I had no great antipathies to conciliate.

This Cawnpore life was an old friend with a new face. If the face had not been quite so hot, so muddy, and so dusty, I am fain to admit I should have liked it the better. At two o'clock, there came the great ordeal of lunch, or tiffin, in the mess-tent—more curries and chops, and cold meat and pickles, and pale ale. You knew it was very wrong, but it was also very nice; and whatever a man's liver says next day, it is a remarkably complicitous witness, and its evidence is very *ex post facto*. Surely the Strasbourg goose would die pleasantly if he could but share the fate of his Indian-influenced brother. Where in the world does *foie gras* present itself to the ultimate victim of its aggrandizement in so attractive a form? where is pale ale so like the finest ideal of nectar—bright, clear, Rabelaisian—a cool Niagara of wit and pleasure, rushing, with insouciant glee, down into the great abyss, in a foam of sick-certificates and abscesses? A bottle of beer!—Why, it is nothing. I know men who take three at tiffin. I know men who declare they know men who take a dozen bottles of beer in the day, and that they—the takers—are all the better for it.

Just as the sun is setting, round come the nags to each tent-door, and there is a rush out into the dust, until the darkness is felt. Then there is a helter-skelter home, and a hasty bath, and dinner. The tent-table is spread with a clean cloth, and lights, numerous if not dazzling. As at breakfast, each member has his own fork, knife, spoons, plates, and other paraphernalia. The soup is served, as it only can be had in India—hot as the sun, thick with bones and meat—a veritable warm jelly. Then comes the fish—roach, or some cognate Cyprinus, hateful to me as Ganges-fed; then joints of gram-fed mutton, commissariat beef, curries of fish, fowl, and mutton, stews, and ragouts, sweets of an intensely saccharine character, with sherry, beer, and soda-water, and now and then a pop of Simpkin, or champagne. Our mess usually consists of Colonel Pakenham, Deputy-Adjutant-General of the Queen's Forces; Major Norman, Deputy Adjutant-General of the Army; Major Stewart, Deputy Assistant-Adjutant-General; Captain Allgood, Deputy Quartermaster-General; Major Apthorp, Postmaster; Captain Johnson, Deputy-Assistant Quartermaster-General; Captain Tombs, Paymaster of the Force; Colonel Young, Judge-Advocate; Captain Robertson, Deputy Judge-Advocate; Captain Fitzgerald, Chief of the Commissariat; Lieutenant Goldsworthy, President and Commissariat officer of Head-Quarters' Camp; Mr. Clifford, 9th Lancers, Surgeon to the Chief and Head-Quarters; to whom were subsequently added Dr. McAndrew, Principal Medical Officer; Dr. Tice; Colonel McPherson, Quartermaster-General; Captain Seymour (Her Majesty's 84th), Assistant Adjutant-General. One of the mess had an exterior which I find thus described: "figure, lean and angular; narrow round shoulders; big splay feet; hair fiery-red, dishevelled, and matted in snaky masses; beard and whiskers, if possible, more red and fierce than the hair; forehead low and receding, but broad and bumpy over the

SCHOOL OF DIALECTICS. 187

brows, which are two elongated white knobs, from which spring a few red hairs; eyes feline; nose large, coarse, aquiline; mouth huge and coarse, covered as to the upper lip with red hairs, growing wildly in carrot-coloured spikes and garnished with a few massive fangs, the intervals between which are filled up with small metal spikes, on which teeth had once been fixed by dentistric art." But this queer outside belonged to a man of ability, though his mortal structure was unquestionably of an unusual sort. He had read a good deal, and had mastered the outward works of the Aristotelian logic. He always commenced at first principles, and set argument on a right basis, by questioning every statement made, in the most general and uncontroversial spirit. Of course this failing was a source of much quiet amusement to us. Suppose one said at table. " I think the Zemindars are against us," there was one voice heard at once, " Why do you think so? I think the contrary. I call on you for proofs :"—or that it was remarked, " Jones nearly rode over a boy this morning close to the church," our friend would remark, " Nearly is a relative adverb in reference to time or space; and, from what I heard Jones say, I believe it was several hundred yards from the church; nor is it established that it *was* a boy." Of course there was a school of dialectics thus established, in which there were many pupils for the fun of the thing. But, on the whole, our life was placid, peaceable, and animal in those early Rechabite times.

The good old hookah days are past; cheroots and pipes have now usurped the place of the aristocratic silver bowl, the cut-glass goblets, and the twisted glistening snake with silver or amber mouth-piece. It was somewhat expensive, as it had special attendants attached to it. It seems as if the facility of communication with England deorientalizes men—they acquire less of the habits of the country and retain more of those of their own. They spend less money; for they look forward to enjoying themselves on a lengthened leave in England, or in accumulating comfortable additions to their pensions. The race of Eurasians is not so freely supplied with recruits. It is now very rare and shameful for an officer, civil or military, to live in a state which was normal last generation. The mode of building bungalows has altered. There is now no beebee's house—a sort of European zenana. But yesterday, in again visiting the slaughter-house at Cawnpore, the friend who was with me said he thought it had been a portion of the house of some officer or official, and that the compound had been the residence of some native woman. There are now European rivals to those ladies at some stations. It was the topic of conversation the other day at mess, that the colonel of a regiment had thought it right to prohibit one of his officers from appearing publicly with an unauthorized companion at the band parade; and the general opinion was that he had no right to interfere. But the society of the station does interfere in such cases, and though it does not mind beebees or their friends, it rightly taboos him who entertains their white rivals. European equipages have been substituted for palanquins and their numerous attendants. Instead of inclining to settle in India, the European looks more to home than ever he did; and the number of those who fix themselves for the rest of their days in some pleasant "sunny" angle of Bengal is diminishing.

Next to my griffinish wonder at the want of white faces, has been my regret to perceive the utter absence of any friendly relations between the white and the black faces when they are together. Here comes a trooper—a tall fine old fellow, with face as fair as that of many a sunburnt soldier from England—he carries a despatch for the Lord Sahib— he has ridden with it fifty miles through a country full of rebels. The old Sikh asks for the tent of the Chief; he dismounts, sticks his lance in the ground, fastens his panting horse to it, and stalks in his long leather boots—his heels, perhaps, stuck up in a crease of the leather six inches above the sole—through the camp. It is ten to one if a soul notices him, and if he goes to a wrong tent he is saluted with an adjuration, and a request to go to a place far beyond the limits of the camp, by the angry young gentleman who has been disturbed in his "Pendennis," or in the contemplation of a fine "ash." The old soldier will follow his own sahib to the last; but for strange sahibs he has not much regard, and he thinks it's their nature to be rough and rude, and so he shuffles forth on his cruise, looking hopelessly about for the dera, till some kind mortal compassionates his distress. What is the old trooper's revenge? Why, he sticks in our service, saving up money and remitting it to his family—retires on his pension, and then, when his last hour is near, his last act is to try and get his name "scratched," so that he may not *die* in the service of the stranger.

Of course there are many exceptions, or rather

these cases of discourtesy were the large exceptions to the rule in dealing with the natives. Some of our officers appear to possess their confidence to a most extraordinary extent. I say appear, because, after what has happened, few can be sure of the feelings of these men. Look at the domestic servants in camp; the tones in which they are spoken to have rarely one note of kindness, often many of anger in them. Look at the boxwallahs, who come round with all kinds of nick-nacks, stationery, perfumery, and such things, and see how hard it is to bear the cruel and unmeaning practical jokes to which they are exposed, by men who have ceased many years ago to be school-boys. Our camp is full of significant, if small, indications of a mocking and unsympathizing spirit which, no doubt, the native reciprocates. There is no such enemy to a black skin as your Anglo-Saxon who has done so much for liberty. In his hands, slavery, which the Spaniard, the Portuguese, and even the Frenchman, made compatible with some degree of friendly feeling of intercourse and of mutual good-will, became so hard and dreadful, that his own love of freedom revolted at the results of his involuntary prejudices. We see the exercise of those antipathies developed in the anti-slave-States of the Union, as well as the Carolinas; whilst in South America, as I am told, the relation between master and slave is like that which prevails in Russia between proprietor and artizan serfs. It may be that the native is more to blame for the gulf between us than we are; for his religion digs it deep. He will walk with us, talk with us; but, like Shylock, he will not eat with us, drink with us, or pray with us. Still there is no

Curtius' spirit among us to leap into the chasm. How unlike all this up-country life is to Calcutta, where I was asked to dine with a large party at a rajah's, and where the wealth of the natives, and the long denationalization of the Europeans, smooth the way to larger and more liberal relations between them. But again: how utterly unfit to rule, or legislate for, or comprehend India, or anything Indian but Calcutta, must the Calcutta European be!

For several days I have nothing to put down of any consequence. The Ava has sunk, and with her my first letter from India. The second was merely leaves of my note-book, and some loose pages written to save a mail, on my arrival in Cawnpore. I have been very anxious to find out all particulars about the Cawnpore massacre; but as yet all is obscure. The excellent chaplain of the station, Mr. Moore, brought up an old woman who was ayah in Sir Hugh Wheeler's household, and was present at the massacre at the boats; but she gave a very confused and incoherent account of all that passed, and at last burst into tears, which put an end to her story. One fact is clearly established; that the writing behind the door, on the walls of the slaughterhouse, on which so much stress was laid in Calcutta, did not exist when Havelock entered the place, and therefore was not the work of any of the poor victims. It has excited many men to fury—the cry has gone all over India. It has been scratched on the wall of Wheeler's intrenchment, and on the walls of many bungalows. God knows the horrors and atrocity of the pitiless slaughter needed no aggravation. Soldiers in the heat of action need little excitement to vengeance.

I had almost forgotten, so very little is his presence remarked in camp, that Sir Archdale Wilson of Delhi is here in charge of the artillery. He has a little mess of his own, consisting of Major Johnson, Colonel Hogge and Biddulph; and he is rarely seen except in the evening, when he walks about with his cheroot in his mouth. I hear now, that much of the kudos he received was undeserved, and rather that it belonged to his subordinates. He is said to have been vacillating, undecided, and desponding, and at the supreme moment he was overcome, and unable to give any orders—so Delhi men tell me. As an artillery officer, he was for continual hammering, and doing everything by artillery. He is a tall soldierly-looking man, with a small brow, quick eye, and large feeble mouth. But whatever his demerits or virtues, he was commander of the army before Delhi when the place fell, and his honours are due to him, and to his position.

Captain Peel and his blue jackets, with their heavy guns, are in advance on the road to Lucknow; but I see him often in camp. He rides over to confer with Sir Colin, and perhaps to "chide each dull delay" by his impetuous gallant spirit. His white trousers unstrapped, a pair of hunting-spurs on his shoes, a blue undress frock coat, with the post-captain's three gold bands on the cuff, and a cap with a white cover—his invariable rig—mark him as a sailor. There is apparently nothing doing here; but, besides the duty imposed on the Chief of waiting for Jung Bahadoor to enter Oude and to see the Agra convoy safe, there is something yet to be done in the way of getting up matériel. Thousands of coolies, and of men, women, and children-labourers are busy on the works of the *tête-de-pont*, or rather are lazy on them. The dust of the whole neighbourhood for miles round, as these people go to and return from their labour, is distressing. All the country about Cawnpore is covered with the finest powdered dust, two or three inches deep, which rises into the air on the smallest provocation. It is composed of sand, pulverized earth, and the brick powder and mortar of the dilapidated houses; whatever, in fact, can turn into dust. As the natives shuffle along, their pointed slippers fling up suffocating clouds of this unpleasant compound, and when these slippers are multiplied by thousands, the air is filled with a floating stratum of it, fifteen or eighteen feet high, and extending over the whole of the station. Even in the old days, when the roads were watered, the station of Cawnpore had a bad notoriety for dust. What an earthquake to shake to pieces, what a volcano to smother with lava and ashes, has this mutiny been! Not alone cities, but confidence and trust have gone, never more to be restored!

Among those heaps of dust and ashes, those arid mounds of brick, those new-made trenches, I try in vain to realize what was once this station of Cawnpore. The solemn etiquette, the visits to the Brigadier and the General *en grande tenue*, the invitations to dinner, the white kid-gloves, the balls, the liveries, the affectation of the *plus haut ton des hauts tons*, the millinery anxieties of the ladies, the ices, and champagne, and supper, the golden-robed Nana Sahib, moving about amid haughty stares and ill-concealed dislike. "What the deuce does the General ask that nigger here for?" The little and big flirtations, the drives on the road —a dull, ceremonious pleasure—the faded fun of the private theatricals, the exotic absurdities of the masonic revels, the marryings and givings in marriage, the little bills done by the rich bunneahs, the small and great pecuniary relations between the station and the bazaar, the sense of security—and then on all this exaggerated relief of an English garrison-town and watering-place, the deep gloom of apprehension—at first "a shave of old Smith's," than a well-authenticated report, then a certainty of disaffection—rolling like thunder-clouds, and darkening the glassy surface of the gay society till it burst on it in stormy and cruel reality. But I cannot.

"Ah! you should have seen Cawnpore in its palmy days, when there were two cavalry regiments here, a lot of artillery, and three regiments of infantry in the cantonments. Chock full of pretty women! The private theatricals every week; balls, and picnics, and dinners every evening. By Jove! it's too horrible to look at it now!" And so, indeed, it was. But one is tempted to ask if there is not some lesson and some warning given to our race in reference to India by the tremendous catastrophe of Cawnpore? How are we to prevent its recurrence? I am deeply impressed by the difficulty of ruling India, as it is now governed by force, exercised by a few who are obliged to employ natives as the instruments of coercion. That force is the base of our rule I have no doubt; for I see nothing else but force employed in our relations with the governed. The efforts to improve the condition of the

BEGGARS AND WIGWAM VILLAGES. 195

people are made by bodies or individuals who have no connection with the Government. The action of the Government in matters of improvement is only excited by considerations of revenue. Does it, as the great instructor of the people, the exponent of our superior morality and civilization—does it observe treaties, show itself moderate, and just, and regardless of gain? Are not our courts of law condemned by ourselves? Are they not admitted to be a curse and a blight upon the country? In effect, the grave, unhappy doubt which settles on my mind is, whether India is the better for our rule, so far as regards the social condition of the great mass of the people. We have put down widow-burning, we have sought to check infanticide; but I have travelled hundreds of miles through a country peopled with beggars and covered with wigwam villages.

CHAPTER XIII.

Action at Meeangunj.—Sir Colin Campbell and Jung Bahadoor.
—Hindoo temples mined.—Moonlight walk with Sir Colin.—
Notes on the birds.—A bad day for quadrupeds.—Fishing in
the Ganges.—Morning devotions.—Our first haul.—Plan of
attack on Lucknow.—General notion of our plan of attack.—
Astonishment of an old Sikh.—Scene of the Cawnpore tragedy.
Divine service in the ruined church.—A distant cannonade.—
Reports of spies.—The enemy in immense force.—The Adjutant-
General.—A near approach to ubiquity.—Camp of the Agra
convoy.—Rotting corpses.

February 18*th*.—Norman came over to me with an account of a little action at Meeangunj, over in Oude, —a sanguinary affair for the enemy. It was an attack on an old walled town in which were some mutineers and rebels. The place was gallantly attacked; but the men gave way to some license, and Hope Grant had to punish the criminals of Her Majesty's gallant 53rd pretty sharply. The cavalry charged the runaways, among whom were many townspeople, and cut them down indiscriminately. "Indeed, how could they discriminate?"

After breakfast Colonel Sterling showed me some interesting papers relating to the relief of Lucknow. It seems that the necessities of the garrison had from time to time been greatly exaggerated, and that Havelock, Outram, and Sir Colin Campbell have all in turn been deceived with respect to the quantity of supplies in the Residency, and the period for which the be sieged could be fed. Had Sir Colin Campbell known the real state of the case, he could have waited some

ime longer, and have collected such a force as would
have enabled him to have occupied Lucknow, instead
of retiring from it with the women and garrison, and
giving it up to the enemy. Recollecting the statements in the papers just before I sailed, I was much
surprised when I found that Sir Colin had only 4000
men to relieve the Residency. When he announced
his intention to retire, Outram asked if he had the
authority of the Governor-General in Council to do so.
Sir Colin telegraphed at once, and received Lord Canning's permission to act according to the best of his
judgment. Meantime, he had fixed on Alumbagh for
the site of the post of observation, to be left under
Outram, as a kind of intimation to the Lucknow
people that the British were not losing sight of them,
and were coming back again.

Sir Colin paid me a visit in my tent in order
to let me see some news from Jung Bahadoor's
force. He chafes at the delays of the Goorkhas;
but McGregor's despatches showed that there was
no *arrière-pensée* in the ally's procrastination; that,
in his opinion, it was really caused by bad organization and want of everything that the army should
have, such as transport, food, and ammunition. Lord
Canning strongly urges on Sir Colin not to move
without the Goorkhas. He points out that Jung
Bahadoor is dying for military distinction, and that if
we were to operate against Lucknow before he came
up, we might give him offence and drive him back to
his mountains in a huff. Is the power of the man, of
his State, or the aid of his troops so great, that we
should hold our hands for fear of offending him? I see
that Sir Colin, who is accused of dilatoriness, is really

annoyed at all those impediments. He has telegraphed to know positively when Jung will cross over into Oude. Our relations with those gentlemen are rather more difficult in these days than in the less prudish times of Clive. Jung Bahadoor is not over nice in his morals, and is notorious, even among Hindoo princes, for his sensuality. *Eh bien!* He has taken our Commissioner, Colonel McGregor, so completely into his confidence, that he agonizes that excellent Presbyterian and Christian by affecting to consult him as to his domestic affairs. One would like to know what advice our worthy Commissioner gives on these delicate matters.

Met Macdonald, 93rd, our old Provost-Marshal at Balaklava, who told me there was a rumour at Oonao that Her Majesty's 53rd had been attacked by the enemy, and lost men, on their march. As soon as the sun had set into the bank of dust, which rises about 10° above the horizon, I rode out with Stewart to the Hindoo temples over the river, which the engineers are blowing up, as they cover the fire of the guns in the *tête-de-pont*, and, indeed, served to protect the guns which the Gwalior Contingent brought to play against the bridge of boats before Sir Colin crossed over. They are of brick, covered with chunam, and are rather effective in the distance, but on nearer approach turn out to be squalid enough, though massive and strong. Hundreds of coolies were at work pulling down the walls and clearing away heaps of the rubbish; dirty fakeers sat Marius-like amid the ruins, but no one seemed to care at the desecration of the holy places; and the horrid little gods, three-headed monsters of mud stuffed with straw, were lying about under our feet in mutilated overthrow, without exciting the horror or any other emotion, as far as I could see, of their worshippers; nay, some of them threw a four-headed image into the river, and laughed as it sank in the water. What did they laugh at? The mines will soon be tamped, and the whole nest of temples will leap into the air amid fire and thunder. Only one thing proves the people don't like our proceedings; they steal away at night, and it is difficult to procure labourers for the works.

At dusk, groped through clouds of dust to the Rifle Camp, and dined with Newdegate at the mess, where I found some old friends, but very many young and new faces. It was late when we broke up, for our friends had much to say of the old Crimean days; but the moon was shining brightly, and only the road separated the grove, in which the Rifle Camp was pitched, from the sandy plain, in which stood the Head-Quarters' tents: not a soul was visible on road or plain. The tents shone like cones of snow in the light; no sentry challenged as I approached the main street; not a voice could be heard—but on looking towards the end, I saw one solitary figure pacing up and down in silent thought. As I got nearer, I recognized the well-known and peculiar light soldierly step and figure of Sir Colin, who was perhaps, pursuing the same train of thought that Shakespeare attributes to Henry before the day of St. Crispin. We had a long and interesting conversation. He laid the greatest stress on the all-importance of handling soldiers judiciously when they are taken under fire for the first time. "It may take years to make infantry, which has once received a severe check, feel confidence in itself again; indeed, it will never be done, perhaps, except by most careful handling. It is still longer before cavalry, once beaten, recover the dash and enterprise which constitute so much of their merit." I understood him to allude to the conduct of some of the regiments under Windham at Cawnpore, which had been engaged in two unsuccessful assaults against the Redan. The variety of illustration, the keenness and excellence of reasoning, which distinguish Sir Colin's remarks on military matters, render his conversation very instructive and delightful. So eager is he when once engaged in a demonstration, that he cares not for time or place. So, to-night he took me into his tent to show me some papers, late as it was; but he could not find them, and I bowed myself to bed.

February 19th.—A light shower pattered on our tents this morning; but the thirsty earth drank it all up, and in a moment after the last drop fell, the canvas had smoked itself dry, the stones were all blanched again, and the mud flew into dust, the earth, like a half-satisfied drunkard, only craving the more for drink. Ere breakfast I went down to the end of the camp, which is just over the river, and made notes on the birds, which, however, were by no means numerous, though we had our usual whirling clouds of swifts, buzzards, kites, vultures and crows. Some pretty metallic fly-catchers in the shrubs over the stream—great adjutants stalking by the filthy banks —a squalid island covered with human bones—and over, in Oude, a dancing hazy sandbank, topped with trees, were all that met the eye, save a long and lofty column of dust on the left, which marked the road of the convoys out to our camps, on the road to Lucknow. At breakfast prophecies of heat, and certain indications of tough mutton. There are no horses to be had—a universal complaint. To-day I was fain to buy a spiteful, half-broken, country-bred mare, for between 30*l.* and 40*l.*, about three times her ordinary value. When I went out to ride this evening Stewart borrowed her, and I took Sir Colin's fine white charger, a very large, powerful horse, up to anything except making friends with elephants or camels. I visited the old mosques again. On my way back, passing the assembly-rooms, I turned in to hear the band play, and to talk to some of the Rifle Brigade and the 88th, whom I recognized in the distance. I dismounted, and an artilleryman held the horse for about half an hour. What he did to him I don't know; but as I was remounting him, ere I got well into the saddle, he reared violently, and stood straight on his hind legs. An attempt to start him only brought on another tremendous rear, which made me feel as if he was coming right over on me, and so I slipped, with more agility than grace, out of the pigskin, and slid over his shoulders to the ground, where I was received by hard gravel and the congratulations of my friends. The inexplicable thing is, that on mounting the horse again, he went with the greatest quietness, and showed no inclination to rear. Visited the temples again, and found that Stewart had lamed my new purchase—a nail in the hoof. A bad day for quadrupeds. No news from Jung Bahadoor yet. Our preparations are incessant. "Over the river" seems a gulf into which streams of grain, hay, cattle, men, horses, carts, camels, and elephants disappear never to return. Watched otters feeding along the banks this evening. They certainly make fine feasting on the nasty Hindoo-fed fish. One otter made a bold rush at a kind of sea-eagle, which came cruising about after a large fish he had captured and carried up on the bank.

February 20th.—Those otters so fascinated me that I went out this morning early to fish; Pat. Stewart and Baird went with me, and we had chuprassies, with guns, &c., to coerce the faithful. The Ganges has eaten away the bank on the right side, below Cawnpore, so that it forms a steep wall of earth, some thirty feet high; at the Oude side, the waters roll over sandy shelving slopes, which melt gradually into the green fields. There were plenty of boats, large open flat-bottomed craft, like a light Thames barge, and we soon selected one near some nets which were drying on the strip of sand between the course of the stream and the bottom of the bank. The river is here about seven hundred yards broad, and its current is divided by large beds of bare sand, on which were heaps of human bones. These are accumulated from the bodies which come floating down the river, and are arrested by the banks till they are quite decomposed. As one of the islands is opposite the ghaut where the boat massacre took place, I could not help imagining that some of those bones might be those of our poor murdered countrymen, and felt a desire to have them interred, but there were no means of doing so.

Our fishing threatened to be frustrated; for though we had boat and nets, we had no fishermen. However, one of the chuprassies started off to rout out the inhabitants of a few poor cottages near at hand, and we sat down in the shade of a boat on some balks of timber. Presently a lean old man came down to the river near us, and began his devotions, or poojah, for the morning. He unwound his turban and uncovered his head, which was shaved clean at the top in a furrow from the forehead to the back of the poll, so that he looked very much like a clown with two stiff ruffs of hair at each side of his head. Taking his loto, or brass pot, in his hand, he walked into the stream, which is as foul as the Thames at low tide, and having rinced his mouth with the sacred waters, proceeded to pour out libations on his crown and chest, rubbing himself all the time with one hand, and squinting with satisfaction. Then he squatted down till the waters came up to his neck, and began a low prayer, which lasted for a few moments; after which he returned to the shore, washed his turban-cloth, and laid it out to dry in the sun. Then he began a most extraordinary series of evolutions, saying a prayer on one leg, with the big toe of the other foot crooked round his ancle, then on the other; taking up the mud and smearing it on his forehead; next saying a prayer on his belly, and kissing the earth repeatedly; then slowly turning round and ducking his forehead to the ground at each point of the compass, and then reciting in a loud voice a long invocation to "Ram," with his eyes turned up to heaven, and his hands clasped as if in supplication. He then decently washed his dotie, or loin-cloth, put on his turban, again rinsed his mouth, and walked away with the mud hardening, on his forehead, his shoulders, and arms, into a thick yellowish paste. He never took the least notice of us till, in reply to a "chaffing" question, he made a short answer, not ill-humouredly, and left us. Whilst he was praying, several bloated bodies, covered with crows and vultures, came floating down the river close to us, poisoning the air and water, but he took not the least notice of them.

Our fishermen had now come up in custody of the chuprassic, and we rowed out to one of the islands, whilst the net was spread in a wide curve from the shore, the fishermen wading and beating the stream with long sticks, to drive the fish towards it. Our first haul was quite enough for me. It brought up a number of very hideous fish, a little longer than herrings, with long bodies, large silver scales, with light yellow bellies, large black eyes, and very long pectoral fins, provided with sharp spines, with which they hopped actively on the ground. Another sort, a little larger, were fish covered with a slimy skin, greasy and pustulous, with mouths like that of a shark, from which projected long worm-like feelers. A third sort had very sharp spines at the gill and back fins, and made a croaking noise like a frog when taken out of the water; but, worse than all, the net brought up parts of human skeletons, some with flesh upon them. A few *coups de filet* were quite enough for me, and we went back to breakfast. Our fish were cooked; but they were to me a forbidden dainty. Others, more philosophical and less nice, who declared that whatever fish ate became fish, and partook of our spoils, said they were exceedingly rich and good. I have resolved never to eat fish whilst I remain in India. I almost forgot to say, that at one draw a fish, which seemed to be three feet long, dashed right through the net and made across the bank *with one of the fishermen* after him: but the fish swam faster than the Hindoo could run, and got off triumphantly. Attempted to write, but found the heat very great. The perspiration, dropping from my forehead, blotted the letters, and my hand steamed literally as if I had just come out of a Turkish bath.

Saw the Chief, and got a general notion of our plan of attack. We seize on the Dilkoosha, a palace with large enclosed park, on the Goomtee, at the south-east of the city, and thence proceed against the works which the enemy have thrown up, enclosing the city from the Goomtee by the line of an old canal up to the bridge which Havelock and Outram crossed on their advance into the city. The great mass of the city—a wilderness of lanes and narrow tortuous streets, nearly as large as Paris—lies to the north and west of this bridge, from which a road leads to the Residency. Sir Colin is determined to have no street fighting. He will batter down their mud walls and shell the palaces, which form the strongholds and centre of the enemy's position. They are on the east side of the city, and extend almost in a line parallel with the route to the Residency, north and south from the suburbs to the river Goomtee. The line on which Sir Colin advances is familiar to him, for it is that which he took on going to the relief of the garrison. It seems that all the reports we heard in England of the strength of the force under Sir Colin on that occasion were absurd exaggerations. This comes of the Venetian secrecy of the Indian Government. Misapprehensions, which may often give rise to serious inconvenience, are thus caused at home; for the public are obliged to rely on the misinformation of the Calcutta press. When Sir Colin advanced on Lucknow—I saw the figures and returns this very day—he had a force of 5,536 infantry and cavalry, (946 horses,) of which nearly 1,000 men were left in the Dilkoosha, when he advanced to fight his way to the Residency: Windham had 2,402 men left with him at Cawnpore; Outram had 2,683 men and 527 horses when Havelock and he forced their way to the Residency. It was very fortunate that the Chief did not delay at Lucknow; for if all I hear be true, the garrison of the *tête-de-pont* at Cawnpore was in a demoralized state when he reached the other side of the river. The Rev. Mr. Moore, with whom I had some very interesting conversation to-day, said that the men got quite out of hand after their retreat. They broke open the stores, took the wine provided for the sick, smashed open the officers' boxes—many of them were inebriated. This is a sad picture! An old Sikh, who was standing at the gate of the work, lifted up his hands in wonder when he saw the men running past in disorder, and said aloud, "You are not brothers of the men who beat the Khalsa!" He patted some of them on the back and said, "Don't be afraid: there's nothing to hurt you." The fact is, that the men—young soldiers, many of them half-drilled, belonging to a great number of regiments, were seized with a panic when the retreat became necessary. They were crushed by the heavy fire of the enemy's artillery. They were— but who is to tell all the truth? Some men and some regiments fought as well as the best on the best of our fields. Others appear to have recollected only the bad handling of the 18th June and 8th September, 1855. The first thing Colonel Napier saw when he got into the entrenchment was one of his boxes, which had contained all the records of his long services, lying broken open, and some of the papers scattered all over the place. The others were lost, never to be recovered. Nothing more to say to-day, except that just as we were going to blow up the principal mosque on the river, it was discovered it belonged to a well-disposed native, and Sir Colin gave orders that it should be spared.

February 21st. Quadragesima Sunday.—Ere the sun got hot, took a walk to the ghaut where Wheeler's garrison was attacked on embarking, and was cruelly slaughtered, with the exception of the unhappy ladies. It is a place of horrid memory, well-suited, by its position, for the atrocious stratagem. Had our soldiers not been taken by surprise, they would, no doubt, have carried the guns, swept the assassins out of their lurking-places, cleared the beach, and covered the embarkation effectually. The road by which the procession marched to the boats goes past our camp; I followed it, past ruined bungalows, till I came to a bridge over a dry watercourse, by the side of which a path, deeply indented in the earth, struck off to the left, down to the river. The nullah expanded as it neared the stream, and its naked sides assumed an appearance of verdure at its junction with the Ganges. A temple (I have called the Hindoo pagodas "mosques" several times, owing to old Turkish associations) stood on the high ground over the river, embedded in trees, thick groves fringe the slope of the banks, and hide the few native cottages which overlook the current. Here the guns were masked, and the ambush was planted. My imagination completed the details of the dreadful picture: the waters flowed red with blood—the air was filled with the smoke of musketry—the thick white puffs, through which rustle flights of deadly grape, roll from the trees—the despairing screams of women rise above the hellish tumult of the murderers and their victims —streams of black smoke rise from the burning boats! I turned and left the spot with every vein boiling, and it was long ere I could still the beatings of my heart.

Divine service in the church, which is all in ruins. Where is the memorial church of Cawnpore? It seems to me almost a mistake to re-establish our station here. We could easily move it a few miles away, and let the city perish altogether; but the railway station will determine that point. The lesson for the day seemed to me, in the state of mind in which I was, to have peculiar significance, though, perhaps, it was not more applicable to Cawnpore than to any place wherein it was read to-day—" We will destroy this place, because the cry of them is waxen great before the face of the Lord."

February 22nd.—Went once more to the ghaut, and thence returning, went to the Rev. Mr. Moore's bungalow (in ruins) and breakfasted. Found there Maxwell, 88th Regiment, and Mr. Dangerfield; Maxwell has an Arab for 100*l.*, but it is too light for me. This evening bade good-bye to Mansfield, who is going home wounded, and to Alison, who has lost his arm. The latter did his best to stay; but his wound is in a very bad state. He is well-informed, well-read, and clever, and Sir Colin will feel his loss.

The old ayah whom Mr. Wheeler sent for, told me Sir H. Wheeler's head was struck off as he leaned out of his dooly, at the ghaut; but she does not seem to be a very good authority. In spite of the heat, I managed to write a good deal to-day, and sent off my letters before the evening.

February 23rd. — Camp hours are invasions of civilized life. Long ere dawn, lights shine in our tents, horses are brought round, and cups of tea, held under one's nose, stimulate us to meet the cold mussack. Just as I was out of bed, Sir Colin was good enough to visit me with some papers relating to that terrible impedimentum, Jung Bahadoor, who is evidently the present *bête noir* of our General's life. Sir Colin has at last prevailed on Lord Canning to permit him to move without waiting for the Goorkhas; but the permission is given in very vague terms. He then went off to view D'Aguilar's troop. One of his favourite themes, in regard to Horse Artillery, is the neglect of the Royals to carry a proper quantity of ammunition; and the fact that Maude's troop had only twenty-four rounds a gun, on the memorable 25th October, at Balaklava, has evidently made a lasting impression on his mind. Walpole's brigade came in this morning, and occupied the ground of the regiments which crossed into Oude, and we also received cavalry reinforcements, which bring up our strength here to 1,300 sabres. Just as we were lighting cheroots and pipes in the mess-tent, after breakfast, I heard, as I thought, the dull beat of a heavy gun far away; I listened, and in a moment more three or four reports followed in quick succession. "Listen to the firing!" "Where?" "Don't you hear it?" "No:

it's only a nigger knocking against the tent." But I was positive; and in half-an-hour the sounds were heard by all in camp, and lasted till mid-day. There is nothing to rouse one like the sound of a cannonade: it's a tremendous electrifier, and the oldest soldier pricks up his ears at it.

It is strange that surprises now seem more common than in ancient warfare; for the tumult of musketry and guns sets every one on his feet in an instant, and in old times a general might move an army, almost without a sound, close to his enemy. It is probable that outposts were further advanced, and that the duty of vedettes and picquets was very carefully performed. Surprises could not, however, have been as serious as they are now, when guns can be brought into play, and a heavy fire opened, with destructive effect, on unprepared men. I take it the old mercenaries could be scarcely taken unprepared. Each man had his arms at hand; now, guns have to be limbered up, horses harnessed, ammunition served out, &c., &c. The firing is at Alumbagh, some forty odd miles away.

Went over to the Commander-in-Chief's tent, and found him busily engaged with Colonel Napier (not one of the Napiers; but as good a soldier as ever lived), looking over plans and maps of Lucknow, and referring, now and then, to the reports of the spies from the city. How feeble these were—a very small quantity of bread to an immense outpouring of watery sack. "Abdoola Khan is in charge of a moorcha (battery) at the Roomee Duwarza, with 4 guns, 1,000 sepoys, and 3,000 nujeebs (irregulars). The Begum is greatly pleased with Mummoo Khan, and says he is the only man who fights the infidels; but she reproaches Ram Buksh, and says his heart is of water; last night there was a great sermon by a holy man from Mecca; a magazine blew up, but I don't know where, though I believe it was done by a man to whom I offered a reward,"— and so on.

It is quite evident the enemy are in immense force, and that the works around Lucknow are really formidable; but Sir Colin relies on his artillery, and will not waste life in street fighting. It becomes a question now, whether he or the Governor-General was right in their respective plans of campaign. Here are both Rohilcund and Oude in the hands of the enemy; whereas, if the General's plans had been followed, we should have only Lucknow to deal with, though, no doubt, the Rohilcund people would have flocked to augment the garrison. I heard to-day, for the first time, from the lips of the General, that " the Governor-General of India has absolute control over, and command of, the army in the field, so far as the direction of the campaign and the points of operation are concerned." Having had a sight of the plans, I was glad to get back to my tent. Whew! how hot it gets at noon now. The silence is oppressive, almost; nothing but the neighing of horses, and the screams of the kites and buzzards; the slow guggle of the natives' hubble-bubbles, and now and then a native orderly inquiring for the "Lord Sahib ka dera" (the Commander-in-Chief's tent), breaks the lazy repose in the street; but inside the tents nearly all are busy, for there are few drones, except the aides, whose lives alternate between spasmodic excitement, activity of the most energetic character, and intervals of novel-reading. The heads of departments are always busy. No one near General Mansfield has a sinecure. Norman, the Adjutant-General of the army, is a sort of steam-engine, made of bones, flesh (very little of that), blood, and brains; and his tent, to any one but himself, might bear the inscription of the Inferno. Colonel Pakenham pours out his soul over schedules all day long, and may be seen wandering, now and then, in the precincts of the Sahib ka dera, in the hope of securing a few moments' consideration of those important, but rather sawdusty, documents. Colonel Pakenham was, for a long time, head of the Adjutant-General's department in the Crimea, and it is certain that in that department there was little to blame, for if not always *suave*, he is certainly indefatigable in office work, and endowed with a quaint humour often found in combination with a correct, if hard, judgment, and with serviceable sagacity; now, by the fortune of war, he finds himself, as it were, playing second fiddle to a lieutenant in the 31st Bengal Native Infantry, who is Adjutant-General to the whole army — Queen's troops and Company's—though Colonel Pakenham is the official organ for the former. As to little George Allgood, no nearer approach can be made to ubiquity than, by the aid of thorough-bred Arabs, hard-riding, and incessant work and exertion, he manages to effect daily. If you look for him in his tent, he is there; take a hard gallop in ten minutes after, and you see a not over tall youngster, with a heavy blond beard, tremendous solar topee, and long riding-boots, which recall that lucent original in which pussy gazed delightedly at her reflected visage, taking angles and bearings in some remote field, and then scampering across country, straight as an arrow, to some other point of stratification. He is the Quartermaster-General; lays out the camp, makes plans, procures information. Then there are the doctors and the officers of the Commissariat, whose life is one long report. No wonder, as the sun turns into a great red-hot cannon-ball, sinking rapidly to rest through a haze of vapour, they all rush gasping to their horses, and take a canter, in clouds of smoke-like dust, till darkness and dinner-hour arrive.

This evening, Stewart, Lord Seymour, and I, rode over to the camp of the Agra convoy, which is pitched on the plain near Wheeler's entrenchment. It was a wonderful sight! The tents, of all shapes and sizes, were barricaded by gharrys, buggys, gigs, palkees, and the air was shrill with the voices of women and children; ladies in hats and bonnets, once the envy of up-country stations, flitted across the canvas streets, and fair children, borne by black-faced ayahs, or escorted by their bearers, prattled on all sides. I hear that there is, in this little canvas city, as nice an observance of the rules of society, and as fine gradations of social position, as in the oldest cathedral-town, or the newest watering-place. "The women had such jolly rows all the way down from Agra," quoth a merry little sub., but a very ungallant one; and I'm sure he must have maligned the ladies. Some of the officers had been present when Greathed permitted his "avenging column" to be surprised. They assured me he did not even post picquets; and that the enemy's cavalry were in on them before they dreamed of an attack. The women, children, and civilians had been shut up in the fort of Agra for months; but the rebels never ventured within range of the guns. All the country, they said, was disaffected; but the Indian agricultural population do not join in the conflicts of the armed classes, and accept the rule of the conquerors passively. A rifle officer told me, that in their recent patrol, they came upon several topes full of rotting corpses, which indicated the places where the Special Commissioners had been executing justice—an *in rei memoriam* not apt to be speedily forgotten

CHAPTER XIV.

The army massing itself.—A living *corpus delicti*.—Sir J. Outram attacked.—Buy a gharry, a horse, and coachman.—Our army on the move.—Destruction of Hindoo temples.—Reply to a priest's intercession.—War, and no quarter given.—Indiscriminate executions.—Striking tents.—Camels and their burdens.—A welcome invitation.—Cross the Ganges into Oude.—An apparently illimitable procession.—A notion of Old World times.—"Master's mess buckree."—Ruined villages.—Orders for marching.

February 24th.—The enemy are becoming very uneasy at our gradual, workmanlike, and, as it were, mechanical advance; the army is massing itself all along the road from this to Bunnee — a column marches from Cawnpore to Oonao, the troops at Oonao move on one march nearer to the front—the regiment in that station goes on to Bunnee,—and so the movement progresses like that of a snake, gathering up fold after fold, till he is ready for his spring. What fine active young fellows are all around us! Sir Colin evidently likes young officers, but keeps them well in hand—not a move is permitted without precise orders—every march is regulated by Mansfield, and the effect of almost every step is weighed by him and the Chief. Invited to dine at the mess of the civilians to-day—they have a big bungalow to themselves, and mess together in consideration of the hard times. Formerly, each man would, of course, have had his separate establishment on a large scale. There were at dinner Sherer, magistrate and collector; Batten, judge; Power, assistant judge; the doctor;

Willock, civilian ; Glyn, of the Rifle Brigade; some anonymous "uncovenanted;" a travelling gent.; and an officer who had just returned from a Jack-Ketch expedition, in which he had great and deserved success. A very pleasant evening, with much discussion of Indian matters, which might have been very instructive to a griffin, were it not that all the authorities differed from each other on every one point. I perceived that the stupid men were sanguinary, shall I say in direct ratio to their stupidity ? One story told of a magistrate, not very far off, was amusing enough. A woman was brought before him charged with the murder of her little daughter, by throwing her into the Ganges: the culprit confessed the crime, alleging that she could not maintain the child, and wished to save her from shame. Sentence of death was passed, and as justice hereabouts is rapid in all its movements, the woman was next day taken forth and hanged with a full company. As the magistrate sat in his cutchery that morning, lo! there came before him a little child, who demanded of the sahib, what he had done with her mother! It was a perplexing question ; for the woman had been executed. It turned out, that the child had been carried down by the current and had been picked up by a fisherman, who kept her till she was sufficiently recovered to walk to the station to find her mother. Maxims of law are not disregarded with impunity; and here was a living *corpus delicti* in a most unpleasant form. What became of the girl I know not; and I suppose the judge, a very well-meaning, excellent man, took to reading Blackstone.

February 25*th*.— Distant cannonading — a telegram from Sir James Outram to say he was attacked by a large force from Lucknow. The result, of course, excites not the smallest conjecture, for it is certain and invariable. Again: an outburst of firing at midday—said to be from Russoolabad, in Oude—which Hope Grant was expected to attack. The Mecangunj affair has struck terror into the outlying rebels. The news from Sir Hugh Rose is not very hopeful. He is obliged to halt from sheer want of supplies. The authorities knew, months before, that he was about to make this march. It shows either that they were apathetic, that the country is hostile, or that it is barren. Sir Hugh has a fine force, is full of work, and is accompanied by Sir Robert Hamilton, and we hope to hear that he will clear all before him when he does move, though it will require hard fighting to do so, as the enemy are strongly posted at Jhansi and at Calpee, the country is exceedingly difficult, the people wild, fierce, and barbarous.

Bought for 60*l.* a gharry, a horse and coachman from an Agra refugee. Well, the coachman is an exaggeration; but he came quite naturally with the horse, and squatted himself down, with his wife and three children, in the rear of my tent, as a matter of course, and just looked as if he were part of the bargain. He belongs to the horse, and the horse belongs to the man who owns the gharry. My next proceeding was to send my white mare *to be broken*; for it appeared that little preliminary had been neglected in early education. Dined with General Mansfield, where there was a small party—no "shop," and very agreeable conversation: the chief not well pleased at the mention of two officers' names as being the first in at the attack on Meeangunj, for he thinks this race after the Victoria Cross is destructive to discipline, and is determined to discountenance it. However, all these things will be forgotten for the moment. We are on the verge of the great move—another forty-eight hours, and hurrah for the Oude campaign!

February 26th.—Busy writing and preparing for the march. Since dawn, a long cloud of dust, rising from the sandy plain across the Ganges, and the roll and tramp of endless wheels, and feet, and hoofs on the bridge, show our army is on the move. Simon's legs are quivering with anxiety and packing up; but there are no cares for carriage, no trouble about transport. See! There are elephants, camels, and oxen at call! Make requisition on that inexhaustible Commissariat! and if the rupees are in your purse, there will be no difficulty about *impedimenta*. In the evening went up to the Ghauts, where the Engineers are, positively this time, about to blow up Siva and her shrines. These latter present a front to the river about as long as that of the Temple Gardens, but they stand at a far greater elevation, being forty or fifty feet above the stream, which is approached by broad flights of white steps. The little nests of temples, which look so fine in the aggregate, are mean enough in the abstract; massive low domes rising from dumpy walls, and covered all over with lotus leaves —dark foul chambers, full of withered flowers, hideous idols, and lignam altars : that which was, perhaps, refined and elegant in Greece, is horrible in Hindostan; but it is not indecent. Last night there was an Engineer "sell" on a great scale; indeed, they are great practical humorists all over the world—nothing diverts them so much as getting together a great crowd to see something blown up, and then not doing it—the docks, or houses of Sebastopol, mines at Chatham, or temples on the Ganges—it's all the same. Last night we had all our trouble for nothing; and indeed I should be sorry to say how often it was the same case before. This evening one old temple obstinately refused to be blown up. Its companions were, however, less resolute, and two of them gave a kick, as it were, upwards in the midst of a column of dust and smoke, and, with a grumble which shook the ground, collapsed into heaps of brick, white plaster, and earth. None of the natives came to look at it, except the coolies engaged in the works and a few fakirs, who looked as if they thought the lightning from heaven would blast us. It must have been a great triumph for them when the stubborn old temple had its own way. And why not? The Russians showed me a gate of the Kremlin which was split by French gunpowder just up to the edge of a picture of the Virgin—*there* the force of the explosion was arrested.

Two of the mines were fired ingeniously by Pat Stewart this evening. He had some Jacob's shells for his rifle, and, standing quite out of danger, he fired one at some loose powder on a stone, whereon the end of the fuse was lying. The shell exploded, fired the powder, and ignited the fuse, and, after a second or two, the temples, spitting fire and smoke out of their mouth-like 'gateways, were seized with sudden convulsions and dropped to pieces. Alas! dirty fakirs and Brahmins, your triumph was but short. Like the mediæval miracles which saved the lives of holy men many times only to let them become martyrs at last, so Siva's interposition is transitory, and her temple is doomed. Some of those priests interceded for the safety of their shrines: "Now listen to me," Robert Napier made reply. "You were all here when our women and children were murdered. You were at those shrines and temples which we are about to destroy, not for vengeance, as you know well, but on account of military considerations connected with the safety of the bridge. If any one of you can show he did an act of kindness to a Christian man, woman, or child—nay, if he can prove that he uttered one word of intercession for the life of any one of them, I will promise you, and pledge myself, the temple where he worshipped shall be spared." Well said, brave Robert Napier! There was no reply, and the temples were destroyed. On our return to dinner, found the general orders had been fulminated at last, as I suspected they would yesterday. The Head-Quarters' camp marches to-morrow at day-break for Oonao; but, as the chief wishes to set all things straight at Cawnpore ere he leaves, and to sweep the army before him, Sir Colin, and Mansfield, and their immediates, wait here till we have arrived within a march of Lucknow. In pursuance of his usual policy, Sir Colin had not permitted any one to know his intentions till the orders were out, but it was surmised by the natives several days ago, and the Commissariat gomashtas, from signs in their sky, known only to themselves, had predicted the movement to a moment. Very annoying to the General, but almost unavoidable.

The animation of our dinner to-night is remarkable—great clatter of tongues, and I think more popping of corks and clatter of knife and fork than usual. Our luxuries are not many, for the sherry is pronounced to be queer, the port is groggy, and our drink is beer, claret being reduced to a short supply of *ordinaire*. The soup still maintains its gelatinous robustness; our curries are leathery as ever; and our great resources are mutton, and ineffable pastry. Tonight, the great mess-tent, which will be borne by four camels and an elephant, will be packed up, with our apparatus of tables, plate, crockery, bitter beer, and provisions, and the army of servants which belong to it; and we take the field, very much as his majesty Louis the Great would depart from Versailles, for the theatre of war. As for myself, I am delighted at the prospect of escaping from this monotonous dreary dusty Cawnpore, and the very hum and no drum sort of life I have been leading. Oude is, they say, the garden of India; here everything is blighted, burnt, and ruined. There are no courts to see, no schools, no intercourse between the people and the authorities, except such as spies conduct, or the ruder relations of justice and punishment, which are surely very unedifying. I shall see beside, though in a cruel, exterminating form, in which no quarter is given on either side, all the pomp of eastern warfare, which, if now it has no glory, has at least circumstance enough. It is horrible to be engaged in such a war. Wherever the rebels meet a Christian, or a white man, they at once slay him pitilessly. The natives who conceal these do so at their peril. Wherever we meet a rebel in arms, or any man on whom suspicion rests, we kill him with equal celerity, and without any greater show of pity. Foreign nations are watching us as closely as they can; but there is a long space of land and sea to cross, and little or nothing is known at Calcutta, where there are, it is said, some correspondents of a few French journals. A French general, in a letter to Sir Colin, expressed his regret at certain violences attributed to some of our officers in cold blood—I presume alluding to Hodson shooting the princes at Delhi, and things of that sort; but he should know that here there is no cold blood at the sight of a rebel. His military apophthegm "*que les représailles sont toujours inutiles,*" would be applicable in a state of war; but we consider ourselves engaged in suppressing a rebellion and a mutiny in which the actors have perpetrated great crimes. When Neill marched from Allahabad, his executions were so numerous and so indiscriminate, that one of the officers attached to his column had to remonstrate with him on the ground that if he depopulated the country he could get no supplies for the men. Sir Colin is utterly opposed to such extreme and reckless severity, though he is the last man in the world to spare mutinous soldiers with arms in their hands.

February 27th.—When I entered my tent last night I found all my things packed up, sword cleaned, pistols laid out, and everything ready, according to my servant's notion, for a dreadful campaign full of personal encounters. But the commencement, at all events, was to be made in peaceful guise. All things considered, Stewart and I thought it was best to proceed into Oude triumphantly in our gharry. Many things induce us to take this resolve—the heat of a late march, the dust, and our wish to stay in camp as late as possible. About an hour after midnight, the camp, which is usually profoundly quiet till the first signs of dawn, was disturbed by a strange noise which at first sounded like the clatter of many horses' hoofs on a hard plain; but as it neither advanced nor receded, it became quite necessary to find some other solution, and on getting up and putting my head out into the moonlight I saw all the Kelassies in a state of unprecedented activity, hammering away at the numerous tent-pegs with billets of wood, to loosen them in the ground that they might be readily pulled up when the tent is to be struck. No one but a very old Indian warrior could sleep in such a noise. Besides that, the scene was so novel that it fixed my attention at once. In a bright blue sky, wherein a cloudless moon sailed serenely through the twinkling stars, there rose up, far and wide, innumerable columns of smoke, now white in the light, or black in shade, from the camp-fires, around which the camp-followers were warming themselves, in the keen pure night air. Far as the eye could reach across the plain —whereon stood, like skeletons and gallows, the leafless and branchless stumps of trees—the fires wavered and sparkled, each a Phœbus to a world of black spirits all clad in white, and worshipping the rays of their luminary. In the remote distance, rose in front, the ruins of bungalows, the shells of the church and Assembly Rooms and Masonic Hall, and the ragged low outline of the native city. Behind the camp, the Ganges, for once picturesque, rolled and gurgled in a broad twirling sheet of silver, between us and the Oude horizon, now blackened into a coarse framework of forest. The bridge of boats which spanned it looked like the trunk of a giant tree; but the hum of voices and the creaking of cart-wheels directed the eye to its outline, and then one could make out, against the silvery course of the stream, an incessant dark jagged thread, which moved onwards and across into Oude.—The camp-followers and the bazaars were already moving towards the next camp. As I watched, a wonderful ingredient was added to the tumult, which had been waxing higher every moment, in the camp. This was an aggregate of prolonged angry grumbling grunts, swelling by degrees into a storm of furious sound, which raged far and wide over the camp. I had never heard the like before; but the cause was not doubtful. In the rear of each tent were couched three or four camels, which had been brought up noiselessly from their own part of the world, and were now expressing their resentment at present and their apprehensions of future wrongs. The moment the dood-wallah pulls the string, which is attached to a piece of wood passed through the cartilage of the animal's nostril, the camel opens its huge mouth, garnished with hideous blackened tusks, projecting like *chevaux-de-frise* from its lips, and from the depths of its inner consciousness and of its wonderful hydraulic apparatus, gets up groans and roarings full of plaintive anger, the force of which can only be realized by actual audience. When solicited by the jerking of their noses, they condescend to kneel down and tuck their legs under them; they are prevented rising by a rope which is passed under the fore-knee and round their necks. All this time their complaints wax furious as the pile grows upon their backs, and do not cease till long after they have risen and stalked off with their loads in endless file, the nose rope of one being fastened to the tail of another, and so on $n + 1$. I do not remember any traveller who mentions this riotous conduct on the part of the camel, though there are some who have done full justice to their unpleasant odours. I was so interested in the scene that I remained out till the sky began to warm up in the east. Long before that time, some twenty tents of our little city had tottered to their fall, and others were fast collapsing, or were being made up in detached round cylindrical rolls to fit on the camel's back. Their tenants, fortified with an early cup of tea and a cigar, had ridden away for the bridge; and when I turned in there were only some five or six tents standing in isolation on the ground: the rest had vanished, and left no trace behind.

The sun was high and hot when I awoke. My camels were waiting for their load; and in two or three minutes my habitation lay prostrate, and was being dissected into separate members by the Kelassies. Whilst Stewart and I were preparing for our start, the chief came out of his tent and asked us to breakfast with him—a very welcome invitation. He seems quite pleased at getting off at last; and if the work is to be done, it were best done quickly.

Major Herbert Bruce, who is employed in the Intelligence Department and has done good service, came in whilst we were at breakfast, and gave some interesting accounts of Hope Grant's flying column and of the Meeangunj affair. He says they very nearly captured the Nana in an expedition they made to a fort in Oude, opposite Bithoor. The stories about his crossing the Ganges and the main trunk-road are false. It was a relative of his who got away, it is supposed, to raise disturbances in the Calpee and Etawah districts. The native policemen who were stationed near the ford, at which the rebels crossed, have been seized, and several of them have been hanged by Captain Bradford, the police-officer. It is suspected they allowed the rebels to cross without giving an alarm. At all events, there is no doubt of their punishment. Bruce says all the Oude people are against us; but he thinks we shall catch Nana Sahib as soon as Lucknow falls. The whole thing will be over then.

At one o'clock, having sent off all our traps, Stewart and I took refuge from the heat of the sun, which is becoming daily stronger and less bearable, in my gharry; and in a scene of dire confusion and tumult, proceeded over the bridge of boats across the Ganges into Oude. It was in the Crimea I first heard of the annexation of Oude, which was represented not only as an act of the highest political wisdom, but also as a political necessity. Now, near the spot, I hear wise men doubt the wisdom—and see them shake their heads when one talks of the necessity—of the annexation. The ex-king, who is in captivity at Calcutta, has acted with a firmness which one could not have expected from a mere sensualist, as he was said to be, half-idiotic and entirely base. I am told that his conduct at the time of the annexation astonished our officers; that it was characterized by dignity and propriety. Up to the present moment, he has neither consented to his deposition nor taken one farthing of the annuity which the Company settled on him, nor has he given the least ground for believing that he has participated in the mutiny and rebellion. But empires never make restitution; they have no consciences. The Chancellor of their Exchequer never has to acknowledge the receipt of conscience-money. Oude is British as long as England holds India.

Our road lay in a straight broad line of elevated causeway, just over the sands of the river-bed, now at its lowest; and thence through a country as level as the sea, bearing the marks of high cultivation, and diversified by numerous topes or large clumps of trees, so numerous, indeed, as to hem in the horizon all around, with a framework of rich green foliage. As soon as we had advanced a few miles from the Ganges, not only the broad road, but the broad track at each side of it, was thronged by an immense and apparently illimitable procession of oxen, hackeries, horses, ponies, camels, camp-followers on foot or riding, trains of stores, elephants, all plodding steadily along in the burning sun under the umbrella of dense clouds of white dust. The road, cut up by the passage of *matériel* of ammunition and guns, is broken frequently into deep ruts full of fine dust from the "kunkur," or the limestone nodules, which, hardened into a sort of concrete, rolled down and watered, formed the usual macadamization of Indian highways, and are, when new, the finest metalling in the world. The pathways are in a condition equally favourable for the formation of the veil, which rises like the smoke from endless batteries. What an infinite variety of sights and sounds! What a multitude of novel objects on every side! What combinations of colour, of form, and of sound! As we jogged along, half-choked and baked, in our inglorious chariot, with a syce, running as *avant-courier*, shouting all kinds of mendacious assertions as to our rank and position, as a sort of moral wedge to open the way for us—I, for one, looked with ever-growing wonder on the vast tributary of the tide of war, which was surging around and before me. All these men, women, and children, with high delight, were pouring towards Lucknow to aid the Feringhee to overcome their brethren. From India, wider than the regions which the Romans regarded as the world, come the representatives of hundreds of dark-faced tribes, whose speech is a symbol of conquest and of a life in camps—the camps of the conqueror; but that speech is almost their sole bond of union. The sight gave me a notion of the old world times, when nomad tribes came from east and north to overrun and conquer. These people carried all their household wealth with them. Their houses were their tents; their streets, the camp-bazaar; their ruler, the bazaar-kotwal; their politics, the rise and fall of rice, and such commodities; their fate, that of the host they adhere to, like mussels on the sides of a ship. The old men, perhaps, had been with Lake, or had followed Scindia, or Holkar; the young men could talk of the Punjab or Scinde: the children were taking up their trade with the campaign of Oude. Bred in camps, but unwarlike—for ever behind guns, and never before them—the aptitude of myriads of the natives of Hindostan for this strange life is indicative of their origin, or, at all events, of the history of their country for ages. Most of those people are Hindoos from Bengal or the north-west provinces. Some are from Central India,

There are not many Mussulmans, except as domestic servants; the huge-limbed Affghan, with his enormous turban and fair complexion, toils alongside his camel, which is laden with dried fruits; the Sikh, whose whiskers are turned up and tied in a knot on the top of his head, protects the precious hairs from the contamination of the dust by tying a handkerchief under his jaws, and is marching with a light cat-like tread on his long thin sinewy legs to join his comrades; the fat bunneah hurries on in his bamboo-car to see his store-tent pitched, leaving his dependants to make the best of their way after him; the wives of the binneahs who sit straddle-legged on the tiniest of donkeys, with their toes almost touching the ground, several children in their arms and across their loins, and such a heap of bags and baggage, that all which may be seen of the creatures that carry them, is a disconsolate face, long ears, a ragged mangy tail, and four little black hoofs, bent outwards, with fetlocks quivering at every step; the shrewd-looking, slender Madrassee, in a turban of the grandest dimensions, and a suit of fine muslin or of gaudy stuff, sits grinning and laughing with a select circle of his own set-on "Master's elfent" (or hathee); whole regiments of sinewy, hollow-thighed, lanky coolies, shuffle along under loads of chairs, tables, hampers of beer and wine, bazaar stores, or boxes slung from bamboo poles across their shoulders. Now comes a drove of milch-goats and sheep, which your servant announces as "Master's mess buckree." A flock of turkeys is destined to fatten for her Majesty's — regiment; and this long line of camels presents side-views of many boxes of beer, pickles, potted meats, and soda-water, for the use of the officers of another equally fortunate corps. Monkeys, held captive on the backs of camels or ponies, chatter their despair or fear at every jolt. Parrots scream from recondite and undiscoverable corners of hackeries or elephants. Tame deer pant and halt in their ungenial march; and kennels of pariahs precede, accompany, and follow the march, which presents also some exemplars of their more favoured domesticated compeers, each with a domestic attached to him.

The crops are cut, and there is little to destroy; but intrepid foragers penetrate into the distant villages within sight of the column, and carry off even sticks for firewood, or cut down branches of trees to feed their camels and elephants. None of these villages were inhabited; possibly the people had fled on the first advance of Havelock, and had not returned since. The houses are built of mud; and as the roofs are gone, the villages have an exceedingly miserable aspect. Here and there the walls of some old serai shine as brightly as decaying whitewash can make them; or a pagoda just lifts its domed summit above the tops of the trees. The villages are placed by the sides of muddy tanks or large ponds, surrounded by ragged banks of brown earth baked as hard as bricks, and the friendly shade of a grove is generally close at hand. Some of them have been surrounded by walls of mud, the ruins of which are visible here and there; and sometimes an old crenelated bastion shows that the inhabitants were not always on good terms with their neighbours. At one of those villages, a few miles from the river, the enemy had made a stand against Havelock, but he took them by a flank movement, carried their position, and captured their guns. The name is illegible in my diary, and I have no books to refer to. I walked round the old mudwall and the embrasures which commanded the road with interest. The only traces of the fight were on the parapets, which were still blackened by the fire of the guns. Where the dead were buried, no one knew.

The heat was great, the dust suffocating; ears, nose, mouth, eyes, and clothes filled and covered with white powder. It was about 5 o'clock P.M., when a wheeling multitude of kites and vultures soaring above the dust, announced that we were near an encampment, and very soon the joyful sight of a plain full of tents met our eyes. The large distinctive flags, hoisted by the bazaars of each regiment, for some time confused our little party, which was in search of the Lord Sahib's camp; but at last the well-known Jack caught our eyes in the midst of a fine street of tents; and as we drove over a plain profusely strewn with bleached beef and mutton bones, and charred by camp-fires, and ragged with tulas or native cooking places, our servants came out to meet us, and I alighted at my tent-door, which seemed as if it had never moved from Cawnpore. On entering everything was in its place just as I left it. Our mess-dinner was precisely the same as at Cawnpore; and it was hard to believe we were in an enemy's country. As we were at dinner, the orders were brought in. "The Head Quarters, with the following troops, will march to-morrow; first bugle at 2 A.M.; the troops to march off the ground, at 3 A.M. precisely, in the following order," &c., &c. There was small time for rest, and at 9 o'clock, we were all in bed; not a sound to be heard save the chatter of the natives, or the gurgle of their pipes outside the tents.

CHAPTER XV.

The first bugle.—The head of the column.—Sunrise.—Bullocks, camels, and elephants.—The white mare.—Sinking down into a gulf.—"Are you kilt, sir?"—A fast-trotting camel.—False alarm.—Camp grass-cutters.—Sir William Peel and his heavy guns.—Left behind.—Kavanagh.—A joyful surprise.—Orders to march.

February 28th. — The camels and the Kelassees began their abominable noises soon after midnight. At the first bugle Simon was at my bedside with a cup of tea, and by the aid of a feeble candle, I got into long boots and a great-coat, for it was too cold to face a mussack at that early hour, and the water did not smell very sweetly. On looking out of the tent, I was glad to find the moon shining brightly. Whilst my back was turned my charpoy was taken out and fastened on a camel's back, bed-clothes and all: the tent was cleared out, and in a few minutes more fell flop to the ground, and was stowed away. The sight around us was most picturesque; Salvator would have had years of work in fixing on his canvas the wonderful groups of black wild faces, which contending rays of moonlight and blazing camp-fires lighted up in the sombre shadow of the trees. The plain was studded with innumerable fires; and the incessant yells of the natives, as they called for lost friends or relations, made a perfect pandemonium, arched over by a roof of smoke, through which the moon forced its light with difficulty. My own little bit of Wouvermans stood before me, in the shape of the vicious white mare, which was kicking and plunging to get away from the syce, and evincing the wildest antipathy to camels and elephants.

How to find one's way was no easy matter. The ground looked pitch-black, and was covered with cooking-places, and my horse went plunging from one to another, and dancing amid red-hot ashes in a most unseemly manner. My friend Stewart, mounted on a camel, came to guide me to the head of the column, which we reached, after wandering through a wilderness of bazaars and natives for nearly an hour. We got out on the road; where, in silence and order, the Rifle Brigade was plunging with steady tramp through the dust. As the moon sank in the heavens, the line of our march became more like some dream of the other world, or some recollections of a great scene at a theatre than anything else. The horizontal rays just touched the gleaming arms and the heads of the men, lighted up the upper portions of the camels and the elephants, which resembled islands in an opaque sea, whilst the plain looked like an inky waste, dotted with starlike fires. The sun soon began to make his approach visible, and an arc of greyish red appeared in the east, spreading, but not deepening, till the Far-darter himself rose like a ball of fire in the hazy sky. The band of the Rifles struck one of the old familiar steps, and as the light increased, I was able to make out some of my old friends—Ross, Fraser, Reid, and others—and jogged on, side-by-side, as well as the white mare would let me. Her dislike to camels increased every moment, and the approach of one was the signal for a rearing-match. Pleasant beast for a march! Here, for the first time, I observed the significant attendants on our march—the doolys in the rear of the regiments—a long train of covered litters hung from bamboo-poles, and carried by coolies, who, with their reliefs, form a large portion of the column.

The sun was just beginning to make himself disagreeable, when, after several halts, we caught sight of some tents partly hidden in trees. "Thank goodness! there's our camp. Canter over, and get some breakfast." And there, sure enough, was our mess-tent pitched; the tables covered with snow-white cloths, our plates, chairs, knives and forks, all ready—the curries smoking, and the array of servants standing with folded arms waiting for their masters.

After breakfast each man repairs to his tent, and is not loath to make up by a stretch on his charpoy for the brief repose of last night. For myself, I wrote; and then after some hours' work strolled out to the camp of the Rifles, but was glad to get back again from the sun. I particularly admire the picturesque scenes in the bazaar; but they lose their charm on near inspection, and the annoyance of other senses effectually counterbalances the gratification of the eye. The splendid bullocks, which draw the guns and a large portion of our baggage, are special favourites of mine. I have never seen eyes so soft and beautiful, and I would willingly save the poor willing brutes from the cruelties of their present mode of yoke. They are driven by means of rope-reins passed through the cartilage of the nose, and the yoke is a triangle of wood placed behind the hump, or boss, on the neck, which is frequently galled by the friction. The camels are led by the same means as the bullocks; and my favourites of all, the dear, unwieldy, cunning-eyed old elephants, are compelled, I regret to say, by a stout bar of iron sharpened into a spike at the end, with a hook like an ancient partizan, which is unmercifully dug into the base of the creature's ears, from which it sometimes returns with bits of fat and blood upon it. Dinner was very welcome after to-day's work; and the charpoy most welcome of all, for we march at the usual hour to-morrow morning.

March 1st.—Marched from Oonao to Nuwabgunj by moonlight early this morning. After we had been an hour on the road, there closed over us a storm of thunder and lightning (the cart is always put before the horse), which, as it rolled over the march in the mingled light of the moon and of the early dawn, was inexpressibly grand. In the midst of it, however, I had a little adventure, which very nearly put an end to my Diary and the writer. The white mare had been unusually fidgety and vicious all the night, rearing, plunging, and kicking; and having in vain tried to overcome her repugnance to camels and elephants by coaxing her up alongside them in the dark, I took the opportunity afforded by what looked like a fine open plain in the early dawn, to give her a rattling gallop, and take the game out of her in a burst alongside the column. Giving her a touch of Maxwell's best, I set off across the open. The beast gave a little whimper of pain and anger, lashed her heels in the air, and set off at a rate which I considered my weight would have rendered impossible.

She flew past elephants and camels now, bucked over every rut in the plain, and for two or three miles went as straight as an arrow. Then I tried to get a pull on her; but I might as well have attempted to hold a steam-frigate. She had got the bit in her teeth, or had dipped her mouth in iron, and all I could do was to keep her head straight, and saw at her till my arms were sore. Suddenly a low black line appeared right before us: what it was I knew not. I hoped it might be a wall, and not a watercourse. As I neared the line it grew higher and blacker. In vain I tried to turn the mare right or left, or to pull her up. The black line now seemed a huge wall, with the shadow from the moonlight falling at its base. It was within six feet of me. I sat firm, gave the mare one sharp prick of the spurs, let her have her head, and her own way, and in an instant felt myself sinking down into a gulf which seemed bottomless. My shoulder struck against a hard bank, the mare sank from under me, her hind heels were silvered by the moonlight as my head fell between their furious lash out, and for a minute I lay stunned in the bottom of the watercourse, full twelve feet deep; though I can remember now the neigh of the poor beast as she scrambled to her legs and rushed along the bottom of the course towards the column. "Are you kilt, sir?" was the next thing I heard, as two soldiers dragged me up the bank. I was so sorely shaken, I could scarcely answer; and I felt my bones in perfect wonder. Not one broken! only a tremendous shock which made head and eyes swim.

My good friend Stewart, on his fast-trotting shootee sowar camel, had seen the mare run away, and had followed me as fast as he could. He was a good deal astonished when we disappeared, and more when he found me seated on the bank of the tank which the watercourse led to. The Wouvermans had gone, saddle, bridle, pistols, and all. We were still six miles from our next halting-place at Bunnee bridge. Alas! poor dood, down with you on your knees! At the word of command, the sowar forces his beast to kneel. I mount up on the pad, Stewart clings behind me; the sowar gets upon some undefined space between the neck and the pad, and so we proceed, at a long sling-trot, to regain our position. *Ah, le maudit!* how I suffered! Though it was not my first trot on a camel, it was my first essay in long riding-boots. My legs oscillated violently to and fro, and at each rub the boot made a fair progress in raising a blister, and as I was unable to hold myself quite upright, owing to my bruises and shaking, my head was knocked about like a shot in slings.

Thus we proceeded to the bridge at Bunuee, where a small but deep stream runs under a hump-backed bridge, which had been partly broken by the enemy, but is now repaired. This is defended by a sort of field-work and a *tête-de-pont*, which is occupied by a detachment of Madras Infantry, with field-guns and a body of native police. Our good friends, the Madrassees, are slighter and smaller men than the up-country fellows, but they are quite as tall as our average infantry. Their head-dress, for it cannot be called a shako, is like some gigantic vegetable—a monster bulb, with another growing out of it; but their attachment to it is so great that any attempt to interfere with it might cause a mutiny, like that at

Vellore. The use of the top is popularly supposed to be that the men may carry their extra provisions and loot in it. The officers, of whom the number seemed small, were collected, with those of the police, at the roadside to see us pass, and to one of the latter we gave some particulars of the missing horse, which had vanished in the darkness and been seen no more. He shook his head; "but," said he, "perhaps we may hear of it, if it does not fall into the hands of the budmashes" (the evil-livers, blackguards, rebels). The police, who were under an officer named Carnegie, were wild budmashy-looking fellows themselves, armed with swords, shields, and various fire-arms, dressed in quilted cotton tunics, large turbans, and jack-boots. A few miles beyond this station is Buntheerah, where our camp was pitched, under a fine tope of trees, near a mosque, or pagoda, and a small deserted village.

We have now closed upon the main body of our force. The plain is covered with their tents. Peel's blue-jackets are close at hand, and I hear the skirl of the bagpipes which announces that we are not far from the Highlanders. (The details of our force will be found in the Appendix.) The mess-tent is open to receive us. Breakfast over, and a little quiet gossip over a cheroot disposed of, I retired to my tent to write my daily record, and was just nibbing my second pen and listening placidly to the great monotonous "thudding" through the trees of the big guns from Outram's fort at Alumbagh, when suddenly a tumult breaks out in camp, cries of alarm, and a tramp of feet. I start to the tent-door, and there I see natives of all kinds, grass-cutters, syces, and servants, and bazaar people, streaming across from the front in the wildest terror. In hot haste the Staff were running out; but Sir Colin has just galloped past alone. What on earth can it all mean? There is no firing. Stewart comes up with a smile on his face. "We are going to be attacked," said he; "the grass-cutters have been driven in by the enemy's cavalry."

"Really! and which side are they?"

"Oh! I think it will turn out to be a sham; I don't mean to stir."

"But if they sweep round into the camp, how the deuce is one to know them from our own natives?"

"Shoot every fellow in white that you see. You may be quite sure, if he's on horseback and has a sword, he's a sowar of the enemy."

I had no horse to get ready; and Stewart and I could scarcely have gone forth to battle on our camel; besides, all the Staff, except the aides-de-camp, were taking it quietly; and as we discussed the matter, the stream of fugitives diminished and at last dried up.

In about half-an-hour, Sir Colin came past, with a look which told one his temper had been tried. You must know, that when the camp is pitched, the grass-cutters at once spread themselves all over the neighbouring country to cut grass for the horses— a process which they effect with a tool something like a shoemaker's cutter, by cutting the roots of the grass quite below the surface of the ground. Some of these people either got into an altercation with the villagers, or really came across a party of sowars. At all events they fled towards one of our pickets, commanded by a young officer not very well acquainted with his duty, who at once mounted his horse, rode into the camp, dashed up to the Chief's tent, and reported that "the enemy are upon us!" Sir Colin at once galloped away, turned out the cavalry, got the troops under arms, and made a reconnaissance, which proved it was a false alarm. We had great fun, laughing at McNeil's imitation of the alarmist: "They come! they come! The foe! the foe are upon us!" Sir Colin took occasion to give all the officers he came upon some energetic lessons respecting their duty when in face of an enemy. In fact it was quite practicable for the enemy's horse to have swept round out of Lucknow, and to have cut in upon a careless camp; but the sowars have not got any qualification of good cavalry; they have no dash, no enterprise, and are only efficient in guarding themselves against surprise.

The rest of the day passed quietly; revolvers were put away and swords hung up. In the evening I went over to see Peel exercising his sailors with the heavy guns. Sir Colin was over there also. Peel was in high spirits, for the news had come that he was Sir William; but he would scarce believe it as it was only known by a vague telegram. It was worth while to make a long journey to see the wonderful way in which he had trained his men. To the tap of the drum, or by word of command, they laid hold of the rope-traces of the huge battering guns, and roused them along as if they were toys, wheeled, took them into action, yoked them on again, and rattled off, "with a stamp and go," so lightly that one could not credit the weight of the guns till he saw their broad wheels had cut deep into the hard earth. Thence I walked across to the Highlanders and visited Cameron, in command of the 42nd, Taylor, of the 79th, and some of the 93rd, whom I found on parade, not looking the worse for Secunderabagh. On my return with Col. Cameron to the sailors' camp, I found Sir Colin was still there. He rode over and told us he was "going with part of the troops early to-morrow morning to look out for ground for a camp near the Dilkoosha. The orders will be issued this evening." To my great disappointment, he added, "I think you had better stay here. I shall leave all the Head-Quarters' departments behind, and I am merely going to pick out a place for our camp where we shall be out of range." Of course I must obey; but I cannot, for the life of me, understand why I cannot go, or what reason there is for including me among "the departments."

March 2nd.—This morning, ere full day, Sir Colin, taking with him a force of field-guns, cavalry, and infantry (see Appendix), marched off for Lucknow. I saw them start, and only that it would have looked like begging for a horse, I would have begged to be let go with them. About 6 o'clock we hear a few heavy reports, which become more frequent at 9, but they are more in the direction of Alumbagh than in that of the column which has passed to the east and south of that position. The sky darkens, and a thunder-storm, attended with a heavy fall of rain, falls on the camp. No one is pleased at being left behind. Our ears are straining for noises all day. Patience! to-morrow we too shall be before Lucknow. I sit and write all day. The pools of rain are soon dried up—the heat becomes intense. Cruel old Indians tell us, " This is nothing! Wait till we get a good warm day in May, with a hot wind blowing." I hope I may be able to wait. I write with a pad of blotting paper under my hand. How I envy those lean, lank, red-faced fellows who gulp down the Commissariat ale with impunity! It is true they carry pepper-castors full of carbonate of soda, and dust their pottles therewith till a mighty effervescence arises; but they declare " it's delicious!"

As I sat in the shade of my tent purdah a party of the Rifle Brigade marched past, covered with dust, under Glyn (Richard) and Thynne. How well the fellows looked! Brown as berries; and Thynne, from a slight, tall, handsome lad, grown into a powerful handsomer young man. We had a brief shake-hands and a halt for a few minutes; but the storm was coming on, and they had yet to pitch their tents. They have come up behind us with a convoy from Lucknow. Ere their tents can be set up the rain is down upon them, and the dust is turned into mud. Soon after, there comes into camp Kavanagh, of the Civil Service (uncovenanted—a " covenanted" might have hesitated), who has gained an undying name for the courage and devotion with which he volunteered to go out of the Residency, disguised as a native, through the swarming city, full of cruel enemies, and communicate with Sir Colin Campbell, who was then some miles outside, at the Martinière. How he could ever have made himself look like a native I know not. He is a square-shouldered, large-limbed, muscular man, a good deal over the middle height, with decided European features; a large head, covered with hair of—a reddish auburn, shall I say?—moustaches and beard still lighter, and features and eyes such as no native that ever I saw possessed. He was dressed in some sort of blue uniform tunic—that of the Volunteer Cavalry, I believe —white cords, and jack-boots, and felt helmet, and was well armed—heavy sabre and pistols. He is open, frank, and free in manner; and I believe those grand covenanted gentlemen who did not mention his name in any of their Lucknow reports, regard him as "not one of us." But Mr. Kavanagh may console himself. He has made himself famous by an act of remarkable courage—not in the heat of battle, or in a moment of impulse or excitement, but performed after deliberation, and sustained continuously through a long trial. If the Victoria Cross were open to civilians (and why should it not be?) there is no one who deserves it better than this gentleman. And, indeed, I believe, from his conversation to-day, that the hope of wearing it was one of the main-springs of his devotion. He left wife and children in the garrison, and went out on his desperate errand, which, even to the sanguine, seemed hopeless.

A joyful surprise! This evening comes a native trooper into camp with a chitty for "Russell Sahib Bahadoor," and with what was more important still, a certain white mare, saddle, bridle, and all, which had been found near Bunnee grazing, yesterday, and was sent over to me by Captain Carnegie. The saddle alone was worth its weight in gold.

At dinner, orders are ready for us to march at daybreak to-morrow. Wilkin, of the 7th Hussars, who is dining with me, is summoned to fall in with his regiment soon after midnight. As we get near the place, we hear great reports of the enemy's strength. There are, it is said, at least 60,000 regulars of all sorts, and about 70,000 nujeebs, militia, and matchlockmen. All the great chiefs of Oude, Mussulman and Hindoo, are there, and have sworn to fight for their young king, Birjies Kuddr, to the last. Their cavalry is numerous, the city is filled with people, the works are continually strengthened. All Oude is in the hands of the enemy, and we only hold the ground we cover with our bayonets.

CHAPTER XVI.

March for Lucknow.—A vision.—Jellalabad.—Sepoy skeletons.—
An old Sikh officer.—Sergeant Gillespie.—Site of our new
camp.—The Martinière.—The Dilkoosha.—A breach of etiquette.—View from the roof of the Dilkoosha.—The enemy's
trenches.—A round shot.—Striking beauty of Lucknow.—A
young langour.—Visitors and guests.

March 3rd.—With heavy guns, Highlanders and Head-Quarters' departments marched from Buntheerah for Lucknow this blessed fresh morning. How pleasant it is to get free! I recalled the sensations of our first reconnaissance in the Crimea, when we got out of the mud and into the sweet grass and fresh flowers. Mr. Kavanagh had my white mare; and I succeeded in borrowing a less lively creature, at which I was much rejoiced, when I saw Mr. Kavanagh now rushing furiously past the column, now performing the more intricate manœuvres of the manège unwittingly, and as full of anxiety for his seat as a member with an election petition against him. * * * *

A VISION.

As I think of it now, it seems a vision—a waking dream! For some days I wrote no entries in my diary; and all that I could write was sent to "another place," and so I can only trust to memory for that morning march. First, a sea-like plain of sandy soil, which looks much as the ocean does, when seen from the deck of a ship under a dark grey sky. In a right line across this plain, a stream of infantry, cavalry, and cannon, guarded by sailors, and drawn by many oxen, stretches away to a black point on the horizon, which is just fretted by a border of trees. Then patches of tall sugar-cane, towards which our flankers, looking like dots on the surface, ride exploringly; then groves of trees like islands; beyond, by the side of a large lake, a solitary fort, with crumbling bastions, on which, however, glance the bayonets of our sentries. This is Jellalabad; the extreme point held by the garrison of Alumbagh. The engineers have filled it with their stores. More than once the enemy have assailed it; their scaling-ladders lie about in the brushwood. See: there is a skeleton in the remnants of a sepoy's uniform. Why does that officer ride his horse over the bones? Brave men do not war with the dead. Thence we come to thick woods, through which our road winds out to more open country. Far away, above a field of wide-spread cane, we see a white tower. That is part of the Alumbagh. We pass under the walls of Jellalabad, and through more woods; once more we come upon a plain where skeletons are lying with red rags sticking round them—sepoys killed by Outram's cavalry in some skirmish between his post and Jellalabad. Then the column halts and closes up, and the camp-followers creep close in to us. Amid the high grass and under the trees on our left, we see white figures moving; they are the enemy's sowars.

Stewart and I push on the front, and find the head of our column halted at a narrow wooded lane, close to which there is one of the enemy's field-works to cover a couple of guns, which Sir Colin probably disposed of yesterday. The lane opens on a plain, which is skirted on the left by woods and sugar-cane cates. It is quite uncultivated, full of deep dry watercourses and nullahs cut in the stony surface. No one knows where the chief is: not a soul is to be seen. We must be close to Lucknow, and still closer to the Lord Sahib's camp; but the extreme end of the plain in front of us is a rise which conceals everything from our view. Presently a clump of lances appears on the brow, and a small body of cavalry appear on the ridge, and makes over towards us, led by two officers. As they approach I recognized Johnson, who was coming to look for the heavy guns, and to guide the column. "The chief's camp is about a mile ahead. I will give you my sowars; make the best of your way across the open ground, for the enemy have horse and foot in the cates and woods on your left." Stewart and I at once started off at a sling trot, followed by an old Sikh officer and some dozen of lancers, and as we went along, the old Sikh, stroking his beard, which flowed almost down to his saddle, told us tremendous fibs—"How the Lord Sahib had taken the Dilkoosha, the Martinière, and was half-way into Lucknow. How the Sikhs and Artillery had slaughtered many hundreds of the budmashes and taken all their guns; and how he and his men had swept their sowars to Hades." He was a noble-looking old economist of the truth; and his men were the wildest, finest-looking fellows possible—part of Probyn's detachment of Punjaubee Irregulars (Watson's?).

Now and then we looked to the left, but not a sowar showed himself, though once or twice it seemed to me the sugar-canes had white tops to them. The ground was very hard, broken, and, as a friend of mine says, "ravinous;" but as we got to the top of the ridge, we saw an old rubble wall, evidently guarding a large enclosure of trees, running in front of us, with many dry nullahs intervening. Down one of those we rode, and on turning a corner, I heard a voice from above, in a broad Scotch accent, "Save us! is that you, Mr. Russell? Well, sir, I never did think of seeing you here; but indeed I'm glad to see you." The speaker was an honest non-commissioned officer of the 93rd, Sergeant Gillespie, who was for a long time Provost-Sergeant of the Head-Quarters' camp in the Crimea, and in charge of the Russian prisoners. The camp, he said, was just inside the wall, "a bittock away. We weren't in the Martinière yet, but we'd soon be, whenever Sir Colin liked to say the word." And so we parted.

A little further on met David Wood, commanding all our Horse-Artillery, and his aide-de-camp, and he volunteered very kindly to lead us the right way. It was a long one; but at last we turned an angle in the old wall, came into a fine open wood, and before us were the tents of the Highlanders. It was now breakfast-time—past it; a long fast since dawn; a hot ride. Welcome was the voice that cried out "Hadn't you two better stop and have some breakfast?" And not one, but two, and many voices, for every one knew Pat Stewart, who hailed from north of the Tweed, and not a few of the 42nd knew his companion. We did wisely, under the circumstances; first we went to one tent, and sat outside, consuming at the little table all the breakfast of Cockburn, whilst Colonel Cameron's servant was preparing another meal for us. The regiment was turning out; there was great buttoning of white gaiters and filling of flasks, so that our hosts had to leave us, and saved our blushes. Breakfast No. 2 was announced—rashers of cow-beef, tea, and bread; but there was no milk, as the honest Scot announced to us, "The gates (goats) were as dree as a stane;" yet, wonderful to relate, we nevertheless exhausted his banquet, and then set off for our tents, which were in an adjoining enclosure.

The site selected by the Chief was in a series of magnificently-wooded parks, attached to several palaces, or country houses, of the royal family of Oude, south of the Dilkoosha. The trees were of great age and extreme beauty, affording us a fine shade and cover to innumerable langours, or black-faced long-tailed monkeys with white hair and whiskers. Some deer which were captured also lived here. When we arrived, the tents were just being pitched. The precision with which this is done in India is admirable. I recollected our first attempts in Bulgaria, and thought there was one part of military life, at all events, which our Royal officers might learn from the Company's. It is in this wise: take Head-Quarters, for instance, there is a tindal, or overseer of Kelassees, whose business it is to keep up with the Quartermaster-General's officer charged to pitch the camp. His men carry the Commander-in-Chief's standard, and small flags affixed to short iron spears, which vary in colour according to the regiment or department, and rackets of cord. On arriving at the ground, the Quartermaster-General fixes on the best site for the Lord Sahib's tent; the standard is at once planted and displayed, showing all within view where the Commander-in-Chief's camp is. Then each tent is marked off; the cords are fixed in parallel lines; the boundaries of the tent-spaces being distinguished by the flags which are fixed in the ground; the coolies set to work to level all inequalities, to cut down shrubs or grass, to fill up trenches; the train of camels approaches; each Kelassee sees the place marked off for his master's tent; the camels and elephants kneel down, are unloaded; are led off to feed; and then cone after cone of canvas rises rapidly, till the city is complete, the two principal buildings being the Chief's mess-tent and that of the Head-Quarters' Staff. We were pitched in the park of the Bibiapore, and just outside that wall is the Dilkoosha. It is occupied by our men, who also hold some walls in front of it, within musketry-fire of the trenches and rifle-pits of the enemy in front of the Martinière. "No one is to go to the Dilkoosha unless on duty there." An order settles that matter.— "Head-Quarters, Bibiapore, March 3rd. By order of his Excellency the Commander-in-Chief, the bearer of this pass, Mr. Russell, is permitted to enter the Dilkoosha, to visit the outposts, and to go to and fro as he pleases. (Signed) W. H. Norman, Adjutant-General."

Stewart, who is on duty, for he is to work up the telegraph to the Dilkoosha, starts with me. We walk under an avenue of mighty trees, bordering a drive which leads to a gateway in the wall, arched over, and ornamented by pilasters. There is a slight irregular fire of musketry going on outside. On emerging from the gateway there extends a wide, broad plain, right, front, and left, which contains some remarkable objects; on our right, at the end of the park from which we have just emerged, is a walled garden filled with cypresses, summer-houses, plaster statues, with kiosks, and pleasant walks 'mid orange trees. Beneath it flows the Goomtee, about 500 yards from us, coming down with many a curve from the city of Lucknow. Beyond it, on the right, is an expanse of meadow and corn-fields, bounded, as usual, by wood. One small hamlet and a few cottages are all the signs of habitation we can see here, but in a break in the trees far away we can make out an arched bridge, which is the viaduct of the road from Lucknow to Fyzabad, over the Kokraal stream and nullah. Directly in front of us is about 1200 yards of broken ground, intersected by two ruinous old walls, which run down to the river, and seem to have been parts of an outer enclosure of the Bibiapore. Above those walls there rises the most curious structure I ever saw. At first glance one exclaims, "How beautiful! what a splendid building;" at the second, "Why it must have been built by a madman!" At the distance of more than half a mile we can make out the eccentric array of statues, the huge lions' heads, the incongruous columns, arches, pillars, windows, and flights of stairs leading to nothing, which are the distinguishing features of the Martinière. The centre of the building is the most grotesque; the wide sweep of the wings and their curve inwards from the triad stairs leading to the entrance has a fine effect. But the statues! they are perched on every angle, drawn up as close as they can stand all along the roof, fixed on the pinnacles, and corners, and pillars, in all directions. In front of the whole building (rising from a sheet of water in shape of a letter T) there is a tall pillar, not unlike the monument to the Duke of York.

At the proper left corner of the Martinière, there is just visible the embrasure of a low earthwork. On the proper right of the Martinière, there are a few one-storied white houses, a wall which stretches a long way to the right, inside which there is a park full of dense trees, which completely screens the city and the line of the enemy's works from where we stand. Bounding the landscape, about 400 yards away, on our left, is the Dilkoosha, which is nothing more nor less than a good specimen of a French château of the beginning of the last century, improved by an Italian artist. Where is the city of Lucknow? Somewhere over there beyond the Dilkoosha, and thence stretching behind the park of the Martinière.

There is a group of officers standing under a tree to our right on a little mound: we join them, and look placidly at the line of our men just in front, who are firing, through the wall they have loopholed, at the enemy's trenches, from which comes an irregular dropping fire. "Those fellows have sent one or two round-shot from the angle of the Martinière towards our camp," quoth one. I was looking through my glass at the time, and I distinctly saw the gunners laying the piece for our humble selves just as he finished speaking. It is an unpleasant thing to look down the muzzle of a hostile gun with a glass. "I think," said I, modestly, "they are going to fire at us." As I spoke, pluff came a spirt of smoke with red tongue in it—a second of suspense, and whi-s-s-s-h, right for us came the round-shot within a foot of our heads, plumped into the ground, with a storm of dust and small stones, beyond us, and then rising rushed over the wall into the Chief's camp.

It's not etiquette, strictly speaking, to bow to a round-shot on duty; but we were not on duty, and we all "bobbed," gently, pleasantly, and unconcernedly, as it were. Each man smiled as he looked at his neighbour. "Begad, that was a near shave for some of us; we'd better get from this tree—we're only drawing fire." A sensible remark, and each man stalked away, very savage with the enemy, and affecting great indifference. Just some twelve inches lower, and where had been the brains of some of us, or the subtler part. Of all horrid sights, I know none so bad as seeing a man's brains dashed out like froth by a cannon-ball! One would never feel it one's self—for the time is come, when brains are out, that men will die. "My telegraph wires will be exposed to fire," said Stewart; and so we sauntered on to the Dilkoosha, which was filled with Highlanders. No one asked for our passes—we crossed the court-yard, ascended the flight of steps to the hall, and thence, through heaps of ruin, broken mirror-frames, crystals of chandeliers, tapestries, pictures, beds of furniture, mounted to the flat roof. A vision, indeed!

A vision of palaces, minars, domes azure and golden, cupolas, colonnade, long façades of fair perspective in pillar and column, terraced roofs—all rising up amid a calm still ocean of the brightest verdure. Look for miles and miles away, and still the ocean spreads, and the towers of the fairy-city gleam in its midst. Spires of gold glitter in the sun. Turrets and gilded spheres shine like constellations. There is nothing mean or squalid to be seen. There is a city more vast than Paris, as it seems, and more brilliant, lying before us. Is this a city in Oude? Is this the capital of a semi-barbarous race, erected by a corrupt, effete, and degraded dynasty? I confess I felt inclined to rub my eyes again and again. But let us analyse. On our right is the Martinière. Behind it is a high parapet of earth, which, beginning at the Goomtee, sweeps away to the left till it is lost in the foliage of the trees. This is the great outer line of works, which the enemy have raised with such trouble, and (for them) such energy. Here there is a raised redoubt, which we call the Cavalier; there is a battery; further on there is a gun *en barbette;* and on the left there seems to be a strong work in front of a large, two-storied, high-peaked house, called "Banks' Bungalow." Behind this parapet and the trees, which seem to run through the streets of the city, is the wilderness of fair architecture which renders the place a marvel to us. Near us is the Begum's Kothie, on the proper left of Banks' bungalow; beyond is the little Imambarra—a mass of minarets, flat roofs, and long, ornamented frontage; then the Mess-House; on the right the angles of the racket courts. On the left, in a blaze of gilding, spires, cupolas, domes, stretches the vast Kaisar-bagh. Then beyond are the Tara Kothie on the right; the Residency on the left; the Chuttur Munsil, the Mohtee Mahul, the great Imambarra : the Badshah-bagh in a park at the other side of the river; the race-stand, a wide suburb, and the Kokraal viaduct.

Close below us we look into the enemy's trenches and rifle-pits, extending on the right of the Martinière down by the park wall. They are filled with men in white, and, here and there, a few red-coated sepoys, or telungas. These trenches are wonderfully extensive, and are for the most part mere covered ways, intended for approaches to rifle-pits, or rather sunken pits, for musket and matchlockmen. As we look, a great commotion takes place among them in the pits—little waves of men are seen flowing from under the park wall into the various trenches, and presently a large zigzag fire of musketry goes twitteringly along the lines of the trenches, like a long train of gunpowder. This fire is directed at the Dilkoosha—the balls hum over us now and then, or flatten here and there against the roof, but the greater part of the fire is wasted, and the ground in front of us, marked by puffs of dust, shows where the bullets strike. *" Grace à Dieu!"* the enemy have only "Brown Bess." A few years more, not one of us could have stood here, for all our good friends in the trenches had been armed with the Enfield, or some other rifled musket. " Sergeant, just let a few men fire at those fellows under that tree!" From the west door of the Dilkoosha a road ran straight away towards Banks' bungalow, and about half-way down the enemy seemed to have made a cut across it, for we could see men's heads moving to and fro, and some six or seven fellows got out on the road, and under cover of a large tree, were firing towards us. "I think," said the sergeant, "that ye'd best mak it seven hundred yards, Macalister." "I'll just tree them at sax hundred and fafty." Ping went bullet! Our friends at once ducked their heads, and bolted for the trench. One of them, as he gained the top, threw his arms into the air, and fell into his haven of refuge. "I thocht I nicked am that time," quoth the sergeant, ramming down another cartrigde.

The contagion of the fusillade had spread. From all the windows of the palace, as well as from the roof and its queer turrets, a sharp fire was kept up by our men, before which the smoke from the hostile trenches melted away as though it were in a strong breeze. Do what they would, the sepoys effected nothing more formidable than hitting the walls with a falling bullet, whilst the tops of their pits were pelted, as it were, with constant puffs of dust where the conical balls whizzed sharply through the sand. Presently, however, a thick puff of smoke rose from behind the trees on the right of the Martinière, and a round-shot rushed over the turret on which I was standing. At the same moment another gun opened from Banks' bungalow, and the shot, ricochetting three times, rolled at the last bound up to the door of the Dilkoosha, and dispersed a crowd of idlers. The gun from the left angle of the Martinière was all this time firing about ten or twelve shots an hour, and the balls rushed past us on the right towards the Chief's camp. Suddenly, our firing, which was exciting enough, ceased in the lower story. A subaltern appeared on our flat. "The Commander-in-Chief has sent orders that there is to be no fire from the Dilkoosha, except by orders, or in case of actual attack." Indeed, it was useless expenditure of ammunition, and drew fire upon us from artillery. Only one of our men was wounded—a bullet flew through a window, and had still force enough to break the bone of his arm.

As we were looking at the city in quiet—for the evening's renewed fire was too contemptible to notice —Sir Colin, Mansfield, and Lugard, with some of the staff, came upon the roof, and Sir Colin, going into one of the turrets, proceeded to discuss a large map with Colonel Napier. Although the heat in the sun was very great, I was so interested that I bore it all, in order to get the picture into my head as well as I could. It is there, never to be effaced as long as the canvas lasts; but I find, alas! I cannot make copies, therefore I cannot give them to others. Not Rome, not Athens, not Constantinople, not any city I have ever seen, appears to me so striking and beautiful as this; and the more I gaze, the more its beauties grow upon me. The city is said to contain about a million of people, and 150,000 armed men at the very least. It is thirty miles round. We have, however, only to gain the south-east angle, and all falls to our hands. The spies report great preparations for its defence— three inner lines of works—many cannon in position. But there are dissensions in the city. The presiding genius of the defence is Huzrut Mahul, Begum of Lucknow, whose son, a boy of fourteen years of age, is the puppet-king of Oude. The Begum has a favourite, one Mummoo Khan. The opposition is led by a Moulvie, or Mahomedan priest, who is said to be a vigorous fanatic.

Of the result of the siege no one doubts. We have a very powerful first-class siege-train; plenty of eight-inch guns, ten-inch guns, and mortars; a compact, well-disciplined army; a very cautious, skilful soldier at their head, aided by lieutenants of ability and intelligence. As an ingredient in our calculations I may mention that Jung Bahadoor is at last marching as fast as he can towards Lucknow, and may be expected here in a few days more.

Sir Colin takes long looks through his glass; he says he is surprised at the size of the works. They look, indeed, like heavy railway embankments. From the top of the Dilkoosha, I went down to the wall in front of it, through which about thirty file were firing, their comrades lying under such shade as they could make with their greatcoats, whilst their native cook-boys were dressing their dinners. A very pretty scene; none of the horrors of war in sight. One man only hit in the leg, and gone off in a dooly. Now and then a round-shot, making a very remarkable noise in the air, which showed it was *not* round, went over towards camp. The Martinière full of people passing to and fro. Some finely-dressed rascals, in gay silks and shawls, visible through the glass. The fire of the place is very weak; if they had good guns and plenty of them, they could pound us out of the Dilkoosha, and force us to open regular trenches.

Towards evening, walked through our gateway into our camp. Simon informed me, "Much cannon-ball come here, sar"; and in effect we learn that several round-shot have cut the trees overhead and plunged into the ground among the tents; but lately the enemy have knocked off their unpleasant practice. The men, busy in hunting the poor langours, which had a very hard time of it. One of my servants got hold of a young one; it looked the picture of sorrow, and I would have let it go, were I not sure that it would receive cruel lapidations, and perhaps a death-blow. It was tied by a string to my gharry. Our first interview to-day was distant; when I approached to shake hands, it made an ugly face, chattered, and caught me by the whisker, which it pulled very viciously. Repeated advances on my part, aided by demonstrations of roasted Indian corn, at length established a friendly feeling between us, and ere· long it had learned to take my hand and look into it for food.

Dinner passed just the same as usual. We were all talking of heavy guns, battering, and storming, for half-an-hour, and then dropped into our usual quasi-controversial conversation. Our condensation increases the number of our visitors and guests, and the mess has as many as five or six-and-twenty covers laid; plates of all patterns, flanked by fifty or more little salt and pepper turrets; a silver Lucknow on a waste of table cloth. To-night some guns are to be sent up to the ridge, behind the wall, on the right front of the Dilkoosha, to open on the angle of the Martinière to-morrow morning. Sir Colin and the chief of the staff are in constant intercourse. Bruce is busy with spies, Napier with plans. We have no politicals in camp.

CHAPTER XVII.

A narrow escape.—Under fire.—A kind of club-meeting.—Horsford and the yellow eunuch.—*Personnel* of our officers.—Reconnoitring.—A prettily-adjusted brass shell.—Sepoys' courage.—The yellow eunuch again.—Floating bridge across the Goomtee.—Habitual use of a telescope.—Advance of the enemy.—A brisk cannonade.—Brijeis Kuddr.—Daily Avocations.—General order from Bahadoor Khan.—Fly-fishing.—A dignified retreat.

March 4th.—This morning had very nearly seen the last of my penmanship, and put an end to a member—very humble, indeed—of that republic which young Prince Esterhazy assured me, at Moscow, was worse than the Rouge—the "proletariat of letters." I had sauntered out with my glass under my arm, and went down to the garden which I previously mentioned. It must have been a very pretty spot—opening on the river by a flight of steps, with alcoves, covered walks, orange-trees, kiosks, abundant statuary in plaster, a platform for dancing, an orchestra, the ornamented roofs covered with gilded bosses and spires—tall cypresses and tamarinds bordered the orange-plantations, and a wilderness of flowers sprang up in their neglected beds. Everything was fast going to decay; the irrigation-canals were choked up, the fountains were dry, the statues falling to pieces, the lattices in the kiosks broken. Walking out of the garden, I went down to the broken ground close to the river, and proceeded to take a good view of the Martinière, which seemed quite close at hand. On my left front was our wall, with two guns and two howitzers in position behind it, and the red-coats firing through the loopholes. About one hundred yards behind me was a small tree, under which some officers were sitting and standing. A stout, round, little gentleman, *en bourgeois*, whom I have remarked lately about Head-Quarters, rode out of the Bibiapore park on a white pony, and joined the group. I was looking at the Martinière through my glass, soon after, and observed a fellow from behind the wall of it stretch out a coal at the end of a stick, or long pincers, to the gun, little dreaming that it was laid right for me, but in a second I heard the rush of the ball coming straight at me, and the wind of the shot made me *wink*. I turned instantly to see where it was going, and in the place where the group under the tree had been, I saw but a pillar of dust and earth. As it cleared away, the white pony appeared describing veritable scenes in the circle, with our stout friend on his back; but his *entourage* had dissolved. The shot had struck right under the horse's belly; and it is no imputation on the chief clerk of the Adjutant-General's Department to say, that he moved slowly away from ground which the enemy had so accurately measured. The wind of a shot has no physical effect except creating a current of air; its moral effects differ according to one's nervous or mental constitution.

The moment the enemy fired, bang! bang! bang! bang! went our two guns and two big howitzers at the angle of the Martinière. Large blocks of the plaster and brick tumbled down where the shot struck; the shells burst, in two balls of smoke and fire, right over the embrasure of their gun; but in three minutes another round-shot from the corner flew into our camp. Again our guns went at it. This lasted all day; the corner of the Martinière suffered, but the gun was not touched. After breakfast, which I enjoyed all the better for having a head on my shoulders, went to the top of the Dilkoosha, where I spent the day, hot as it was. The advantages of the site, as a look-out, made it a general rendezvous. Sir Colin came up about eleven o'clock, and spent half-an-hour on the roof examining the place and talking to us. Lugard has occupied some of the lower rooms as quarters for himself and staff (a round-shot passed through his breakfast-room this morning). I was glad to be away from camp, as it has to be moved to-day. The enemy find they annoy us, and have learned from their spies, the Lord Sahib is there. I should not be surprised if they mistook Mr. Hogan, on his white pony, this morning, for the Commander-in-Chief on his white horse. This morning a round-shot pitched close to our mess-tent, at breakfast-time. A little later, as I was in my tent, preparing to go out, another rushed through the crashing branches close to me, and I thought some of us must suffer. There was a short and a slight commotion among the natives; on going out, I found the shot had gone through the tent of Sir David Baird's servant, and had broken *his pipe;* but had done no other damage. Nothing makes people so uneasy as being shelled or under fire in their camp. The oldest soldiers can't stand it. No one knows when or where a shot may come. Sir Colin had, in fact, put us too near, as we were only a couple of hundred yards from the Dilkoosha. There were some casualties from the fire in the Highlanders' camp. The sepoys give their guns a great elevation, don't mind the strain on carriages, and fire away.

There was a kind of club-meeting on the top of the Dilkoosha all day. I met Colonel Evelegh, of the 20th—an old neighbour in the camp near Cathcart's Hill—a gallant and excellent officer. He looks browned, hale, and hearty. Macdonell and Horsford, of the Rifle Brigade, were also there. The latter engaged in a duel with a rascal in the Martinière, who was dressed very conspicuously in rich yellow robes. He sat in a window, and now and then took a rifle from his servants and fired it at us. From the blackness of his face, and the richness of his dress, it was imagined he was one of the African eunuchs of the palace, whose skill, as marksmen, had caused us great loss during the siege of the Residency, and to one of whom Neill's death is attributed. After the second or third shot, Horsford's rival disappeared. Napier, of the Engineers, also came up and surveyed the place. His manner is charming, kindly, quiet, and free, and his eyes have a serene, *good* expression, which invites confidence and demands respect.

I could not but be struck with the admirable *personnel* of our officers as they stood chatting in groups to-day. Sir Colin, spite of a slight stoop, is every inch a soldier in look and bearing—spare, muscular, well-poised on small, well-made feet, to which some utilitarian boot-maker has done scant justice, and given plenty of leather; one arm held straight down by the side, with clenched fist, the other used with easy gesture; his figure shows little trace of fifty years of the hardest and most varied service beyond that which a vigorous age must carry with it; the face is marked, indeed, with many a seam across the brow, but the mouth, surmounted by a trimmed, short moustache, is clean-cut and firm, showing a perfect set of teeth as he speaks; the jaw, smooth and broad, is full of decision; the eye of the most piercing intelligence, full of light and shrewdness. General Mansfield, taller than his chief, well made and broad-chested, gives some indications of his extraordinary attention to the labours of the desk and study in a "scholar's slope" about the shoulders. His face is handsome—a fine oval with a vigorous jaw; compressed, arched lips, full of power; a well-formed nose, and a brow laden with thought; his sight is not good, and he is obliged to wear glasses or spectacles, which he holds rather aloft, giving himself the air of our friend at the banquet of Nasidienus, "*omnia suspendens naso.*" It is this, probably, which has made some people think the general is supercilious: but I am satisfied no one will find him so who has to approach him on business. Horsford is the *beau idéal* of an English officer. Look at all these men, and you will find there are not above two who have the least "swagger," or swash-buckler air, whilst they all look like soldiers.

Pat. Stewart introduced me to some of the Bengal Engineers—Taylor, Brownlow, Greathed, &c., men of remarkable intelligence, and distinguished by past services, though they are yet quite young. Probably each of them has seen, in a year, more active service than Lieutenant-Colonel Harness, of the Royal Engineers, who commands them as senior; though I don't quite understand how he is placed with regard to Napier. He is most active and zealous, and now, towards the close of his life, he is realizing in service what before were but scientific dreams or the theories of the lecture-room. His aide-de-camp, Beaumont, who is noted for mechanical skill, has probably seen more service than his chief. It was amusing to see Peel, to-day, picking out ground for his guns. He walked about in front of the Dilkoosha, and away towards Mahomed Bagh, as if he were taking stock of a new farm. The enemy caught sight of him, and blazed away from all their rifle-pits; but their balls fell short, for the most part, and he went on squinting through his pet naval glass, unheeding their polite attentions. Presently he came up to the top of the Dilkoosha, and I said, "I think that some of those fellows must have gone very near you." "Pooh!" said he, laughing; "they can't shoot straight; besides, I was 500 yards away from the nearest of them, and these matchlocks won't carry more than 400 yards, as I have proved to my perfect satisfaction." However, their fire against his guns, close to us, became so sharp towards the afternoon, that he sent up to the Engineers to say he wanted a breastwork thrown up to protect his gunners.

After Peel had made his *reconnaissance*—which, by the bye, drew some dozens of the enemy to sneak across the road towards the Mahomed Bagh, in order to get a pot-shot at him—we saw a horseman emerge out of the wood near the Martinière, and ride at a walk along our left point, a proceeding which the enemy resented by an incessant fusillade; it turned out to be Kavanagh, who was doing a little reconnoitring on his own account. Scarcely had he slowly retired from the scene, when out came Colonel Harness, with two or three other officers; but by this time, orders had been sent to stop those little expeditions, and to our infinite amusement we saw an officer running after the chief of the Royal Engineers, to prevent his doing what he was specially bound to do.

The enemy, by this time, had got perfectly savage at our insulting promenades upon the open. Just as the colonel and his little party were regaining the cover of the Dilkoosha, a heavy gun was fired from Banks' bungalow, or near it, and once again the sepoys showed how well we had trained our Native Artillery, for the shot struck so close to the group that it covered them with earth and dust. As yet, Peel is not satisfied with his ground, and our fire this evening had not done more than make holes in the Martinière, bite away the angle of the wall, and frighten the statuary. Just as we were leaving this evening, the enemy, who had sent two shots into the building this morning, and plenty over and short of it, fired a very prettily-adjusted brass-shell, which burst with a "smack" over our heads, within a yard or so, and sent a hatful of fragments whirring through the men in the court-yard, with no more serious result than wounding a sutler's pony.

When we got back to camp, found we were in new ground in a park at the back of Bibiapore, which has a fine French château-like house in it. Here Sir Colin and his staff have taken up their quarters. Norman and the department have also found shelter there for their offices; but the chief sleeps in his tent. Had a large party at mess, many of whom had been in recent "dours," and I heard a good deal of "potting pandies," and "polishing-off niggers." It seems quite settled, that the enemy never fight well unless when they are in a position in which a civilised enemy would not fight at all. It is amusing to see the old Indians waxing angry at attacks on the courage of their sepoys, "*olim tam dilecti*," in which they find taunts secretly directed at themselves, and yet, in their anger, obliged to admit that the pandies do not fight as they used to do, now that they are faithless to their salt.

Sir Colin and Mansfield declare they always had the same opinion of the sepoys that they have now. " God forgive me, it was the only time I ever wilfully lent myself to an untruth in my life, when I expressed myself satisfied with their conduct." Why did our officers lend themselves to such deceit? It is a long answer to an embarrassing question. It was "the mode;"—more than that, an officer would be persecuted, hunted down and ruined, who dared to tell the truth. I am assured, in the old days, a Queen's officer who ventured to express an opinion that the discipline of a sepoy regiment was not perfect, would be insulted till he was forced to fight, and then had a host of enemies ready to put him under the sod with a bullet, or to stab him with their pens in the Indian press, which was quite dependent on the services, with few exceptions, of volunteer writers and correspondents.

March 5th.—To get through my work in a profitable way, I took up writing materials, and luncheon of salt beef and rum-and-water, to the top of the Dilkoosha to-day, but it was not quite a good place for study or composition. In the first place, Peel had got four heavy guns into position on the left, close to the house, which, with the two guns and two howitzers on the right, augmented now by two more guns, keep up a constant fire on the Martinière and on the suburb near it, as well as on the enemy's rifle-pits. To this the pandies are replying from their old gun at the Martinière, reinforced by another piece, apparently a nine-pounder, and by guns placed in various holes and corners along their works, so that the cannonade shakes the château, and the balls in reply, screaming and roaring overhead and alongside, disturb one's attention. Again the enemy have got the range of our camp, and our tents are to be once more removed and pitched further back. Great escapes and some wounds from lobbing round-shot already. It is fortunate and comfortable that the enemy have not got mortars or iron shell, or, if they have, don't use them. Just imagine a thirteen-incher, or a "whistling dick," coming into our mess-tent; or, worse, into one of the hospital tents!

Our friend, the yellow eunuch, showed to-day at the Martinière; but he and his friends bowed and retired when a ten-inch shell popped into their gallery and paid them a flying visit.

Dined at the Engineer mess this evening, which is in possession of a very large tent. The long tables were completely filled by some twenty-five or thirty members of the mess—Royals and Bengals, and their friends. Astonishing bills of fare; considering latitude and longitude, reflected great credit on the khansamah, or the superintendent, and the preparation was highly creditable to the cooks; claret, champagne, and military wines in abundance. Whilst we are feasting, the fanatics in Lucknow are listening to their Spurgeon, who has come from Mecca, and is to preach a great sermon to them this night before the Kaiserbagh! But the mass of the enemy in Lucknow will, I suspect, be fiddling or being fiddled to, for as yet our movements have caused them no greater uneasiness than to increase the animosities of their party fights, and to acuminate the Court intrigues. Let us see what a start they will get in the morning.

As we were sitting over pipes and cigars, after dinner, a disconsolate young artillery officer and an aide-de-camp come in to us from the adjoining Head-Quarters camp, and ask "Where the bridge is?" They have to bring down some guns to the river, and cannot find their way. Thus the secret is known. The engineers are at work on the Goomtee, throwing a floating bridge across, and these guns are going down to defend it. The night is fine, clear moonlight. Who will come and have a look at the bridge? It is near 10 o'clock—late for camp, and so only some four or five of us start off with the artillery. It is not very easy to find the way, for the wood is thick, and the moonlight falls fitfully and uncertainly through the dense branches, but at last we emerge on the meadows, which lie between Bibiapore and the river, and we see its waters like a strip of mirror in one bend, as it whirls through the dark plain. At one place there is a black, ant-heap-like body, which resolves itself, as we approach close, into a body of sappers, some carts laden with empty porter casks, and native drivers and coolies. They are close to the river, which is here about forty yards broad, with deep banks on both sides. Not a very silent party, for there is a row of voices and creaking of cart-wheels, which could be heard a mile away. Already the men have cut down the bank and made a rough roadway to the water's edge, and the first raft of casks is in the stream.

Nicholson, who is in command of the engineers, and is charged with the execution of the bridge, is an old acquaintance, since the days when he was wont to spend his energies in the preparations for blowing up the docks at Sebastopol. He thinks the bridge will be ready to-morrow. It is to be practicable for heavy guns. All this means that Sir Colin has devised a very masterly plan of turning the enemy's line, of taking them *en enfilade*, and even in reverse by throwing a strong corps across the Goomtee. There is not a soul on the enemy's side of the river. A few riflemen or infantry, in the long grass at the top of the bank, could have impeded the operation immensely. The native drivers would have run away, and we should have had to wait till morning. After an hour spent very pleasantly in watching the progress of the bridge, and seeing the practical application of the lessons taught at Chatham, I walked back to camp and turned into bed. Late as it was, General Mansfield was at work in his tent as I passed.

March 6th.—At dawn was up, and went down with Stewart and some others to see what progress had been made with the bridges. One floating raft was completed from bank to bank, and a party of the 38th under Hume, were across the stream as a covering party. The second bridge was not ready, and so some of us sat down and watched the progress of the men, and others enjoyed their morning smoke and a dish of gossip with their friends. It was a pretty sight—the red coats and white cap covers dotting the little mounds in our front, the earnest sappers rolling casks, pulling planks, cording, belaying, and floating off the portions of the bridge; the smooth stream; on our left the Martinière and the line of the enemy's works rising above the long, level line of meadow, and on our right a wide expanse of cornfields rolling away against a shore of deep rich green mangoe topes. Now, if there is one thing more than another which I have learned in my odd campaigning career, it is the use of a telescope, and a constant habit of using it. Many, many a dreary hour have I beguiled with my Troughton and Sims in the dreary winter days at Cathcart's Hill, by resolving the dull outline over the Tchernaya into groups of Russians, and huts, and men on the march, and long convoys of provisions. I was now at my old work once more, and was busily searching the mangoe topes, when my eye was attracted by a white flickering line, just visible in the space between the top of the corn-fields and the branches of the trees. I looked more intently. There could be no doubt of it! A body of horse was moving down on our right flank. See, there are the heads of some bullocks! "What do you see?" "Oh, you'll find out soon enough! Here are the enemy coming down on us with guns and cavalry." Every eye was now directed to the wood. Our artillerymen, in charge of four pieces on the other side of the river, jumped up and stood by their guns. Presently, from the wood in front of us, emerged the head of the body of cavalry, a magnificent "swell," as he was called, in yellow shawls, with a green turban, mounted on a white arab, leading them. He was followed by a sort of staff, and then came a body of sowars in white, riding in threes, and carrying lances, who were at once recognized as belonging to one of the revolted cavalry regiments. "The infernal scoundrels!" growled an Indian officer near me. "They murdered their colonel, and they are the d——t cowards unhung." On they wound in a fair show, edging towards our right, till they were within 600 or 650 yards of where we stood. The bravado was too much for some of our young soldiers. Instead of waiting till the sowars had come within 300 or 400 yards, the picket on the right rose, and began to fire at haphazard. Never was there such a rapid change as came over those gallant cavaliers. They had been curvetting, prancing, and bahadooring with their swords in the air, till the first bullet, whizzing in front of the leader's horse, knocked up a light puff of dust. Down went his sword at once, in went his heels, and off went the arab in a cloud of dust, followed by the whole ruck of horsemen, who never drew rein till they were a good mile away. "I'm sure I saw a gun with them," said I.

"Pooh, Correspondent! You are giving us a false alarm."

"But I do see two. One under that tope in front, unlimbered, and the other—— There! Here it comes!" A column of smoke rushed out of the tope, and a round-shot, fired at the picket close at hand, touched the top of the mound in their front, and, rising, went right into our camp among a crowd of natives. Another and a heavier gun opened on our left front, and the ball dashed up the water of the river near the bridge. It was evident at last that the enemy had opened their eyes, and were trying, too late, to stop the work. "Clear the ground in front of our guns" was passed across the river. And, with a joyous humming cry, away went a 24-shell from a howitzer to the enemy's first gun, and a 9-pounder ball skimmed smoothly away, and covered the front of No. 2 with dust at the second ricochet. The enemy stuck to their pieces, however, and made very good practice, hiding their actual position behind the trees, so that our young gunners and their officers could not dismount or silence them. The sepoys also brought up another gun to the angle of the Martinière, and by giving it and their famous old ordnance, which had lasted under all our fire, very great elevation, threw shot up to the bridge. Soon, however, two big guns came trundling along from our park, and were placed on the banks of the river, between the garden and the bridge. The cannonade became brisk, and the smoke obscured our view, so we went back to breakfast with a running accompaniment of round-shot flying before us into our camp. Some natives and some bullocks and camels had been killed and wounded among the tents, and there is talk of shifting our ground again if the fire continues.

It will be observed that this is no siege. So far it is a disappointment, because it seems as if we shall be obliged eventually to make an assault on some part or other of this big city, and drive the enemy through streets and houses, in which we are certain to suffer loss. Sir Colin will avoid this if possible. The size of Lucknow puts an investment out of the question. The enemy have chosen one side to defend, as it is that which we are likely to attack, and they have drawn up a great railway-looking embankment from the Goomtee on their left to the Charbagh on the right, using the line of an old canal, or water-cut, deeply indented towards the Charbagh as a wet ditch and rampart. Inside this is another line of defence, including Begum's palace, barracks, and mess-house, and sweeping round to the old palaces on the river and the Residency; and inside this, again, is the fortified palace of the Kaiserbagh and its dependencies. There is no regular work to attack — no battery to silence — no wall to breach. Therefore we have no trenches, and the engineers' work is not of a scientific character. The principal strength of the enemy is in their great numbers, and in the possession of a huge and populous city, in which all our troops could be easily lost. My impression is, that they are very weak in artillery. They have shown no heavy guns, their shells are brass, and the outer works in front of us are armed with only five guns, as far as I can make out. If they had heavy guns well served they could make the Dilkoosha untenable. The Russians would have battered it down in twelve hours, and covered the ruins with a rain of shells. The great bulk of the sepoy army is supposed to be inside Lucknow, but they will not fight as well as the matchlockmen of Oude, who have followed the chiefs to maintain the cause of their young king, Brijeis Kuddr (*i. e.* "Dignified or exalted as the planet Mercury"), and who may fairly be regarded as engaged in a patriot war for their country and their sovereign. The sepoys, during the seige of the Residency, never came on as boldly as the zemindarree levies and nujeebs. This Begum exhibits great energy and ability. She has excited all Oude to take up the interests of her son, and the chiefs have sworn to be faithful to him. We affect to disbelieve his legitimacy, but the zemindars, who ought to be better judges of the facts, accept Brijeis Kuddr without hesitation. Will Government treat these men as rebels or as honourable enemies? The Begum declares undying war against us; and in the circumstances of the annexation of the kingdom, the concealment of the suppression of the treaty, the apparent ingratitude to the family for money lent, and aid given at most critical times, has many grounds for her indignant rhetoric. Mummoo Khan, her guide, philosopher, and friend, is said to be a poor creature. It appears from the energetic character of these Ranees and Begums, that they acquire, in their zenanas and harems, a considerable amount of actual mental power, and, at all events, become able *intriguantes*. Their contests for ascendancy over the minds of the men give vigour and acuteness to their intellect.

As I am transcribing these bits from my diary, I find a note which shows the nature of my daily avocations; it is a loose slip from my memorandum-book referring to some weeks past, and consists of a series of questions with which I sallied forth on the unfortunate heads of department, and attacked General Mansfield or the Chief in their morning or evening walks. It runs thus: the questions, which are in ink, being followed by answers in pencil. "Walpole's column, where?" "Kunouj." "Jung Bahadoor, when last heard of?" "Bustee." "Franks' column?" "Singarmow." "Rose?" "No intelligence. He is delayed by want of supplies and transport." "Where is the convoy?" "At Mynpoorie." "Where is the Madras column?" "It is very slow, but is supposed to be near Jubbulpore," and so on. I begin to suspect I and my note-book must be nuisances at times. Up to the last accounts, Rose was exhibiting great activity. He had taken Garrakota, without firing a shot, a fort which had, in 1818, defied 11,000 of our men; and was moving, at the rate of three marches in two days, through Bundelcund, which is described as a sort of Switzerland, and directing his column against Jhansi, where the Rance is determined to hold out to the last.

Sir Colin showed me a sort of general order emanating from old Khan Bahadoor Khan, of Bareilly, in Rohilcund, which bears marks of sagacity, and points out the most formidable war we could encounter—a genuine guerilla. He says: "Do not attempt to meet the regular columns of the infidels, because they are superior to you in discipline and bunderbust, and have big guns; but watch their movements, guard all the ghauts on the rivers, intercept their communications, stop their supplies, cut up their dâks and posts, and keep constantly hanging about their camps; give them no rest."

As there was nothing to see or to do, I resolved to take out my rod and try for a fish in the Goomtee, in which we were assured that many marseer, and other fly-taking fish, abounded. I went back to camp, and, preparing tackle and flies, started with Stewart for the river, and attended by my man Simon. Found the river full of people bathing—camp followers, horses, camels, and elephants—so we moved further down to a place where a bend in the river took us nearer to the town. I was fishing away assiduously, with no success, when Stewart's servant cried out, "Deko! Sahib! deko! Budmash hai!" (Look, sir, look, there is a blackguard!)—pointing with his finger to some high corn growing on the opposite side of the river. Stewart was bathing—his clothes were on the bank—I seized them up, and allowed him to come out after me, as I knew, if he stopped, and the budmashes really were so close to us, he would most likely be "potted" on the spot. There was no doubt the corn was agitated, and so, with as much dignity as was consistent with a proper retreat, we retired from the bank just in time to avoid the fire of four or five sneaking scoundrels who had crept down to pot us, and who were not aware we had got off till they came close to the river banks, when they stood up and fired an impotent volley, which hit the ground about us, but made no indenture in our body corporate. It appeared as if we excited some attention, for a whole string of long-legged rascals were trooping down towards us, and we were amused by witnessing a duel which took place between one of them and an officer on our side, at the distance of two or three hundred yards, without any serious consequences to any one. I was consoled for the termination to my fishing by knowing there were no fish to rise. I recollect being once molested by some vagabond Cossacks, just in the same manner, when fishing in the stream near Baidar, and being obliged to retreat precipitately, with my flies streaming in the air, or catching in the grass, but I bore off my rod in triumph.

CHAPTER XVIII.

Sir Colin Campbell's plan of operations.—A beautiful sight.—Unjust estimate of men's actions.—The enemy swarm.—The Bays, the Artillery, and the Rifles.—The day's work done.—Outram's camp.—The enemy active and unhappy.—Little Miss Orr.—Preparations for Outram's advance.—Kite-flying.—Warfare and cruelty. Native milk-women.—Outram's advance.—My Caubulee pony.—A terrible game of cricket.—The storming party.—"Pandy" and "Smith."—Assault of the Martinière.—A canter to the newly-gained post.—Butler, of the Bengal Fusiliers.—Pandy's deserted trenches.—Sikh Barbarity.—The Begum still undaunted.

March 7th.—Yesterday, which commenced with a little excitement, has set my diary all out of order. After writing for an hour or so, I went to the top of the Dilkoosha, where Sir Colin soon came up; and, taking me into one of the little turrets out of the sun, he was good enough to explain, map in hand, what was his plan of operations, which up to that moment was a dead secret. "Outram, with a complete corps of infantry, cavalry, and guns, crosses the floating bridges, or rafts, across the Goomtee, and marches straight for the road which leads over the Kokraal viaduct that you see there beyond the Martinière. This road leads, in a line nearly parallel to the course of the Goomtee, to the Iron and Stone bridges—and now, mind that this is kept quiet. Outram will be placed so as to command the rear of the enemy's line, and to take their works in flank and reverse, whilst our attack is pressed with vigour from this side against the Begum's kothie and Banks' bungalow as soon as the Martinière is taken—a movement being made against it the moment Outram's success is developed." As Sir Colin was talking to me, I was amused by a little incident. A round-shot, passing by the turret, plunged with a great squash into the front of the courtyard below us, which was full of men, and involuntarily I said, "That's done harm, I fear!" Sir Colin never raised his head apparently from the plan he was showing me, and merely interpolated the words "none whatever" in the structure of exposition which he was raising for me, and went on; all the time our guns kept up a furious fire on the Martinière, and on the whole line of the enemy's works.

See, there is, indeed, a beautiful sight! The head of a column of British troops is emerging from the woods which surround our camp, and is marching upon the bridge. The bright scarlet of the Bays shines brightly in the sun. What a storm of lightning points—flashes of bright steel—bursts through the cloud of dust. There go the artillery—thirty guns. There go the Rifles—the dear old brigade. Will the column never cease? Hour after hour it has been passing over, and all the time we are in the hot sun and blinding dust on the top of the Dilkoosha. What swarms of camp followers! What a mighty *impedimentum* of baggage, deserts of camels, wildernesses of elephants, all pouring along towards the river, and then following in parallel lines the folds of the serpent-like column which is winding away through the corn-fields till it disappears in the woods on the horizon. The column and its dependencies were four hours crossing over; as to the baggage, it was not clear of the bridge even at night.

The enemy began to swarm out of the city long ere

the appearance of the column gave the construction of the bridge its true significance. It was curious to watch them through the glass; far as the eye could see, were men singly, in twos, or threes, or fours, without any formation, walking, as they listed, along the road to the Kokraal and in the fields alongside, till they were hid by the trees which border the very road along which Outram is to advance, and amid which lies the famous village of Chinhut. How unjust the world is in its estimate of men's actions! Or is it just to apply to them success as the sole rule and the only criterion? Sir Henry Lawrence, persecuted by the "war party" in the Residency, went out to disperse the rebels at Chinhut. The native troops and gunners defected, he was obliged to make a painful and disastrous retreat. The world exclaims "What a foolish expedition to Chinhut!" Had he beaten the enemy, the world would be *almost* equally ready to exclaim, "What a glorious expedition to Chinhut!" So with Windham at Cawnpore. Had he beaten the Gwalior people on the second day as he had done on the first, he would have been cried up as the greatest of generals and of soldiers as of fighters. We should not have heard one word of disobedience of orders, of rashness, ignorance, imprudence, &c., &c. On the other hand, had he let himself be shut up in the *tête-de-pont*—had he given up the city to plunder—had he permitted the enemy to bombard the entrenchments—to cannonade, and possibly destroy, the bridge—what should we not have heard said of him? These remarks come to my mind as I think of what the world would say if Outram there fell into an ambuscade, or got terribly mauled by an overwhelming body of the enemy. How Sir Colin would be decried for "acting in opposition to the principles of war." How the Club strategists would point out "the absurdity, by Jove, sir ! of any man dividing his army—small enough in itself—in the face of a powerful enemy, and putting one part of it out of reach beyond an unfordable river, by gad, sir, as if he wanted them cut to pieces !" Then you would hear it hinted that he and Outram were not good friends, &c., &c. Just as an old Engineer officer, talking of Cawnpore last night, said, "Windham talked so much on coming to India that he made lots of men—if not enemies—quite delighted, at all events, when his boasting was turned into confusion." One of the greatest miseries of an unsuccessful general is, that he can never tell the truth in his own defence. Indeed, what general can ? There is always much to be blamed, which cannot be openly denounced. Never mind the bulletins, but watch a general's conduct after a battle. See how he selects corps or men, and be sure that it is the real way of getting at their value. Where am I getting to ?

The enemy are going out to fight Outram. There goes a gun drawn by three pairs of bullocks. There goes a "swell" in a gilt palanquin, preceded by men carrying gold sticks and maces—real gold and silver sticks in waiting. There is another dignitary mounted on an elephant, with a silver howdah, shadowed by a great umbrella, which shines in the sun. There are numerous horsemen also well mounted, and curvetting through the meadows; and the swarms of footmen, all in white — turbans, dhoties, or tunics—with black cartouche-boxes, are formidable in everything but organization. The day is wearing away. I had pointed out to Sir Colin two guns that the enemy had brought up and placed under cover between the Goomtee and the Kokraal road—my telescope was more powerful in resolving objects than his binocular—and also that they had withdrawn one of those with which they had been hammering at the bridge, when we saw a faint cloud of dust rise up among the trees in the direction in which Outram might be expected to appear. By this time the Dilkoosha was tolerably well crowded by staff officers. "Sister Ann! Sister Ann! do you see any one coming?" There is a cessation in the number of footmen from the city. The dust is evidently approaching towards us, and is becoming denser. Through the perpetual thunder of our own guns just below us I think I hear the report of distant firing. Look!—look! The woods are alive with men in white running back towards Lucknow! See that stream of horsemen rushing towards the Kokraal bridge! Hurra! there comes the swell on the elephant! Hollo! see there how the fellows are cutting along with that palkee! What a dust! What a mass of men running for their lives! Outram must be close at hand. In another instant out dashes, in the utmost disorder, a squadron of the Bays, distinguishable as our cavalry only by their red coats, their swords gleaming as they brandish them among the fugitives, from whom comes a dropping fire. The great mass of the runaways are dodging through broken ground between the Kokraal and the river, where the cavalry cannot pursue them. In another second or two out bounds from the wood a hungry troop of horse artilery—unlimbers—the little black specks flush for a moment with fire, and then we see the ground among the fugitives dotted with denser dust clouds where the round-shot and grape are flying through them. The artillery cannot see or cannot get at the bulk of the enemy, to whose flight the reports of our guns have given increased speed. Our cavalry have disappeared behind the trees at the Kokraal nuddy, but they are now returning. Some heavy guns have opened on them—the round shot are ricochetting through them away towards the other wood, from which the Rifles have now emerged. Outram has made good his ground, and is to encamp on the position he has taken. The day's work is done. But poor Percy Smith lies dead somewhere in the heat and scuffle of that charge in which the men and horses got out of hand. Outram's artillery limbers up; the main part of his force is concealed by the woods, but we can make out the Rifle pickets posted in front, and cavalry videttes under the trees. It is melancholy that the people should think we are their enemies. Amid the fugitives from our advance to-day were women with children in their arms, and men carrying charpoys and bundles on their backs.

To-day (the 7th) was one of the most disagreeable I have yet encountered in my lifetime of six-and-thirty years—that is, so much of it as I remember—a blazing sun—a cold high wind, clouds of dust, sharp, blinding, and offensive. I rode out early on a Caubul pony—a new purchase, which a friend was kind enough to let me have for £50, and I was literally driven in by the dust and could not get over, as I intended, to Outram's camp. Berkeley, his chief of the staff, arrived here from Alumbagh last night, and we arranged that I was to meet him at the bridge soon after daybreak, where he would have a few sowars waiting for an escort, and would scamper over to the camp as fast as possible so as to arrive in time for anything that may be going on, but I was blinded by the dust, and found on my return that Berkeley would not go till later in the day. He is quite recovered of the wound he received in a charge on the enemy from Alumbagh, and looks "harder" and better than when he was in the Guards — a good officer he is admitted by all to be, if a little hot in temper, and as brave as steel. Just as we were recovering the effects of breakfast, the sound of firing from Outram's position summoned all idlers to the front. The enemy had set fire last night to the high jungle grass about the Kokraal nullah, and were enabled to form a guess respecting Outram's strength and the situation of his camp. I went down to the battery in front of the Dilkoosha, and saw through my glass a very feeble attack made upon him under cover of rather a smart cannonade. Some cavalry came down on his flanks, and infantry in very loose order, sheltering themselves under the thick topes around, fired in a desultory way on the advanced posts and pickets. If they intended to drive Outram back it was a miserable demonstration. We could see the tops of Outram's tents just over the trees, and our men pushing steadily through the cover— our guns opening from time to time, and the poor vexed earth seamed with unkindly furrows by the rude ploughing of shot and shell. At last the enemy fell back, finding that Outram was *inébranlable*. To-night he is to receive a fine park of twenty-two heavy guns with elephants to draw them, and *matériel*, so that he is about to play a most important part in the operation, as he has done all along in his fort at Alumbagh. The enemy are active and unhappy. Spies bring into Major Bruce's tent quaint rolls of paper which contain the accounts of what passes in the city; but they are so puerile and feeble in all points, that Sir Colin now seldom reads them, and only listens to Bruce's analysis. "To-morrow" is always to be the day for victory. They are to make two attacks on us to-day; so it was determined yesterday, because they did us the injustice to suppose we would be busy with our prayers. We are short of chaplains, and there is little chance of Divine service to-day. One of those attacks has just come off, the other is now going on. It is directed as if against Franks' divisions and against the Mahomed Bagh. I have quite forgotten Franks, by the bye, who joined us the other day with his fine division, after a triumphant *promenade militaire*, which, however, had not so good a close, for the very day he joined us, he was obliged to haul off from a small mud fort that he attacked without his heavy artillery, and had three officers wounded (one mortally, it is feared) in the attack. He is a fine-looking, tall, soldier-like man, of frank, easy manners, well known for his personal gallantry, but reputed to be severe as a disciplinarian, which is the soldiers' phrase for unpopular. It is thought at Head-Quarters that he cannot have a very just organ of number, as he certainly overrates both the number of the enemy as well as their losses in his recent actions. There can, however, be no doubt about the number of the guns. Young Havelock, his aide, son of the General, has distinguished himself very much by his forwardness and dash, but he is by no means spoiled, for he seems to have inherited the gravity of his father; is quiet, modest, and rather reserved, most eager and keen after work, and promises to be an excellent officer, as he has proved himself already to be a gallant soldier. In person he is slight, but muscular, and well set. His face is rather stern for so young a man, but the expression is agreeable. Sir Colin is rather hard upon him because of his receiving the Victoria Cross for an act which the Chief regards as subversive of discipline and offensive to a gallant regiment—the 64th—whom he was represented as leading to a charge when he should have confined himself to the delivery of his orders to advance. The act will be regarded with more indulgence by his countrymen; but one cannot help sympathizing with the gallant officers of the regiment, who feel that it is an imputation on them to confer the Cross on an aide-de-camp for leading their regiment in a service of great danger.

A little child named Orr was sent in to-day by a friendly native who had concealed her in the city, where there are still two or three English ladies hidden by the same man. The poor little girl was carried out through the enemy in some disguise, and delivered at the Alumbagh post. The body of poor Percy Smith was found to-day—*headless.* No doubt the scoundrels carried his head into the town, and proclaimed that they had won a victory. His nephew was killed a few days before in one of Franks' actions. It is reported that an inquiry will be instituted as to the cause of the extraordinary loss of horses in the

Bays. What can it be but want of training and bad riding in a bad country? We could see the dismounted men running to the rear in all directions, or walking leisurely over the ground.

Monday, March 8th.—This morning ride to the Dilkoosha is now a little more exciting than it used to be, for that abominable gun at the Martinière, which Peel cannot touch any more than the Royals or Bengals, opens on us the moment one or two horsemen show out of the enclosure. A chance shot, Pandy thinks, may kill the Commander-in-Chief. To-day there are great preparations for Outram's move to-morrow. Stewart is busy making a telegraph to communicate with him from head-quarters. We can see a wide plain across the Goomtee, on which there is an odd-looking yellow building, called the Chuckerwallah Kothie, and which, I am told, was the stand-house of the old racecourse. Then nearer to the river is an Italian villa, beyond and behind which are dense-looking groves; and then nearer to the city is a very large park-like enclosure, full of trees, with buildings inside displaying turrets and castellated gables—this is the Badshahbagh, or the Garden of the Badshah, or great king. Beyond it again is a suburb of poor low houses, through which the road leads to the Stone and Iron bridges. The Badshahbagh is strongly occupied by the enemy. Near is a graceful mosque, with two slender minarets, embosomed among noble trees. This is the line of his march. How lovely Lucknow looks to-day! The sun playing on all the gilt domes and spires, the exceeding richness of the vegetation and forests and gardens, which remind one somewhat of the view of the Bois-de-Boulogne from the hill over St. Cloud. But for the puffs of villanous saltpetre, and the thunder of the guns, and the noise of balls cleaving the air, how peaceful the scene is! Up above the gilded spires of the Kaiserbagh are to be seen many kites serenely floating in the air, giving infinite pleasure to the gentlemen who are directing their movements. They are the true composite of monkey and tiger, those Orientals. Any one of those amicable kite-flyers would probably disembowel you—cut off your head if you fell into his hands and could not defend yourself. We tortured our Jews once on a time as the Hindoos and Mahomedans mutilate their Christians now, and I presume our Crusaders—if not the knights, at least their barbarous followers—gave scant grace to the Moslem. Even as it is, we give no quarter to the enemy. Our auxiliaries, those savage Punjabees, would rival the Poorbeahs in cruelty if they dared.

Talking of this matter some days ago, Norman remarked that in the Punjab war our men were mutilated by the enemy whenever they fell, dead or alive, into their hands, though we, on the contrary, took their wounded into our hospitals, and treated them with every care and attention. But war can never be purged of a dross of cruelty and barbarism. It is all very well to talk of moderation in the hour of victory, but men's passions do not cool in a moment, and in every army there must be ruffians who rejoice in a moment of licence, when killing is no murder. Soldiers do not always spare a wounded foe. Indeed, I have been struck by the prominence given to the conduct of those who have done so. We all have eard of the French officer at Waterloo who, perceiving that the antagonist at whom he rode in a harge had lost the use of his sword-arm, threw up is sabre, saluted, and rode on. It is not the grace f this act so much as the act itself that has made it o well known. It would have been reckoned cowardly if the Frenchman had passed his sword through is enemy's body, could he have made the latter a risoner; but if the Englishman with his bridle-arm ad shot the Frenchman dead, he would esteem it as a gallant act; just as some of our officers did who got away from their Russian captors at Inkerman by shooting them with their revolvers. Conduct warfare on the most chivalrous principles, there must ever be a touch of murder about it, and the assassin will lurk under fine phrases. The most civilized troops will commit excesses and cruelties, which must go unpunished, as they did at Badajoz. With all its chivalry, the field of Crecy, or of Agincourt, must have been fearful in its cruelty, when, not to mention the slaughter of prisoners, the kernes and churls with their sharp knives went searching out the chinks in the armour of the fallen knights and nobles, and pierced them to death as they lay helpless on the field. It was not much better when our wounded Guardsmen were bayoneted by the Russians in the Sand-bag battery.

To-day there is little doing beyond the ignition of gunpowder. It is very amusing to watch the kirmishing between the sepoys in the pits and trenches, and our soldiers. The latter expose themselves in the most reckless way. One fellow went as he thought under cover, because he held his head down, but the whole of his back was exposed to the enemy, who potted away at him, and at last hit him in the elbow. He immediately stood up, and discharging his piece with one hand doubled back behind the wall. Here the men have made themselves quite comfortable, and protect themselves from the sun by means of matting and wickerwork frames. The milk-women carrying their pitchers of milk on their heads —one of them at least—venture down to this post under the wall, and I can hear the pleasant music of her bangles as she walks, and the shrill cry of "lay dood" as I stand on the roof. "Come here, Miss lay dood! I want you for a dhrink ov skim milk," cries a soldier, and smilingly she jingles over to him and fills him a cup of the compound which, to my mind, neither cheers nor inebriates. Her husband, a jealous Hindoo, hovers over the scene behind the artillery parapet under pretence of selling tobacco and lights. The "lay doods," equivalent to our "milk-ka-alow," generally go in pairs, and disturb the quiet of our camp till they are warned off by the Chief's sentry. By the bye, his Excellency always trusts his person to natives. The Commissariat officers also prefer native guards for their treasure chests and tumbrils. Very recently, when in charge of European regiments, two of these tumbrils on two separate occasions were afflicted with an extraordinary leakage of rupees. The British soldier unquestionably suffers from an "*auri sacra fames*" in India. Why should he not? He sees around him a vast social fabric to which the same desire is a great moving principle. Every day I hear it said, "If it were not for the rupees I would not stay in the confounded country or an hour." The reason the Chief has natives on duty before his tent is, that they stand the heat better than the Europeans.

March 9th.—We are getting *aux prises* with the enemy. Early this morning Outram moved out from his camp, under a thundering fire of his guns, which tore up all the plain in his front, and drove the enemy out of their hiding-places in mosque inclosures, villas, and old suburbs. Owing to the dust, which began to fly very thickly as soon as the troops moved, very little of the advance could be seen, except the flashing of the bayonets and whirling dust clouds, where the cavalry were moving to the right; but the advance of the musketry-fire was steady, and only interrupted for a short space, during which our men lay down as if to escape from the cannon-shot which the enemy were hurling at them. Our artillery seemed to shut the hostile guns up, and to force them back, and our line advanced again, but it became quite impossible to follow them, owing to the nature of the ground and the obscurity in which the sheets of flying sand wrapped the landscape. I went back to breakfast, and as we were sitting in the mess-tent, an officer, very hot and dusty, and tired, who had come over from Outram's camp, told us he was driving the enemy before him with ease, but that they still held out in the Chuckerwallah Kothie, and that the sepoys looked as if they would fight for it ere we got the Badshahbagh. So I repaired once more to the Dilkoosha, only to find the dust more hopelessly interceptive than before. I mounted my Caubulee once more, and set off to the left of our position, which was in a very large park, with some Mahomedan tombs and praying-places under the trees, called the Mahomedbagh. The angle of the wall of this park, which is some hundreds of acres in extent I should think, was quite close to a suburb of mud-houses cut up by deep narrow lanes, in which were many of the enemy. Our men had loopholed the park-wall, and were maintaining a constant fusillade on the houses, which appeared to be separated from us by a deep trench or dry canal, and the enemy replied with musketry, and now and then with a round-shot. I had fastened Caubulee to a tree, and was looking through one of the loopholes at a lot of sepoys who were creeping along under a wall about 150 yards in my front, when a gun was fired from among the houses; the ball rushed through the wall, sending a soldier's firelock flying to pieces, grazed a tree, out of which it cut a heavy splinter, and pitching right under poor Caubulee's nose, covered him with dust, and, as I thought, knocked him to pieces. I ran up to the spot, but my steed, not liking such rude jokes, had broken away and was flying through the trees as fast as he could, lashing out and neighing like mad. Running is not my forte, especially with the thermometer at ninety degrees something, and my legs in heavy jack-boots, and I was right glad to see a Sikh lay hold of my charger. When I got up to him I found his nose and eyes a little cut by the sand, and the rope of my Peat's feeding-bit gone, and no other damage done. On my return to the Dilkoosha I found all our guns pounding at the Martinière in the most vicious manner. Peel was hurrying to and fro in our front among his blue-jackets. How splendidly he brought up his guns the other day, and I forgot to say a word about it! He had to take them to ground on the left front of the Dilkoosha—a cumbrous train of men, bullocks, guns, and tumbrils; and he might, I think, have gone round the building and come out on the left of it, but he coolly marched round from the right under our noses, and in full view of the enemy. It would have been a pretty sight, had it not been matter of life and death, to see how solidly the blue-jackets marched with Peel and their officers among them, and how the sepoy artillerymen plumped shot after shot right across the line of their march, always contriving, however, to strike the spot over which a gun had just passed, or that to which a gun was just coming. It was a terrible game of cricket, and we were all relieved when we saw the men and the guns safe behind their battery-parapet. As I came up to-day, Peel said, "Well, I think they're getting rather sick of it yonder," pointing towards the Martinière. At this moment a rocket was fired from his battery, which, after a few erratic twists, hissed away for the corner of the Martinière park and burst among the houses. "That was well pitched," said he. I asked, "Well, how are the rockets doing to-day?" "Well! you know rockets are rockets.—If the enemy are only half as much afraid of them as we who fire them, they are doing good service."

I went on to camp, and heard that Outram was making way, but that we had lost two officers at least. Just as I was writing in my tent I got a note—"We assault the Martinière at 2 o'clock to-day." Indeed, as I was going through the Highlanders' camp, several of the officers asked me "what was up," as they were ordered to give their men dinner at 12 o'clock.

So once more I went to the Dilkoosha, where I found Sir Colin, Mansfield, and others, on the top, whilst Lugard, who was to direct the assault under very precise orders from the Chief of the Staff, was getting ready to turn out his division. The 42nd and a Punjaub regiment are to lead. They will be supported by the 38th, 53rd, 90th, and 93rd. The storming-party are to use no powder, and are restricted to the bayonet, but they will advance under a heavy fire from their right flank, and will be covered by a concentrated fire of both batteries on the right and left of the Dilkoosha. Lord, after all, how tiresome is a camp! how monotonous, and yet exciting, are war's alarms—even these small fellows—and how dreary is a siege unless when the enemy are active and strong, and make one uneasily perturbate. The concurritur is changed. There is no "*cito*" now about the "*mors venit aut læta victoria*," and dull scientific method has taken the place of ardour and vigorous enterprise in the day of battle. Here now has been Mansfield writing an order for the attack of the Martinière which is as cold and precise and exact as a bit of Euclid. How the men are to be fed; how so and so are to do this and that; how, when this is done, the other thing is to follow; and how, as this is to that, so is the advance to be the occupation of the enemy's position. And yet it is very nice and exact, and, above all, it saves blood-letting, an object thank God, of great import to us here, though of distressing insignificancy to the bulletin-reader or to the relativeless public, which is always rejoicing in the death of other people's relations—"*gloriæ nomine gaudet.*"

We are all on the top of the Dilkoosha, the trenches near the Martinière are full of the enemy. The rockets, shot and shell, from Peel's battery, and from the artillery on the right, make great holes in the walls, dash down the parapets, send Claude Martin's plaster deities in showers through the air; still Pandy holds on, and when the dust clears away, there is his white turban and his black face visible in the ruin. Why Pandy? Well, because it is a very common name among the sepoys—like Smith of London, or any other generic designation.

The Dilkoosha served as a screen to the troops. Looking down on them as we did, they seemed as regular and stiff as toy battalions. Meantime the guns on our front were maintaining a most tremendous fire on the angles of the Martinière, under which, indeed, they crumbled away in blocks and sections of brickwork. The rockets hissed incessantly into the ruined houses, in which we could still see white turbans moving to and fro. The sepoys certainly stand fire exceedingly well when they are in cover.

At last the time arrives—it is just 2 P.M. Through the din of the cannonade rise the words of command in the courts below us. "Forward!" "forward!" "forward!" tapering away from company to company. As the leading files of the Highlanders appeared on the flank of the Dilkoosha, the guns at once ceased. The enemy understood the whole thing in a moment. Ere the smoke had cleared away from the front of our batteries, we could see them "sloping along" their advanced trenches towards the zig-zags leading to the rear; deserting their rifle-pits, crowding into the main passages, and then flowing in white-crested streams, bobbing up and down in little waves towards the Martinière. But few of them fired as they fled. The moment the leading company of the Highlanders deployed into line, and the Sikhs on their flank began to double, the sepoys made a rush out of their hiding-places. White figures flew down the steps of the Martinière, passed the open doorway, flitted along the corridors. It was a regular race between Sikhs and Highlanders to catch the enemy. As they streamed out, the dooly-bearers of the regiments came trudging in close columns after them. Poor fellows! the fire of the enemy's guns, which was opened from the ditch of the canal, as soon as they discovered our attack, was too late to touch our men, who were already screened from it by the Martinière park, but the round-shot plumped among the doolies, and more than one of the bearers dropped, mutilated and quivering lumps of flesh, in the dust. Just at that moment the 53rd appeared marching in great order, in columns of companies, right for the line of the enemy's fire. Sir Colin, who had come up from the court, was very wroth. "See that fellow, Mansfield! just look how he's taking his regiment into that fire! Here, sir; go down and tell the commanding officer to deploy them at once, and advance in skirmishing order. How men can be such fools!" Well, there must be fools in all professions, and accidents in every operation. See! there is a prodigious dust in the midst of that troop of artillery, which is galloping in the flank of our attacking column. A gun has gone over in the uneven ground bodily, horses and all, and there it lies with the carriage and wheels up in the air. This is but of little moment, for our men are already in the enemy's trenches. There they go,

leaping into the rifle-pits—Hurrah! They're in the
Martinière itself: there they go, up the steps. "Here,
Mr. Russell," said Sir Colin, handing me his glass,
"I'll make you aide-de-camp for the time; your eyes
are better than mine—just look through the trees, on
the right of the Martinière, and tell me who are the
people you see there?" "They are Highlanders and
Sikhs, sir; I can see them clearly. They are firing
through the trees, and advancing very rapidly!"
"Then we'll go over to the Martinière." Our horses
were waiting us below. General and staff and
idlers canter across the open to the newly-gained
post. The enemy got sight of us, and their round-
shot came by with that peculiar noise which cannot
be imagined by those who have not heard it, and
cannot be described by those who have. Not a soul
was touched. Soon we were clambering up the winding staircases of the Martinière, and got out on the
balconies, from which lay an extensive view of the
suburbs of Lucknow, the line of the enemy's works,
the Goomtee on the right, and the flat country beyond
it, consisting of sandy plains and well-wooded fields,
across which Outram's troops were moving in splendid
order, whilst his artillery, unlimbered on a patch of
sand, over the Goomtee, was pounding away at the
enemy behind the canal works. Just at this moment
an aide-de-camp came to Sir Colin. "General Lugard
says there's a battery beyond the Martinière wall
which is annoying him, sir, and wishes for instructions." "Tell him to take it, if he can." However,
there was no need for this, for already Outram's
artillery was ploughing-up the canal entrenchment,
and the cannon-shot were enfilading it from end to

end. At about 1 o'clock Sir Colin sent over an order that this operation should be effected; but I think, with the exception of a few gunners at the Cavalier Battery, the sepoys had fled from the canal parapet soon after Outram moved in the morning, and before we were well into the Martinière. A desultory fire was going on from the walls and houses, which were surrounded with trees and gardens, in rear of the canal parapet. The Highlanders and Sikhs, pushing on, were in the suburbs, and were firing steadily at every object which showed itself. Suddenly we saw a figure rising out of the waters of the Goomtee, and scrambling up the canal parapet, which just terminates at this place. He gets up—stands upright—and waves his hand. "What is he?" "He must be one of our fellows, sir, he has blue trousers and red stripe." And so it was—Butler, of the Bengal Fusileers, had volunteered to cross the river from Outram's force, and to ascertain if the parapet was really occupied. Had it been so, his mission must have been fatal to him; as it was, it was crowned with success. He was soon followed; our men, too, ran across and seized the extreme left flank, being checked, in their extension towards Banks' bungalow, by the fire of the place. There was another escapade to divert our attention. An officer, who had got out in the open, between the suburb and the enemy's end of the entrenchment, could not find the way back again, and rode once or twice backwards and forwards amid a rolling fire of musketry directed at him by the enemy, whilst our soldiers were obliged to do all they could to prevent his being hit by their balls. "Hallo! those rascals are waking up!" A round-shot whizzes past our heads as we are looking on—in an instant after, another smashes the brickwork of a window-frame, and covers us all with mortar and splinters of brick. "All officers are to go below immediately." There sits the Chief, and one or two of his immediate staff, in the shade of a large column, whilst the *polloi* are sent down below. But there was nothing to see now; Outram's bayonets are dancing in the sun above the clouds of dust and smoke, but his tillery is directed towards the city, and his men are moving towards the shelter of the trees, where they are to find their resting-place for the night. The fire of musketry in our front is quite slackened, but a sullen shot from the left now and then expresses the dissatisfaction of the rebels in Banks' bungalow and the western end of the canal works at our success, which they have not the courage to seek to turn into defeat.

I had a canter about Pandy's deserted trenches. The ground is covered with their tulas, or cooking-places, and with little other remnants—no beef-bones and beer-bottles as in the case of the British, or tin cases as in that of the French, or rags and cabbage-stalks as in that of the Russian, are strewed over their camping-grounds. Thence I went over to the Dilkoosha to see how Peel was getting on. I had to wait a little ere I could get into his room, and, in spite of myself, I was obliged to witness the amputation of a dooly-bearer's thigh. I have seen quite enough of those sights, one way or other, but I never beheld greater courage or endurance than was displayed by this man, who appeared to be only twenty years of age—a slight, tall, dark-coloured Hindoo. His thigh was horribly shattered by a round-shot. His large eyes moved inquiringly about as the surgeons made their preparations, but he never even moaned when, with a rapid sweep of the knife, the principal operator had cut the flesh through to the broken splintered bone. The blood does not show so much on the dark skin as on the white. In two or three minutes the black leg was lying on the floor of what had once been the Begum's boudoir in the palace of Heart's-ease—in two or three minutes more the dusky patient, with a slow shiver, passed away quietly to the other world. Some of my friends in camp would deny he had any soul, or, as one of them put it, "If niggers have souls, they're not the same as ours."

I found Peel extended on a little bedstead, pale and feverish, but he would talk of nothing but the attack, and the certainty he felt of being able to get up in time to be in at the finish. His sole annoyance, with regard to the wound, was that it kept him from the guns and the field. The ball has sunk deep in the thigh, and the wound is severe, though not dangerous, so that I don't think his anticipations will be realized; and I know we shall all feel his loss.

Our camp-dinner was very animated; and in the evening I had a long talk with Sir Colin, who explained to me some further points connected with his plan of attack. He particularly insisted on the value of the flank movement made by Outram, and on the effect of his fire to-day; being careful, however, to let it be seen that he had originated the operation, and had kept it so completely to himself, that Outram did not know of it till the very night before he crossed the Goomtee.

Later I saw one who had come over from Outram's camp, and he told us of the great success of the day, and of the fine advance made by the right corps, a wing of an army. Alas! that he should have to tell, too, of the disgusting termination to the attack on the Chuckerwallah Kothie, the yellow house on the racecourse, in which some few sepoys made a resistance, which a national Tyrtæus or Dibdin would have chanted in noble song; their enemies called it foolish and fanatic. What could they do more than fight to the last, and kill or wound every man who approached them? As they had killed a British officer of a Sikh regiment, several men, and wounded more, the troops were withdrawn from the house, and a heavy fire of artillery was opened on it. After the walls had been perforated in all directions with shot and shell, so that it seemed impossible for the little garrison to have escaped, a detachment of Sikhs rushed into the house—some of the sepoys were still alive, and they were mercifully killed; but for some reason or other which could not be explained, one of their number was dragged out to the sandy plain outside the house, he was pulled by the legs to a convenient place, where he was held down, pricked in the face and body by the bayonets of some of the soldiery, whilst others collected fuel for a small pyre, and when all was ready—the man was roasted alive! There were Englishmen looking on, more than one officer saw it. No one offered to interfere! The horror of this infernal cruelty was aggravated by an attempt of the miserable wretch to escape when half-burned to death. By a sudden effort he leaped away, and with the flesh hanging from his bones, ran for a few yards ere he was caught, brought back, put on the fire again, and held there by bayonets till his remains were consumed. "And his cries, and the dreadful scene," said my friend, "will haunt me to my dying hour." "Why didn't you interfere?" "I dared not, the Sikhs were furious. They had lost Anderson, our own men encouraged them, and I could do nothing."*

The fighting on Outram's side was very sharp. The enemy begin to understand that if the bridges are taken their means of escape are much hampered; already they must comprehend that their defences are partially turned, and that their great outer canal-parapet is made useless. In all my wanderings to-day I saw only three or four "pandies" dead or *in extremis*. One of my servants had on a fine cumma-bund this evening. I asked him where he got it. "A dead budmash."

Hodson dined with us at mess. A very remarkable fine fellow—a *beau sabreur*, and a man of great ability. His views, expressed in strong nervous language, delivered with fire and ease, are very decided; but he takes a military, rather than a political, view of the state of our relations with India. I should like to see Hodson at the head of his horse try a bout with the best Cossacks of the Don, or Black Sea; not that I would willingly have the fight, but that if it must be I should be sorry to miss the sight of it.

As we walk up and down in the stately avenue of trees, beneath which lies our camp, the car is saluted

---

* I saw the charred bones, some days after, on the plain.

with the pattering fire of small arms across the river. Now and then a big gun spoke out, and the shot cleft the air on its mission of mischief, or a shell twinkled in long ellipse as it flew into the city. Bruce tells me they are in dreadful alarm there to-day. Penthesilea, the Begum, is still undaunted. The Kaiserbagh is the stronghold, but, after all, it is merely a series of open courts and stucco-palaces, and the Chief is going to treat them copiously to vertical fire ere he assaults.

CHAPTER XIX.

Outram's great success.—Jung Bahadoor's arrival announced.—Poor Garvey!—The Begum Kothie.—The Maharajah's reception.—The Begum Kothie taken.—The rush of the 93rd.—Horrors ineffable.—The Secunderbagh.—General Outram's camp.—"The Bayard of India."—The Badshahbagh.—Cunoujee Lall.—An old curiosity shop.—Death of Hodson.—Tremendous bombardment.

March 10*th*. — Outram's success is greater than we had ventured to anticipate. His column actually got as far round as the second or Stone bridge yesterday, but the general thought he was too weak to occupy such an extended position, and so he contented himself with establishing himself strongly at the Iron bridge, and he is in secure occupation of the Badshahbagh,. a large walled garden and enclosure, amid one of the finest of the King of Oude's summer palaces. The river only separates us from the enemy, and, as Sir Colin advances, the two columns will get the rebels and their principal works between two fires. From what Sir Colin said to me the other day, he must have expected difficulty and a stout resistance in taking the Badshahbagh. My bearer is much gratified with our proceedings. "In ten days' more time master will sleep in Kaiserbagh." I had just settled down in my tent to write, as I heard it would be a *dies non*, when tap! tap! tap! began the Kelasses, and Simon announced, "We change camp to the other place" (not liking to trust himself to Martinière). In order to be near our work, Head-Quarters are to be shifted to the edge of the great tank in front of the Martinière, and close to the recent trenches of the sepoys.

Jung Bahadoor's arrival is announced at last, and the Chief sent out two squadrons of cavalry and two guns to welcome him. He is by no means pleased, however, with the intimation made by McGregor, the British Commissioner with the Goorkha camp, that the Nepaulese expects a royal salute, and would "*like*" one for each of his brothers. "And he an artillery officer, too," says Sir Colin, "to entertain a proposition so contrary to custom. He should have told Jung Bahadoor salutes are never fired at sieges." But the Goorkha had his way. Metcalfe, whose long experience of Indian courts, and mastery of oriental vernacular peculiarly qualifies him for a task he has so often filled, is to represent the Commander-in-Chief.

What a pounding the rascals must be getting to-day! Outram is at one side of the Goomtee, with batteries established on both sides of the Iron bridge, and in front of the Badshahbagh, and the roar of his ordnance is never ceasing. A battery of heavy guns and mortars was established outside the Martinière park, and whilst the tents were being moved, I went down and staid by it for some time, watching the shot and the bombs flying into the town. Many of our shells burst short. Just as I was turning to go away, I heard an exclamation of alarm from the men at one of the mortars. As the smoke of the gun cleared away, I saw the headless trunk of a naval officer on the ground. It was a horrid sight. He had been killed by the shell which was discharged just as he rode before the muzzle. He will be buried this evening and forgotten to-morrow.

It is "Poor Garvey! He was a capital fellow. Now then, you men, mind what you are about!" And how can it be otherwise?

Brasyer's Sikhs are in Banks' bungalow on our left, and that officer's conduct has been highly spoken of at Head-Quarters. India is still the ground where the teeth of Cadmus have fairest nurture and most rapid growth. A few years ago Brasyer was a non-commissioned officer. Behind us is the gorgeous mausoleum of Claude Martin, the French trooper, who died a prince in all but name.

March 11th.—Placidly, outside our tents last night, we walked up and down beneath the magnificent trees, cheroot in mouth, and eyes upturned gazing on the twittering flight of the shells from Outram's batteries, and from the Chief's mortars, which shot like showers of falling stars into the city! How different the scene must be inside the Kaiserbagh! Those bombs fall with murderous effect into the crowded courts. And we are quite safe. A few mortars in the enemy's hands, well-worked, could make our position exceedingly disagreeable, instead of its being one of perfect ease and security. *Si rixa est, ubi tu pulsas, ego vapulor tantum.* They well may say so. The shells which burst high in air, as ours often do, are the prettiest to look at, in a pyrotechnic point of view, if the least effective, though their splinters, scattered from an elevated centre, must radiate with deadly results, and search out all the enemy's defences. All night the fire pounded the enemy, whilst we slept securely. This morning the horizontal fire commenced at daybreak from the Shannon's guns and the siege train at close quarters. The shot passed through the mud walls of the enclosures in front of the guns without let or hindrance, and breached the enemy's defences beyond them.

I went out early, and visited the batteries inside the canal, in which there is but little water; but the bridges are broken. Clarke, of the Engineers, was busy repairing that which is above Banks' bungalow. The parapets, which looked so formidable, are in reality rather weak, owing to the nature of the material, which is sand, so little cohesive as to tumble down at the shock of the guns mounted on the parapet. They tried to prevent this by feeble revetments with sods, and by facings of planks. Immense labour had been spent on the loopholes, which were made of bricks, or baked mud, with openings to the right and left, and to the front. On walking down the road towards the Begum Kothie, I found it convenient to turn into the enclosures and gardens on the right, the walls of which had been pierced for the passage of our men, as the enemy were firing up it very smartly. Stewart had a narrow escape. A round-shot cut a tree just over his head, and the heavy branch all but crushed him as it fell. The gardens were filled with our men, Sikhs and Highlanders, who were in readiness to assault the Begum Kothie as soon as the breaches were practicable. This is a block of buildings of great size, forming the southern point of the second line of defence. We could see the elaborately-ornamented gables and entablatures, with minarets and gilt spires, of the palace above the walls in front of us. On the right of this place, there has been an impression made on the enemy already. The 53rd walked quietly into the Secunderbagh, where the sepoys had learned such a tremendous lesson that they did not like to occupy it again. The large mosque, called the Shah-nujeef, which is in front of the Secunderbagh, was also taken; but it was judged inexpedient to hold it, and our men were ordered to fall back upon the Secunderbagh.

I remained spying about, glass in hand, and watching the sepoys, who were swarming in and out of their works like ants in a hive, till the day was far advanced, and it seemed as if the time for an assault had quite passed. I returned to our camp, where preparations were being made for the reception of the Maharajah Jung Bahadoor, by his Excellency. All Head-Quarters' people were warned in general orders to be ready at 4 o'clock in full *tenue* at the Commander-in-Chief's state tent, which was pitched for the occasion. There was a guard of honour of Highlanders, and a cavalry escort told off; carpets were laid down and the Union Jack displayed; and, terrible to be said, the bagpipers of the 93rd, fully provided with bags and pipes, were in attendance. The Chief presented himself to us in his full uniform, and looked every inch a soldier. Although General Mansfield was not present, as he was watching the operations against the Begum Kothie, and had some of his staff with him, there was a fair muster of the staff. The chairs and seats were disposed in a semi-circle, sweeping round the tent from the entrance, the chief place being in the centre, opposite the door, whilst we were seated on his left. Four o'clock came, no signs of Jung Bahadoor. A quarter of an hour passed by; the Chief walked up and down with one hand behind his back, and the other working nervously, like one who is impatient or expectant. At half-past 4 the regular cannonading close at hand ceased, and up rose a startling heavy rolling fire of musketry. We all knew what it meant. The assault on the Begum Kothie was being delivered. Sir Colin listened as a hunter does to the distant cry of the hounds. Louder and louder rang the musketry. Come quickly, Sir Jung, or you will find an empty tent! Just at this moment, however, the agitation among the crowd of camp-followers, and the "Stand to your arms," warned us that the Maharajah was at hand, and, in a minute or so, he made his appearance at the end of the lane formed by the guard of honour, and walked up towards the tent in a very slow and dignified sort of strut, followed by a staff of Goorkhas, and accompanied by his brothers, and Captain Metcalfe. Our eyes were fixed on him, but our ears were listening to the raging of the fight. Sir Colin walked to the door of the tent, met the Maharajah, took him by the hand, and led him inside. Then took place a good deal of bowing and salaaming, as the Maharajah introduced his brothers and great officers to the Chief; and it was some time before the latter was comfortably seated, with the Goorkha chief on one side, and his brothers and the officers in attendance on him on the right-hand side; the British being on the left. The durbar was open. It consisted of fine speeches, interpreted by Captain Metcalfe, whilst the English and the Nepaulese were examining each other. Stout Calmuck-faced, high-shouldered, bow-legged men these latter, very richly attired in a kind of compromise between European and Asiatic uniform. As to Jung himself, he blazed like a peacock's tail in the sun. Nor, indeed, was either of his brothers much inferior to him in splendour. But brighter than any gem the Maharajah wore is his eye, which shines with a cold light, resembling a ball of phosphorus. What a tiger-like, cruel, crafty, subtle eye! How it glanced, and glittered, and rolled, piercing the recesses of the tent. "I believe," quoth one near me, "he is the d——dest villain hung or unhung." In the midst of the durbar an officer of Mansfield's staff comes in to announce to Sir Colin that "the Begum Kothie is taken. Very little loss on our side. About five hundred of the enemy killed!" As we could not cheer aloud, every man did so mentally. Jung tried to look pleased when he heard the news, which Sir Colin announced with great vivacity. The durbar had all along been stupid enough, but when the bagpipes outside were set loose affairs became desperate, and yet no one dared leave. At last the Chief and the Maharajah rose, and then commenced the presentations of the British officers by the former to the latter. On coming to me, Sir Colin said, "Do you wish to be introduced to his Highness?" "No your Excellency, I have no wish of the kind," and so I escaped shaking the hand of a man who has committed cold-blooded murder. His Highness, and his two brothers, mounted the Chief's state elephant, which bore a silver howdah, had its face and trunk curiously painted, and was encrusted with gold trappings; and so, followed by his staff on horseback, Timur-leng moved off. Mansfield came in soon after, and announced that our men were secure in the Begum Kothie: but that he did not think it expedient to attack the Mess-house at so late an hour, though it was not held by the enemy in force, an opinion in which Sir Colin quite concurred. It was getting dark, and, as we had missed the sight of the assault, and should only be in the way among wounded, and could see nothing if we went, our visit to the Begum Kothie was postponed till to-morrow. Hodson is among the wounded.

I had a good deal of talk with Sir Colin in the evening, and found he was much pleased with the rush of the 93rd into the place. He repeated several times, "It will strike terror into them: it will strike terror into them." He thinks that the Kaiserbagh will give a great deal of trouble. "But no matter how long it may take us, I am determined to have no street fighting. I'll not have my men shot down from houses. Now we've got the Begum Kothie we'll work on regularly, and drive them back." The Governor-General is kept regularly informed by telegraph of each day's proceedings.

March, 12th.—Friday.—All impatience for the day. Nearly every soul at Head-Quarters mounting for the Begum Kothie; the enemy still firing down the road from the Kaiserbagh. Turned through the orchards as before, and leaving our horses with the syces, clambered through breaches in the various walls made by our shot till we came out in front of the Begum palace, which is defended by a deep ditch and a broad and thick parapet. Here the traces of the fight were frequent. Patches of blackened blood, parts of soldiers' uniforms, arms, and accoutrements. The ditch itself was filled with the bodies of sepoys, which the coolies were dragging from the inside and throwing topsy-turvy, by command of the soldiers; stiffened by death, with outstretched legs and arms, burning slowly in their cotton tunics, those rent and shattered figures seemed as if they were about to begin a dance of death. We crossed literally a ramp of dead bodies loosely covered with earth. The lower windows and doors of the palace, inside the parapet, were blocked up with brick and baked earth, which was pierced for musketry.

It was through a very narrow breach in the wall of the gateway that we emerged in the court of the Begum Kothie. The place was full of our soldiers moving to and fro in search of booty, or smoking and chatting in the shade; their arms being piled in case of necessity. Lugard was sitting under the shade of a tree, making a hearty breakfast in the garden which bore but little resemblance indeed to that of Eden. He was good enough to send one of his aides-de-camp, Scott, to show me over the place, "and mind," said he, "you don't get potted, for there are some pandies it is suspected, still lurking about." There was good reason for what the General said, as in a minute afterwards a sergeant was shot dead by a sepoy, who, with several others, was hiding in a room from which they were only driven by live shells, and were killed fighting desperately to the last. In the court I met Adrian Hope, and as he had actually led one of the storming-parties, I gladly availed myself of his offer to be my guide. He had got in through a window, through which he had been shoved by his men, and he came headlong on a group of sepoys in the dark room inside, who bolted at once at the apparition of the huge red Celt who tumbled upon them, sword and pistol in hand. Another party had stormed the work on the left of this, and the third had attacked on our right, near the road. The fight was very close and desperate for some time; but the strength of the 93rd and the fury of the Sikhs carried everything before it. From court to court, and building to building, the sepoys were driven, leaving in each hundreds of men bayonetted and shot. The scene was horrible. The rooms in which the sepoys lay burning slowly in their cotton clothing, with their skin crackling and their flesh roasting literally in its own fat, whilst a light-bluish, vapoury smoke, of disgusting odour, formed a veil through which the dreadful sight could be dimly seen, were indeed chambers of horrors ineffable. It was before breakfast, and I could not stand the smell.

* * * *

It is a great step gained. We are now inside the first line of works, and we are beginning to sap up through the adjacent enclosures towards the Imambarra, which is the enemy's next great stronghold. Nearly all their defences are constructed on the hypothesis that we must advance up the street; but our course lies parallel to it about 100 to 150 yards to the left. We thus turn one of the faces of their fire altogether, and the very enclosures by which we advance facilitate our operations, and cover us from the enemy's fire. Mortars are in position, and are playing on the Imambarra and Kaiserbagh already. Napier and Harness are now the active men, and they are engaged in a very rare operation; for seldom, indeed, has a small force like ours ventured to bore its way into an enormous city, defended by an immense regular army, and a hostile armed population. Our plan of action is an improvement on the Napoleon programme for street fighting. As the defences stand, the streets resemble a long double line of curtains connecting strong bastions, such as Begum Kothie, Mess-house, Imambarra, and Kaiserbagh, enclosed by parapets, and defended by batteries. The capture of the outermost bastion, and the lodgment inside the works and one line of the curtain, give us enormous advantages.

Having gone over the Begum Kothie, returned to camp to breakfast; then mounted a fresh horse, and with Pat Stewart rode over to the Secunderbagh by the route which Sir Colin had taken when he advanced on it from Martinière; a ticklish path, through gardens and orchards, with high banks on each side, and then through two villages, so narrow and tortuous that our guns stuck fast more than once. The Secunderbagh is a large square enclosure, with turrets at the angles, and a garden inside with kiosks and summer-houses. In one angle we found H. M.'s 53rd huddled together as far away as possible from the dreadful smell that came from the rotting bodies of the sepoys that were slain there in Sir Colin's last advance. I walked as far as I could venture among the skeletons, to look at the actual scene of the struggle; but I was soon glad to retrace my steps and join the party at the gate. We amused ourselves for some time by watching a part of the enemy in front of us, which was in great agitation, as if in expectation of an attack, and, in fact, the 53rd had already occupied the Shah Nujeef, a very fine mosque inside a serai in front of us, and the Kuddom Russoul, an odd-looking structure on the top of a conical mound, close to the Goomtee. They were ordered to retire, though the engineer officer was satisfied he could maintain his position.

From the Secunderbagh we made for the bridge of boats across the river, and proceeded to Outram's camp. Our ride was by no means agreeable; the heat was great, a hot wind blew clouds of hot sand from the plain into our eyes, nose, ears, and mouth, and the stench of the river, where dead bodies were lying in heaps on the shallows, was suffocating. Paid a visit to Brigadier Walpole, whom we found in a very comfortless sort of ruin, without doors or windows, writing on a plank. His staff were in the same room, and were equally comfortless and hot. Thence we went to Sir Hope Grant's tent, and heard all about the advance the other day from him. His quarters were fixed in a small single-pole tent, and everything inside was covered with dust and sand. Then having beaten up a few more tents, proceeded onwards to General Outram's head-quarters, which consisted of a few tents pitched under some fine trees, close to a pretty mosque that had suffered from our cannon. The general was in his tent, but was about starting for his evening ride, and as he insisted on our stopping to dine and sleep at his quarters, we were glad to have the opportunity of seeing his position; and, above all, I was gratified at the occasion I had long desired of making the acquaintance of such a distinguished statesman, and such a gallant, chivalrous soldier. His forehead is broad, massive, sagacious, but open; his eye, which is covered by a shaggy brow, is dark, full of penetration, quick, and expressive; his manner natural and gracious; his speech is marked by a slight hesitation when choosing a word, but it is singularly correct and forcible; and his smile is very genial and sympathetic. He is of the middle-size, is very stoutly built, and has a slight roundness of the shoulder, as if from study or application at the desk.

We all know of the unhappy controversy which arose between the late Sir Charles Napier and Major Outram, with respect to the treatment of the Ameers of Scinde, and eventually terminated a friendship that had commenced auspiciously, by the application, from Napier's mouth, of an ennobling epithet which, recognized as just at the time, is now Outram's universal soubriquet—" The Bayard of India." Without attempting to discuss the merits of that unfortunate dispute between two great men, I may remark that Outram gave an unusual, but very striking and characteristic proof, of the sincerity of his opinions, for he refused to touch a penny of his share of the Scinde prize-money, although he was not, at the time, in a position to render him indifferent to the acquisition of such a large sum of money. We rode down close to the first battery, which was paying particular attention to the enemy's works at the other side of the river—a long line of parapet extending from the Mohtee-Mahul to the Chutturmunzil and its adjacent palaces. The return fire was very poor, but it was just enough to induce one to stand under the parapet, and thence we could follow, with satisfaction, the flight of our shot and shell into the cupolas of the palaces, or see them bursting, in dust and smoke, inside the drawing-room windows.

Having remounted, we went on to the Badshahbagh, which was occupied by H. M.'s 23rd, under

Bell. In the days of its full magnificence it must have been glorious. Such forests of orange-trees, such trickling fountains, shady walks, beds of flowers, grand alleys, dark retreats and summer-houses, all surrounded by a high and massive wall, and forming, as it were, the approaches to a snug little palace of pleasure, in which were now revelling some of the Welch Fusileers. We mounted up on the flat roof of one of the towers, from which we had a pleasant view of the enemy's works not very far in front of us; and we were rendered aware of the fact that their eyes were as good as our own, by a gentle humming, and sighing, and pinging in the air about us, as though bees and zephyrs were flying past, or birds fanning us with rapid pinion. In one of the rooms was a portrait of the late King of Oude, which I received permission to have cut out of the frame, and carried it off with me; a small bit of loot of very little value.

We returned to dinner, which was spread out on a table before the mosque, sheltered by a giant tree; and the effect of the lamps, the tablecloth, and the "Persicos apparatus" in such a place was very striking. The general had all his staff and many more dining with him. He has saved some soda-water and port-wine from his stores at Alumbagh, and I, for one, found them great luxuries. After dinner, one Cunoujee Lall, a very handsome, intelligent Hindoo, came to Outram for final instructions as to a very perilous enterprise. He is to try the depth of the river near the Iron bridge, in order that we may know if it be fordable or not; but the man is used to services of danger. It was he who accompanied Kavanagh out of the Residency to seek Sir Colin Campbell, and he has since been actively engaged as a spy in our employment. He is working for a high reward; but I do not think the mode we propose of dealing with him evinces much judgment. We know him to be a double-dealer, for he deceives and betrays his own countrymen; but we have promised him a *judicial* and *legal* appointment in the *public service.* How will he exercise his trust?

We retired early, and Stewart and myself found two comfortable beds made up in the corners of the General's tent, and were fast asleep ere he had finished the cheroot and the newspaper with which he retired to his charpoy.

March 13*th.*—It was pitch dark, I am quite sure, when the General woke us this morning, though he maintained stoutly it was daybreak. I know our cheroots glimmered like fire-flies in the tent as we were dressing. A cup of tea refreshed us, and just as the sky was flushing in the east, we mounted and rode towards the Iron bridge; but there were no very agreeable odours which saluted us, no pleasant smell of flowers, no fresh perfume of the early morning. The road-sides were dotted by dead bodies, and when we came to the old cavalry lines, where Outram, in his advance had surprised and cut up a number of the enemy, it required all the powers of tobacco to render the air endurable. From that we passed on to a network of houses, through which we rode in single file; all was silent as the grave. "Just there," said one of my companions, "we saw a pitiful sight the day of our advance. A little boy of eight or nine years of age, very handsome and well dressed, had been struck by a grape-shot in the spine, and was dying.

Beside him was a cage, with a parroquet, which was screaming as if it knew what had happened. We let the poor bird go." It is horrible; but it is true, that our men have got a habit of putting natives "out of pain," as if they were animals. They do it sometimes in charity.

When we got to the street which leads to the Iron bridge, we dismounted, turned a corner, and found ourselves at once under fire. As Outram was first, we could but follow his example, and he walked with the utmost deliberation down to the last house next the bridge, into which we turned, and proceeded to survey the enemy, who were swarming in and out of the houses at the other side. At an extremity there was a barricade, beyond which lay several dead sepoys who tainted the air, and could not be removed by either side. The house in which we took our station had been some old curiosity-shop, and the smell of native scents was almost as strong as that of the sepoys. Our men, behind low walls, were keeping down the fire of the enemy, and at the other side of the way one of our batteries sent an occasional shell or shot over towards the Kaiserbagh and Stone bridge. Outram descending to the street, left most of us under cover, and with two officers walked across to look after the battery. The enemy at once gave them a volley; but they got across untouched. In about five minutes they came out again, and this time ran the gantlet through a storm of bullets. As we returned to the corner where our horses were, we were exposed to a sharp fusillade, which cut the bricks close to us; but again we escaped unscathed, and had a quiet ride back to camp, through another part of the deserted suburbs.

After breakfast under the tree, Stewart and I returned to our camp; but we had set out rather late, and the heat was very trying as we rode over the sandy plains. When I got back, I was shocked and surprised to hear that Hodson died early yesterday, and was buried in the afternoon. Late in the day, after the capture of the Begum Kothie, Norman told me he had been wounded, and was in Banks' bungalow. I was going over to see him yesterday, when one of the doctors told me he was going on pretty well, and that he had passed a tolerable night; adding, "I don't think it would be wise to disturb him, even if his medical attendant let you." Now I hear that I shall never see him more. I felt that we had sustained in India a loss which is really national. I must confess I do not altogether approve of anything but the extraordinary courage and self-possession which marked his conduct in shooting down the sons of the King of Delhi; but at the same time I freely admit that I was impressed so strongly by Hodson's energy, force of character, and intelligence, that I should doubt the propriety of my own judgment if I found it was opposed to his in some matters connected with the treatment of natives. I regretted that an accident had put it out of my power to pay his memory the tribute of respect which Sir Colin and his staff willingly rendered last night.

My servant was in much tribulation at my absence, for which I had not at all prepared him. "I tout budmash kill master and master Stewart."

I lay down and went to sleep in spite of the tremendous bombardment which was shaking the camp. Our sap continues, and we are slowly advancing towards the Imambarra, which is to be assaulted, and of course carried, to-morrow. I saw Sir Colin to-night, and he told me the spies declared the sepoys were leaving the city in great numbers.

CHAPTER XX.

Capture of the Kaiserbagh.—The camp in commotion.—Voilà la différence!—Marks of shot and shell.—Poor Da Costa!—The Huzrutgunj.—Sappers at work.—Discipline after an assault.—Drunk with plunder.—A camel-load of curiosities.—Ready money transactions.—Presents of jewellery.—Camp followers.—Simon and his scales.—Telegraphic messages.—Plundering stopped.—A zenana.—Dinner with General Outram.

March 14th.—CAPTURE OF THE KAISERBAGH.—Well, to be sure, how uncertain are the *certamina belli!* It was only last night that Sir Colin was talking of the hard work there would be in forcing the sepoys out of their great stronghold, the Residency. This morning early I met General Outram, who seemed in good heart at our progress; but said there was a good deal of fighting before us yet. Later still he met Sir Colin and returned to camp with him about ten o'clock, and the two generals, at length, discussed the plan of operations against the Kaiserbagh. It was known that Russell's brigade would make an attack on the Imambarra—a large mass of buildings which lies between the Begum Kothie and the Kaiserbagh, with many intervening buildings and enclosures. Those which were between the Begum's house and the Imambarra had been successively occupied by our men, who sapped through from wall to wall, in a line parallel to the Huzrutgunj, which is the street where Havelock's column suffered so very severely in going to reinforce the Residency; but it was necessary to open a battery to breach the walls of the Imambarra, which are very thick and massive. The breach promised well last night. It was made by guns, which were sheltered by the walls, and fired right through them at the enemy's defences. This morning, if the engineer approved of the look of the work, the assault was to be delivered, and Brasyer's Sikhs and Her Majesty's 10th Regiment were to lead the assault. It was after breakfast, and all the Head-Quarters' people, who were not busy with returns and schedules, were enjoying their cigars or reading the papers. A very heavy fire of musketry, which had sprung up for a few moments, had as suddenly died away. An orderly came up the avenue at full speed, with a small piece of folded paper in his hand. He delivered it at one of the tents. In a second or two, I saw Norman, at his usual canter, hurrying across the street. "What is it, Norman? Have we got the Imambarra?" "The Imambarra! Why, man, we're in the Kaiserbagh!"

Here, indeed, was news. The camp was in commotion. Syces running to and fro, the Chief and all his staff calling for their horses. What a scamper to the Begum Kothie; passing the 42nd, the 38th, and the 90th on our way, who were marching fast towards the Kaiserbagh! We passed from court to garden, and from garden to court; through the walls of mosques and zenanas, and long ranges of low houses, through archways and doors, working hither and thither, along the sap by which our men had advanced through all these obstacles from the Begum Kothie. In our way, strings of doolies, laden with wounded men, showed us the place had not fallen without a blow. A Goorkha or Sikh officer, I never could make out which he was, dressed in a scarlet tunic laced with gold, who was wounded through both legs and had his lower jaw broken by a bullet, was walking to the rear, leaning on the arms of two natives, when, just as he passed me, a chance bullet, flying over the wall, went through his skull and he dropped dead. When we reached the breach of the Imambarra, it was almost blocked up by the men who were pouring into it. It is inglorious work scrambling up second-hand breaches; but it is some consolation to be in good company, and to know that every man has honour in his own place. For one in my position, there would be no honour, reward, or Κῦδος for storming a breach to-morrow. As I said to Sir James Outram, the other day, when we were under a little fire, "If you get killed, it will be said, and truly, that you died a soldier's death — the end of a warrior covered with laurels, who falls in discharge of his duty; but if your humble servant's skull is not thick enough to resist the solicitations for admittance of one of those matchlock-balls, it will be said he died the death of a fool, who was where he had no business to be, and who, in death even, will be covered with ridicule.— *Voilà la différence!*"

Listen to the cheering behind us. Sir Colin is riding up the street. Now he has dismounted, and is marching up the steps of the Imambarra amidst the shouts of the troops. What a scene of destruction meets the eye as we enter the great hall. It is no exaggeration to say the marble pavement is covered two or three inches deep with fragments of broken mirrors and of the chandeliers which once hung from the ceiling; and the men are busy smashing still.

This mischief is rude, senseless, and brutal, but no one cares to stop it. I think of Kertch, and sigh and pass on.

We are on the flat roof of the Imambarra mosque, and a few remote pandies amuse themselves by potting at us, but they are in too great a state of fear to make good practice. Below us, Sikhs and Highlanders are winding in front of the various doors and windows of the buildings around the court, like the denizens of an ant-hill, or, with jubilant shouts, dragging out some miserable pandy from his hiding-place.

There is not a space of four yards square which does not bear the mark of heavy shell blows and dint of iron. The courts are full of the wreck of the Imambarra, mixed with fragments of sepoys' clothing, accoutrements, horns filled with powder, firelocks, matchlocks, shields, and tulwars. Beyond us are the many-tinted domes and cupola-spires, and the multiple-shaped roofs of the Kaiserbagh itself, from which there is still spattering fire of musketry. From the other side of the Goomtee beyond it, puff after puff of white smoke, and the heavy boom of the guns, show that Outram is still pounding away at the enemy, between the Kaiserbagh and the Iron bridge. We are but a few minutes in the Imambarra, and then passing through a very lofty, and indeed magnificent gateway, from the principal court, we find ourselves actually in the Huzrutgunj. It is blocked up with troops, part of the 90th, some of the 20th, the 97th, the 38th, are all there, and the 42nd are behind them, coming up in clouds of dust. I saw General Mansfield, and ran across the street to him. "Is it true we have the Kaiserbagh?" "Well, Colonel Harness and

Napier have sent word that we have turned the inner line of defences. We are in the Kaiserbagh, but whilst this work (alluding to the firing) is going on, we can scarcely be said to have it."

The heat was sweltering, and I pitied our men as they stood under its rays, many of them unprovided with proper protection against the sun, and retaining their old European outfit. I felt the exhaustion produced by the temperature so much, that I could scarcely move a hundred yards without visible distress. The perspiration rolled in streams down our faces between banks of hardened dust, which caked as it settled on our saturated clothes. And these poor fellows might be exposed for hours, not only to this terrible heat, but to a hard struggle and severe fighting. "Water! water! Pane! pane!" was the cry on every side. At this moment an officer, evidently dying, was carried past. He recognized me, and gave a faint smile as he went by. Poor Da Costa! He had been persecuting the Head-Quarters' people at Cawnpore to take him up to the front. He had plied every department with solicitations, used every stratagem, he had even extended his supplications by telegraph to Alumbagh for leave to get to Lucknow. At last he came to me, and begged that I would put him "on my staff!" His regiment was gone in the mutinies, and he was nearly mad with anxiety to strike a blow at Lucknow for certain reasons. If I could take him, the tempter said—and at this time I was indeed in a fair way to fall before such temptation—he would ask my acceptance of that thorough-bred charger which he was riding as he spoke. Somehow or other he managed to become attached to a Punjaub regiment, and he fell early in the day's work.

That we had got so far as the spot where I stood without very great loss was wonderful. All the casemates of the Imambarra, every parapeted house-top on the way to it, every portico, every colonnade in the courts, was blocked up with brickwork, pierced in every direction for musketry. And now we were out in the street, we saw what murderous work it would have been to have forced a passage through what was in fact nothing less than a double line of crenellated parapets and walls, inaccessible to scaling ladders, swept by grape and case from the defences at right angles to the line of the street, and raked by the fire of projecting palaces and gables which would cross their musketry with that from the walls, the whole line of the advance being dominated by lofty mosques, minars, the flat-roofed houses of the street, and such citadels as the Imambarra itself would be when the gates were closed, and the Mess-house and the coachmen's houses. Such was the Huzrutgunj. As I edged along between the troops and the wall, I had many a nod from friends and acquaintances whom I saw for the first time since we had been before Lucknow; a camp is the worst place in the world to meet one's friends, unless one hunts them out expressly, and time rarely admits of that. Ingram, of the 97th, at the head of his men, called out, " Do you know what we are waiting for?" and seemed by no means pleased at my lack of information. Poor fellow, he was all impatience to get to the fatal palace, where, in a little time, he was to meet his death.

Edging on in the shade of the wall, Stewart and

I came at last to an immense earthwork, which crossed the road, with a deep ditch in front, and some embrasures faced with planks, which were burning fiercely. Through the flames peered the muzzles of two guns, most probably well graped, and so we turned sharp to the left, as it would have been neither profitable nor glorious to have been killed by an overheated cannon; and passing along a crenellated wall we turned in through a tall archway, which was nearly blocked up by the rubbish of the tumbled brickwork, through which our sappers had just broken a passage, and found ourselves in one of the courts of the Kaiserbagh! The tail of the small column of sappers was just disappearing under another archway at the opposite side of the huge court, and hurrying at the double. An officer, who had just made his way through the arch, said, "We had better look-out. The rooms round this court are full of sepoys. I can see and hear them." We were quite alone. It would never do to go back, and so, getting as much breath as we could into our bodies by way of provision, off we cantered across the court. It was, indeed, near work. The bullets flew round us, and cut up the ground at our feet, but we all arrived, short of wind and full of laughter, under cover of the archway, beyond which there was another court full of statues, and orange-trees, and shrubs, surrounded by long lines of palazzi in the Italian style, wherein, as one of our friends said, "Hell's broke loose." At one gateway in this court a small body of red-coated soldiers, in some kind of order, were delivering a rapid fire. Everywhere else discord and chaos reigned.

* * * * * *

It was one of the strangest and most distressing sights that could be seen; but it was also most exciting. Discipline may hold soldiers together till the fight is won; but it assuredly does not exist for a moment after an assault has been delivered, or a storm has taken place. Imagine courts as large as the Temple Gardens, surrounded with ranges of palaces, or at least of buildings well stuccoed and gilded, with fresco-paintings here and there on the blind-windows, and with green jalousies and venetian-blinds closing the apertures which pierce the walls in double rows. In the body of the court are statues, lines of lamp-posts, fountains, orange-groves, aqueducts, and kiosks with burnished domes of metal. Through these, hither and thither, with loud cries, dart European and native soldiery, firing at the windows, from which come now and then dropping shots or hisses a musket-ball. At every door there is an eager crowd, smashing the panels with the stocks of their firelocks, or breaking the fastenings by discharges of their weapons. The buildings which surround the courts are irregular in form, for here and there the lines of the quadrangle are broken by columned fronts and lofty porticos before the mansions of the ministry, or of the great officers of the royal household, which are resplendent with richly-gilt roofs and domes. Here and there the invaders have forced their way into the long corridors, and you hear the musketry rattling inside; the crash of glass, the shouts and yells of the combatants, and little jets of smoke curl out of the closed lattices. Lying amid the orange-groves are dead and dying sepoys; and the white statues are reddened with blood. Leaning against a smiling

Venus is a British soldier shot through the neck, gasping, and at every gasp bleeding to death ! Here and there officers are running to and fro after their men, persuading or threatening in vain. From the broken portals issue soldiers laden with loot or plunder. Shawls, rich tapestry, gold and silver brocade, caskets of jewels, arms, splendid dresses. The men are wild with fury and lust of gold — literally drunk with plunder. Some come out with china vases or mirrors, dash them to pieces on the ground, and return to seek more valuable booty. Others are busy gouging out the precious stones from the stems of pipes, from saddle-cloths, or the hilts of swords, or butts of pistols and fire-arms. Some swathe their bodies in stuffs crusted with precious metals and gems ; others carry off useless lumber, brass pots, pictures, or vases of jade and china.

Court after court the scene is still the same. These courts open one to the other by lofty gateways, ornamented with the double fish of the royal family of Oude, or by arched passages, in which lie the dead sepoys, their clothes smouldering on their flesh.

The court we had now reached was exceedingly narrow, a *cul de sac;* one side was occupied by open sheds, in which were broughams, carriages, and harness, and native palkees, with velvet hangings richly gilt, and a lot of trumpery, such as might be seen in a coachmaker's shed—wheels, axles, and such like. The other side was formed by a line of storehouses with rooms above them, and a series of doors, leading out on the court, strongly barricaded. Just where we turned into the court, there was a stone-topped well somewhat in the shade, and close to it was one store-room, the door of which had been left open or forced in by a marauder. On going in we found it literally filled with wooden cases, which were each crammed with nicely-packed china or enormous vases, bowls, goblets, cups of the finest jade. Others contained nothing but spoons, hookah mouth-pieces, and small drinking vessels, and saucers of the same valuable material. I do not in the least exaggerate, when I say there must have been at least a camel-load of these curiosities, of which Stewart and myself, and one or two other officers, selected a few pieces, and put them aside near the well. It was well we did so, for, just as we had put them aside, the shadow of a man fell across the court from the gateway; a bayonet was advanced cautiously, raised evidently to the level of the eye, then came the Enfield, and finally the head of a British soldier. "None here but friends!" shouted he. "Come along, Bill. There's only some offsers, and here's a lot of places no one has bin to!" Enter three or four banditti of H.M.'s — Regiment. Faces black with powder; cross-belts specked with blood; coats stuffed out with all sorts of valuables. And now commenced the work of plunder under our very eyes. The first door resisted every sort of violence till the rifle-muzzle was placed to the lock, which was sent flying by the discharge of the piece. The men rushed in with a shout, and soon they came out with caskets of jewels, iron boxes and safes, and wooden boxes full of arms crusted with gold and precious stones! One fellow, having burst open a leaden-looking lid, which was in reality of solid silver, drew out an armlet of emeralds, and diamonds, and pearls, so large, that I really believed they were not real stones, and that they formed part of a chandelier chain. "What will your honour give me for these?" said he. "I'll take a hundred rupees on chance."

Oh, wretched fate! I had not a penny in my pocket, nor had any of us. No one has in India. His servant keeps his money. My Simon was far away in the quiet camp. He hunted through my clothes every morning, and neither gold mohur nor silver rupee was permitted to remain in any of my pockets; and so I said—

"I will give you a hundred rupees; but it is right to tell you if the stones are real they are worth a great deal more."

"Bedad, I won't grudge them to your honour, and you're welcome to them for the hundred rupees. Here, take them!"

"Well, then, you must come to me at the Head-Quarters' camp to-night, or give me your name and company, and I'll send the money to you."

"Oh! faith an' your honour, how do I know where I'd be this blissed night? It's maybe dead I'd be, wid a bullet in me body. I'll take two gold mores" (mohurs at 32s. each) "and a bottle of rum, on the spot. But shure it's not safe to have any but reddy money transactions these times."

There was no arguing against the propriety of the views entertained by our friend, and he put the chain of great nobbly emeralds, and diamonds, and pearls, into the casket, and I saw my fortune vanish."*

As the man turned to leave the place, as if struck

---

* I have been told that those stones were subsequently sold by an officer to a jeweller for £7500.

by compunction at his own severity, he took two trinkets from a tray in the casket, and said, "There, gentlemen, I'd not like to lave you without a little keepsake. Take whichever you like, and you can give me something another time."

That which fell to my share was a nose-ring of small rubies and pearls, with a single stone diamond drop. My friend was made happy with a very handsome brooch, consisting of a large butterfly, with opal and diamond wings.

This was but an episode. The scene of plunder was indescribable. The soldiers had broken up several of the store-rooms, and pitched the contents into the court, which was lumbered with cases, with embroidered clothes, gold and silver brocade, silver vessels, arms, banners, drums, shawls, scarfs, musical instruments, mirrors, pictures, books, accounts, medicine bottles, gorgeous standards, shields, spears, and a heap of things, the enumeration of which would make this sheet of paper like a catalogue of a broker's sale. Through these moved the men, wild with excitement, "drunk with plunder." I had often heard the phrase, but never saw the thing itself before. They smashed to pieces the fowling-pieces and pistols to get at the gold mountings and the stones set in the stocks. They burned in a fire, which they made in the centre of the court, brocades and embroidered shawls for the sake of the gold and silver. China, glass, and jade they dashed to pieces in pure wantonness; pictures they ripped up, or tossed on the flames; furniture shared the same fate. Suddenly a fellow rushed at us with the long chain of a lustre, made of long green and blue prisms, in his hand, shouting out, "Look here! Look here! Holy mother of Moses, what will you give me for this iligant shtring of imeralds and jewls?" Nor would he really believe our assurance that it was worthless.

By this time, twenty men—mostly English, but some Sikhs—were in the court. The explosion of their rifles, as they burst open locks and doors, had attracted stray marauders. More than one quarrel, which came nigh to blood-letting, had already arisen: things looked threatening: we could do no good: and, as a musbee sapper just happened to look in, we laid hold of him to carry our jade bowls, and got into the outer court, in which there was, on a larger scale, a repetition of the same scene as we had just left.

Oh, the toil of that day! Never had I felt such exhaustion. It was horrid enough to have to stumble through endless courts which were like vapour baths, amid dead bodies, through sights worthy of the Inferno, by blazing walls which might be pregnant with mines, over breaches, in and out of smouldering embrasures, across frail ladders, suffocated by deadly smells of rotting corpses, of rotten ghee, or vile native scents; but the seething crowd of camp followers into which we emerged in Huzrutgunj was something worse. As ravenous, and almost as foul, as vultures, they were packed in a dense mass in the street, afraid or unable to go into the palaces, and, like the birds they resembled, waiting till the fight was done to prey on their plunder.

At last I got to camp. Simon was busy in his little tent weighing gold and silver for natives who had already returned with or got plunder from the soldiers. For days the chink, chink of his scales never ceased. He had a percentage for weighing, and he must have driven a roaring trade. Done up beyond expression, I threw myself on a charpoy, and for an hour slept a sleep of dreams almost as bad as the realities I had just witnessed.

On getting up and dressing, I found it was evening. Sir Colin was walking up and down before his tent. I went over to him, and he told me he had telegraphed to the Governor-General that we were in solid occupation of the Kaiserbagh. I sent off a similar message. The telegraph tent was close at hand. At dinner this evening Sir Colin was rather silent. Perhaps he was thinking that people at home would not be satisfied that more of the rebels had not fallen, for he knew that it was now impossible to prevent the greater number of them escaping.

One blot there was certainly in the day's proceedings. It is true, that the fall of the Kaiserbagh was not calculated upon; but it occurred so early in the day, that greater advantage might have been taken of the success, though it would have been attended by considerable loss of life. I allude to the effect which would have been produced if Outram had crossed the Iron bridge and fallen on the enemy as soon as they were retreating out of the Kaiserbagh. Sir Colin had given orders to Outram to cross the Iron bridge, but they were accompanied with the proviso "that he was not to do so if he thought he would *lose a single man*." The general reconnoitred the enemy in the afternoon, and had everything ready for an attack, but he saw at least one gun laid on the bridge, and the enemy showed their fear of an advance on his part by a peculiarly heavy fire which they opened from guns and musketry on the houses occupied by his men, so that if he had moved he certainly would have lost some of his soldiers, and so have disobeyed orders. The relations between Sir Colin and General Outram, though not unfriendly, are a little stiff on account of past events, and Outram is not the man to act in opposition to the commands of his superior officer. Had Sir Colin not bound Outram's hands so tightly, the advance would have taken place, and a very great slaughter of the enemy must have followed. The breastwork, thrown up at one side of the bridge, was removed,* and all was ready for a vigorous assault, which would have put us in possession of a larger part of the position, with a tremendous loss to the sepoys, when the Kaiserbagh fell. In one place alone they suffered severely to-day. There is a detached building, called the engine-house, close to the Goomtee, below the Chutturmunzil. When our advance from the Imambarra to the Kaiserbagh was established, a portion of our troops swept round to the right, and two parties of Her Majesty's 20th came upon the house, which contained two courts, and rooms full of old machinery. They came upon a body of three or four hundred sepoys who had fled there for refuge. Holding possession of the only means of exit, one portion of the 20th made a furious onslaught on the rebels, shot them down in files, and ceased not till no living enemy was left to kill. The place caught fire. The wounded were burned with the dead. A rapid advance in force might have led to many scenes such as that—and, no doubt, had

---

* For doing this, Lieutenant Wynne received the Victoria Cross.

Outram's column crossed, we might have counted the slain by thousands; but sepoys fight when driven to bay, and our own loss must have been large. As I was returning to camp this evening, I met one who told me the enemy were flying from the city by thousands. Bruce's spies report that the rebels are satisfied Lucknow is lost, though some of them declare they will die fighting in the streets. Allgood's emissaries are unanimous in tales of distress. The Begum alone stands undismayed. A fine dramatic figure, this black Semiramide—ardent, intriguing, subtle, courageous, devoted to her son, and—alas! that it should be so—fond of Mummoo Khan. The Moulvie of Fyzabad, too, assumes grandiose proportions as his resolution, courage, and fanaticism are developed amidst the imbeciles by whom he is surrounded. But the shouts of our men ring from the Kaiserbagh. The enemy's stronghold has fallen, and neither Begum nor Moulvie will ever hold it more.

March 15*th.*—To-day plundering is stopped by order. The place is exhausted. Four friendly merchants, or bunneahs, who were returning to the town, were shot by our pickets. I visited the Kaiserbagh again to-day. Every yard would fill a canvas under the hand of Lewis or David Roberts. The place is full of powder, and explosions are frequent. If the Tuileries, the Louvre, Versailles, Scutari, the Winter Palace, were to be all blended together, with an *entourage* of hovels worthy of Gallipoli, and an interior of gardens worthy of Kew, they would represent the size, at all events, of the palaces of the Kaiserbagh and the gardens inside. The work is evidently Italian; but most hideous, ludicrous, and preposterous are the Hindoo statues in imitation of Italian subjects, which here and there deck the pedestals in the gardens. There are a few really grand marble statues—a charming Venus and dove, a very fine Nymph with hounds, and a severe Apollo, which has been chipped about the stomach by a native artizan, but all the rest, or nearly all, of the many hundred statues, are vile plaster imitations, indecent or grotesque originals. In the north-west angle of one of the courts our batteries of mortars are in full play on the city.

I wandered through a zenana which was full of women's clothes, fans, slippers, musical instruments, flowers, gilt chairs, and damask curtains, very strange pictures, broken mirrors and pendules. A begum of some rank, and remote antiquity, was saved yesterday by General Mansfield's adjutant-general, in one of the houses, and is now in the Martinière. She gave the officer a casket of jewels, which he put in a place of safety; but when he returned, the house was in flames and the jewels were lost. These women say they are sure we shall be beaten in the long run, though they admit the sepoys fought badly; but, say they, "You kill them when they cannot see you, with those great iron fire-balls," alluding to the shells.

The quantity of stuffs, of all kinds of furniture, and every conceivable kind of property taken out of the city by soldiers and camp-followers is beyond the verge of imagination, and gives some reason to believe the statement that there were 1,200,000 inhabitants in Lucknow. Simon is busy weighing money and gold and silver bars and buttons all day; but I cannot induce him to get a shawl for me. When we

old General Mansfield of the storehouse of jade, he
was annoyed at such useless destruction, and. Stewart
went over this morning and succeeded in procuring a
few unbroken pieces for the general.

From the Kaiserbagh I returned by Banks' bungalow, where Outram, who crossed the river with a
strong column this morning, has taken up his quarters, and I stopped and dined with him at a very full
table, for the general would not permit me to go on.
As soon as the place is taken, he is divested of his
military command, which is merged in his high civil
rank as Commissioner of Oude; but as he has been
summoned to the Council at Calcutta, he will only
retain the direction of civil matters in the province
till the arrival of Mr. Robert Montgomery, who has
been appointed as his successor, and is now at Allahabad, in communication with Lord Canning.

CHAPTER XXI.

No rest for the rebels.—The shattered Residency.—A pleasant chat.—A capful of grape.—Street-fighting.—The great Imambarra.—View from one of its minarets.—Shots from all quarters.—A draught of nectar.—Barbarous act of an officer.—Awful accident.—News from Jung Bahadoor.—Pertinacity and Vacillation.—The Moosabagh.—Napier in distress.—Lord Canning's Proclamation.—Rev. Mr. McKay's sermons.

March 16*th.*—The rebels are to have no rest; and to-day they were rudely thrust back into the lanes of the city, and forced from the remaining strongholds which were in their hands. I started from my tent early, and joined Outram (who was to lead the attack) just as he had concluded his dispositions and was finishing his orders to the officers. The Highlanders of Douglas' Brigade, and the 23rd Welsh Fusileers were principally engaged; but Brasyer's Sikhs were also well up to the front. The sun was exceedingly hot, and as the men marched through the narrow streets between the Kaiserbagh and the Residency, the dust, aggravated by swarms of flies, was more than usually offensive. In those streets lay the bloated corpses of natives in all kinds of attitudes. I could not agree with Charles IX. that the smell of a dead enemy was always sweet, and I puffed my cigar more vigorously than ever as I winded one of those abominations. Most of them—there were old men and women among them—had been hit by fragments of shell, which always produce very horrible wounds. As we approached the shattered walls of the Residency, a few shots were fired from the buildings; but there was no show of opposition as the 23rd and 79th extended and entered the inclosure. By a movement of a portion of the force to the right, the Chutturmunzil, the Mohtee Mahul, and the other palaces on the bank of the Goomtee, were occupied.

We passed through the 20th Regiment, which was left in possession of this position, and were soon defiling through the shattered gateway which led inside the Residency. The enemy had not altered it much. The General could give a history to every stone, and Mr. Kavanagh was in great delight, going from room to room in some of the shattered buildings, and reviving his recollections of the events which happened inside during the siege. A halt took place here for some time till the whole force was ready for an onward movement, and wandering from one court to another, all filled with our troops, I came upon the 1st Bengal Fusileers, who were sheltered from the extreme heat by the ruins of the Residency House. Their blue uniforms, to my mind, were not only neater-looking, but better suited for work than the scarlet, which becomes worse and worse every year as the contractors become more bent on sudden riches. An accident here had nigh put an end to my diary. As I was riding across a courtyard, my horse's hind legs suddenly sunk into the ground; lest his whole body should follow, I managed to leap off, and then, by the aid of some dooly-bearers, we got him on solid earth. What a gulf there was! In fact, he had broken through the cement covering of a closed-up well, and but that the chunam was firm, would have carried me down some hundred feet

The officers of the Fusileers were sheltering from the sun, which was, indeed, painfully powerful, under the arches of the shattered house in which Sir Henry Lawrence met his death. They are a very fine set of fellows; but there is, or was, one among them who did a bloody, and a cruel, and cowardly act this day, as perhaps we shall hear by-and-by, and I am glad to know that those who were his comrades feel towards him as he deserves. We were not under fire at this time, and we had a pleasant if not a cool chat, whilst the guns were being brought up to cover our advance. Outram came into the court, and seeing the men of the 79th, who were near us, exposed to the sun, he called to the officers, "Get your men into the shade. Let them go down into the tykanah (cellars) of the house." He is most careful of all the soldiers' comforts, and he seldom gives an order which is not accompanied by a gift of a cheroot, or more, if he has one left. "Oh, ay!" said one of the men, "that's the way with the Giniral; in the Alumbagh he was always kind, and free with his 'baccy."

The 23rd Regiment were now formed-up under cover of the old walls and buildings of the Residency. A battery of Madras guns took up position on our left and opened, at a high elevation, on the magnificent-looking piles of the Imambarra and Hosseinabad in the rear of the Mucheebawun. Outram, mounted on his fine old charger, cantered across the court; the word was given to advance, and with a right good cheer, the 23rd broke into a run, and like a great wave leaped over the low walls in front of them, and swept on towards the left, whilst two or three companies, moving straight out from the Residency on the right, took the road which, passing under its walls, runs parallel to the Goomtee, right up towards the Iron bridge. The instant our men appeared, a scattered fire of musketry was opened on them from all sorts of invisible holes and corners; but the sepoys and matchlockmen were too nervous to take very accurate aim, and each man, having discharged his piece, fled as we advanced. I was trotting along with the 23rd, and looking up the road at a suspicious-looking barricade of wood which was formed at the side of it, when a curl of smoke came flying out of it, and there came a capful of grape right in our faces; most fortunately it was aimed too high; our advance had been too rapid. The iron shower pattered savagely against the walls above our heads; but one man lay rolling in the dust, and presently another came towards the rear, holding his arm, from which the blood trickled. The man who was hit in the arm helped up his comrade, who was wounded in the leg; and as the doolys were not at hand, the poor fellows were obliged to creep towards the rear. Nothing could be kinder or more gentle than the conduct of one to the other. "Lean on me as hard as you like." "Are you sure I'm not hurting the other arm?" and so they returned to the Residency, and after a time got a dooly, and were carried off out of action.

Before the pandies could load and fire their gun again, the Fusileers were at the muzzle, and with a loud cheer rushed into the work, which was a parapet of sand, earth, and planks, bayoneted one or two men, and rushed on towards the bridge, encountering but a slight opposition from some houses on their way. The advance was general on all our line. In all directions the rattling of musketry was heard, and the bullets, fired at great elevations from distant houses, whistled overhead right and left. The 23rd seemed swallowed up in a labyrinth of lanes and narrow streets, and mixed up with the Punjaubees, who were already breaking open houses, and actively engaged in plundering. As Brasyer was leading on his men, he was badly wounded by a shot from a house : a dooly was sent for, and, as he was getting into it, his infuriated Sikhs entered the building, and taking out some men and boys, whom they found there, placed them with their backs against the wall and shot them on the spot. Their cries for mercy were piteous. In a few seconds they were lying below the blood-stained wall a heap of palpitating, quivering bodies. It was necessary to proceed with great caution in this street-fighting, and our advance was gradual but sure. On every side were sights which I would fain have shut my eyes on, sounds which I would not readily listen to again, as well as scenes of wonderful novelty and interest. The dust, the heat, the excitement were overpowering. Emerging from a street full of Sikhs, who were smashing open doors and windows, and pitching the contents of the houses out of the casemates to their comrades or into the street, I saw the 79th's bonnets, like a waving black sea, pouring in a dense flood, crested with bayonets, through a magnificent archway that spanned a broad street. I rode in along with them. The pencil can alone do justice to the general effect of the grand inclosure in which we found ourselves; but there was no time to pause or admire. The cry was "To the left ; right shoulders forward, by the left wheel!" and rushing through another noble portal, pierced with lofty arches, we found ourselves in the outer court-yard of the great Imambarra. Somewhere hereabouts Pat. Stewart turned up. The Highlanders ran across the court, up a magnificent flight of steps, and in another moment, with loud cheers, took possession of the great Imambarra itself. On our right was a noble mosque with two extremely lofty, tapering minarets. With some difficulty we found our way to the doorway which led to the stairs of one of these, and groping our way round and round, and up and up in the dark, till we came on a doorway which opened on a small balcony round the minaret, about 150 feet above the ground.

Alas, words! words! how poor you are to depict the scene which met the eye of the infidel from the quiet retreat of the muezzin! Lucknow, in its broad expanse of palaces, its groves and gardens, its courts and squares, its mosques and temples, its wide-spreading, squalid quarters of mean, close houses, amid which are kiosks and mansions of rich citizens, surrounded by trees, all lay at our feet, with the Dilkoosha, and Martinière, and distant Alumbagh plainly visible, and the umbrageous plains clothed in the richest vegetation, and covered with woodland, which encompasses the city. In the midst winds the Goomtee, placid and silvery, though its waters are heavy with the dead. Across the Stone bridge, in wild confusion, are pouring the rebels, the sepoys, budmashes, matchlockmen, and inhabitants of the place, and from the Iron bridge our guns are opening on them incessantly, and the showers of our Enfield bullets cut the surface of the waters like rain.

All this met our eyes at a glance. "By Jove, that

was a near shave!" This exclamation was drawn from us by a bullet which whistled within an inch of our heads, and flattened itself against the doorway. "I think I see the rascal," said Stewart, "he's in that room; see! the shutter is opening!" As he spoke, ball number two told us our enemy was no contemptible shot. Just at that moment the bonnet of a Highlander appeared in the door. "Lend me your rifle, my man, till I take a shot at a budmash in that house opposite." Taking a long steady aim, the bullet sped just as the shutter was moving outwards for a third discharge. It moved no more.

Our appearance, however, attracted shots from all quarters. Fellows took snaps at us from balconies, from doors on the roofs of houses, from the windows of mosques and minarets. All our balconies were soon filled with Highlanders. Those who could not get through the doorway loaded and handed us their rifles, and we soon got such a superiority of fire that the sepoys slunk away into holes and corners. By this time our advance had reached the Stone bridge, which was in our hands, but many thousands of the enemy had escaped. The arrangements made for cutting them off on the left bank had not succeeded. The force was too far away, and part of the enemy slunk round to the westward between them and the river. Many thousands, however, who went across at first, hearing there was a body of cavalry and guns in front, returned, recrossed the bridge, and escaped into the city. I descended from the minaret, and entered the Imambarra, where our men were already revelling in the cool shade of the great hall; their revels were rather destructive, and glass chandeliers had suffered not a little, but a splendid silver throne, some ivory chairs, and matters of that kind, had been spared, and were placed under the care of sentries.

Anxious to know what progress we were making, I proceeded thence to the great gateway at the other end of the square leading to the Hosseinabad. Here the Bengal Fusileers were established delighted with their success in taking several guns; some of them mere toys, small double-barrelled brass cannon. We could see the enemy in force at the far end of the street, near another gateway and arch which closed it up completely; but they did not fire, and we did not molest them, as we were not prepared to advance further this day. The men looked much done-up, principally owing to the heat of the sun. As for myself, I never enjoyed such a draught of nectar as Salisbury gave me—a cunning preparation of rum and ginger-pop, which, though nearly lukewarm, was inexpressibly grateful. The bheesties, or water-carriers, were in great demand. The thirst of the men was insatiable, and the cries for the "bheesty" from the soldiers must have perplexed very much those willing and courageous natives, who are the best class of camp-followers in India.

The sun was setting, but there was no calm in the evening air. Dropping shots never ceased, and the noise of plunderers was heard in all directions. The dusty atmosphere was streaked with columns of black smoke from burning barricades and houses. It is wonderful the whole city was not in a blaze. Horrid sights encountered us as we returned towards our camp. An old fakeer, whom we had saved from some Sikhs who had discovered his hiding-place in a cellar, was lying with his brains out near the spot where we had, as we imagined, saved him. Many dead bodies which we had not noticed at first were now lying in the streets. After the Fusileers had got to the gateway, a Cashmere boy came towards the post, leading a blind and aged man, and, throwing himself at the feet of an officer, asked for protection. That officer, as I was informed by his comrades, drew his revolver, and snapped it at the wretched suppliant's head. The men cried "shame" on him. Again he pulled the trigger—again the cap missed; again he pulled, and once more the weapon refused its task. The fourth time—thrice had he time to relent—the gallant officer succeeded, and the boy's life-blood flowed at his feet, amid the indignation and the outcries of his men!

To-day's work has not been very successful in causing loss to the enemy. It is evident most of them have escaped. The philanthropists who were cheering each other with the thought that there was sure "to be a good bag at Lucknow," will be disappointed. It must be admitted that it is unfortunate we could not inflict on the rebels such a severe punishment as would ensure their complete discomfiture and prevent their assembling in other strongholds to renew their opposition to our rule. In the evening I saw Sir Colin. He seemed satisfied—"The runaways will go to their homes."

March 17*th.*—St. Patrick's Day. Outram moving round his troops towards Gowghaut. It was extremely hot. No operations going on; therefore, I spent the day in writing. The Commander-in-Chief took occasion to invest General Wilson with the insignia of his K.C.B. for being general of the army at the close of the siege and during the assault of Delhi: a dull ceremony, which did not cause the least interest or sensation in our camp. In the evening Stewart came in full of grief. An awful accident took place. In the inclosures, round the house of Shruf-ood-dowlah, a large quantity of powder was found in tin-cases and leather-bags. By Outram's order this was put on some country carts and sent under guard of a party of sappers and miners, commanded by Engineer officers, to be thrown down a large and deep well. The first case struck the side of the well and exploded violently; the fire leaped along the ground, caught the powder in the carts—two officers and forty men were blown up and dreadfully burnt, so that few are expected to live. Poor Brownlow and Clarke are among the victims. The former a most distinguished scientific officer—a great friend of Stewart's. It was reported to us this morning that the enemy actually had the audacity to make an attack in great force on the garrison of the Alumbagh yesterday at the time Outram was driving them before him in the city. They are inexplicable enemies.

March 18*th*.—This morning, Stewart, sad and sorrowful, told me poor Brownlow and Clarke died in the course of the night. Let us hope their sufferings were light. At 11·30 went over to their funeral at the Kaiserbagh, and saw their bodies and those of the sappers and miners who had died in the night buried in one of the gardens. All the time of the ceremony, and during the funeral service, cannon and musketry resounded incessantly from the city, where they began early this morning, as a force was sent to attack a house where the Moulvie was said to be hiding, which met with stout resistance. The city still full of budmashes. The Moulvie got off, but ere he did he or some of his creatures killed Shruf-ooddowlah, whose dead body lay across the doorway when our soldiers burst it in. We generally employ natives for these expeditions.

Sir Colin is greatly afraid of gunpowder explosions among our men, as he knows how careless they are. I was talking with him last night when news came from Jung Bahadoor on our left, that he had been attacked—had beaten the enemy, had followed up his success and taken ten guns. "That means," says the Chief, "that he found ten guns the enemy had left there. But I am glad he has done so well." After a pause: "We must be very cautious in that city for a long time to come; it's full of powder, and our men won't take precautions." As he spoke several heavy explosions occurred in the city. "My God!" he exclaimed, "see there! I hope those are not mischievous."

From the funeral, which was a very touching and solemn proceeding, attended by all the engineer officers, and many others, Stewart and I rode to the Kaiserbagh, round by the Residency, and under the Mucheebawun, to the Iron bridge, whence we turned up a street on the left, and arrived at the entrance of the Chandnee Chowk, or main street of business, in Lucknow. Guards of our soldiers were stationed at all the thoroughfares, as we came along, to stop plundering; and the camp-followers were obliged to deposit all their spoils in heaps on the ground at those posts. This is, I suspect, a good way of squeezing the sponge. As we turned a corner of the street heard a good deal of musketry, and, pushing on, found in front of us a strong body of Her Majesty's 20th, who were in support of a picket, which was engaged in clearing some houses further down the street, from which the rebels were galling our men. The soldiers were greatly elated, as they had just taken a very fine brass 9-pounder, loaded to the muzzle with grape, which had been abandoned in the street on their approach. Warren of the 20th came up shot through the cheek, and several wounded soldiers limped past us, but they said the houses were cleared. What a strange pertinacity and vacillation about these people! Here they were holding a narrow street after they had fled from the main city; mere profitless waste of life, or rather desire to kill, combined with want of true courage and calculation. Our further progress down the street was stopped by some bullets from budmashes in the houses. Separating from Stewart for a moment, I came across five of them, who were as much startled as I was; however, they all blazed away at me within a few yards' distance, and immediately dashed round the corner of the lane, whilst I retreated in the opposite direction. What I saw of the city was very interesting indeed: as oriental, close, quaint as Cairo, filled with heaps of plunder—all the furniture being in the streets instead of in the houses, for it had been all tossed out of windows.

On our return, took a sweep round by Banks' bungalow and General Outram insisted on Stewart and myself stopping to dinner with him. He sits like a guest at his own table, which is crowded by the various officers his hospitality pours in on his perplexed aides-de-camp. At dinner were Berkeley, chief of his staff; all the officers of the Highland detachment stationed at the bungalow; his military staff; Money, his secretary; Cowper, political; Dr. George Ogilvie, who was one of the Lucknow garrison, and is a man of great energy and ability; and several officers whom the general had invited over as he met them in the course of the day. The house is knocked to pieces with round-shot, and is much dilapidated—scarce a window, door, or pane of glass left; but it is better than the best tent. The dinner was very good "considering," as they say in Ireland; and bottled ale, soda-water, and port-wine were plentiful, which were luxuries we duly appreciated. The general expresses the most liberal views with respect to the settlement of Oude, and is, as I gathered from one or two expressions, shaken in his belief that his advice for the annexation of the province was quite sound, seeing what the results have been. General Outram is one of those men who are great enough to admit they may have been mistaken; he is of that true courage which fears no moral danger from the avowal of an error; and if he really thinks he was wrong in respect to Oude, I am certain that he will confess as much.

Outside Lucknow proper, on the west, and near the right bank of the Goomtee, is a large palace, with gardens and enclosures, standing in the midst of an open country filled with trees, called the Moosabagh. The approach to it lies through a dense suburb on one side, but a road and raised causeway, comparatively free, passes from the Hosseinabad to very spacious walled gardens, and the handsome summer residence of Ali Nucky Khan, late Prime Minister of Oude, now prisoner at Calcutta—beyond which is another way to the Moosabagh. In the latter place the rebels were stationed to the number of 7000 or 8000, with guns, treasure, and ammunition, camels, elephants, and baggage. They were held together by Begum Huzrat Mahul and her son, Brijcis Kuddr, the *soi-disant* King of Lucknow, by Mummoo Khan, and by all the desperate rebels of the country. A considerable proportion of this force was cavalry. Nothing can show the odd nature of these people better than their attitude here; they can have no hope of taking the city, and yet they hang on in untenable positions in presence of their enemy, as if they were quite satisfied they had nothing to fear from us.

It was resolved to attack, and, if possible, punish severely, those rebels. Sir Colin possibly fancied he might be fortunate enough to catch the Begum, the Moulvie, or some other great leader. Willie Campbell, of the Bays, brigadier of Cavalry, was sent round with one body of horse and some guns to cut off their retreat on the south of the Moosabagh. Hope Grant, with a strong force of horse and artillery, moved along the left bank of the Goomtee, so as to dispose of any rebels who might cross it and try to get away at the north side; the Goorkhas advancing into the city from the Charbagh line of road, toward the rear of the Hosseinabad. Thus there seemed fair grounds for believing that when Outram's corps attacked the rebels directly on the front, they would be certain to tumble, in their retreat, across some of the troops on their flanks. *Dis aliter visum est.*

March 19*th*.—This morning Captain Oliver Jones —an enthusiastic naval officer, who has been fighting against the rebels for the last three or four months, wherever and whenever he had a chance, and who was foremost in the attack at Meeangunj—Stewart, and myself, set out for the Moosabagh, which was to be attacked by the Chief and Outram with the dispositions I have mentioned above: but the advance had been rapid, and when we got up to the house of Ali Nucky Khan, the late Prime Minister, which stands outside the town, on the banks of the Goomtee, before one comes to the Moosabagh, we heard the latter had been evacuated and that the fighting was over: rode on, however, and found Napier in some distress, as the heavy guns were stuck in a narrow lane where there was not a soul to support them, and the sepoys, it appeared, had got in between us and the troops in possession of the Moosabagh, some two miles away, so that it was not safe to go along the road. As we were speaking, a rascal started up in the narrow lane close at hand, and fired at us; but his bullet went far wide of the mark, though we were obliged to submit to the indignity of being potted at. It is not too much to say, that fifty determined sepoys, and a few horsemen, could have, at this moment, taken the heavy battery. Soon afterwards a young officer galloped up in some excitement. He had been sent to take prize charge of the Moosabagh; but as he rode along, sepoys started up from the fields of corn and took steady shots at him in the coolest way, so that his escort turned tail, and he eventually very properly followed their example. After a time, a battalion of infantry came up to guard the guns, and as the day was so hot as to put any further excursion amid the list of tortures, I returned with my companions to camp after a canter up to the park of the

Moosabagh. Late this evening I heard the cavalry had made a complete blunder, and that the enemy had got away almost untouched, although we lost one or two good officers in an abortive charge. Pat. Stewart, who is really scarce able to sit on his horse, and is only kept in his saddle by sheer pluck and determination, is going to leave us at last, and now that the place has fairly fallen, he starts for England.

March 20*th.*—The Commander-in-Chief tells me we shall have to wait here till he has placed Lucknow in a proper state of defence. There are copies of a Proclamation by Lord Canning to the people of Oude which has caused much real alarm in camp. Major Bouverie, aide to the Governor-General, has arrived on a mission, which is, I presume, connected with the restoration of the civil power in Lucknow; but if this Proclamation goes forth *pur et simple*, the duties of the Commissioner will become all but impossible of execution. Lord Canning confiscates the land of Oude with the exception of the states of some seven or eight small chiefs. In case of instant surrender he offers favourable consideration, life and honour to the rebel zemindars. This is what Turks and Englishmen call " bosh." These words have no meaning in the ears of natives, and convey no idea to their minds; but at best they are *telum imbelle*, for we cannot really enforce them. Time must elapse ere Oude be ours. It turns out unhappily that the fall of Lucknow has by no means secured the submission of Oude, as Lord Canning must have supposed it would when he hurled his bull from Allahabad. Stewart left for England this evening—*quod felix faustumque sit.*

Sunday, March 21st.—Napier is engaged in drawing up a report on the alterations and defences of Lucknow, of a *grandiose* and very elevated character. It is imperial in conception; but where is the money to come from? We had, for a wonder, divine service in the Mess-tent to-day, at which there was a limited attendance. Sir Colin Campbell is of the Scotch Church; but he might have listened without harm to an eloquent but illogical sermon from the Rev. Mr. McKay, wherein that excellent divine sought to prove that England would not share the fate common to all the great empires of the world hitherto, because she was Christian and carried the ark of the covenant, whereas they had been heathen—*non constat domine!* Our tent was surrounded with Hindoos and Mahomedans. They were our subjects, and part of our State. The Christianity of a Roman Emperor could not save his empire; and as " Sarmatia fell unwept without a crime," so might we fall unwept with many crimes, of which our people know nothing, in spite of our being Christian, with a Protestant constitution and an Empire of all religions in the world. I believe that we permit things to be done in India which we would not permit to be done in Europe, or could not hope to effect without public reprobation; and that our Christian character in Europe, our Christian zeal in Exeter Hall, will not atone for usurpation and annexation in Hindostan, or for violence and fraud in the Upper Provinces of India.

CHAPTER XXII.

Lord Canning's Proclamation.—Visit to the begums.—Mrs. Orr and Miss Jackson.—Frightful wounds of poor Bankes.—The camp of the Seventh Hussars.—Sir James Outram and Lord Canning.—Visit to Sir William Peel.—Munoora-ood-dowlah.—Our aides-de-camps.—The Chief Commissioner of Oude.—My palkee and appurtenances sold.—Sir James Outram's departure.—Doggerel verses and charcoal sketches.—Routed by an elephant.—Sales of captured property.

Monday, March 22nd.—To-day I procured a copy of Lord Canning's Proclamation, which I sent to London, where no doubt it will excite as much disapprobation as it does here. I have not heard one voice raised in its defence; and even those who are habitually silent, now open their mouths to condemn the policy which must perpetuate the rebellion in Oude. In fact, unless there be some modification of the general terms of the Proclamation, it will be but *irritamenta malorum* to issue it.

Having written till I was in a state of liquefaction, I rode over with Major Bruce to see the begums and their attendants, who are prisoners, or at least are guarded in the Martinière. Sir Colin gave me leave to do so; but he has been chary of granting permission to visit those ladies. We found them all in one large, low, dark and dirty room, without windows, on the ground floor, and Bruce's entrance was the signal for a shrill uplifting of voices, and passionate exclamations from the ladies, who were crouched down all round the walls. The begum, a shrivelled, wicked-looking old woman, led the chorus, complained of food, of loss of raiment and of liberty, demanded money and life-allowances, and attendants, and many other things, receiving, at each request, the support of her followers in a sharp antistrophe. One of our difficulties was this—a fair, bright-eyed maid, who sat in the corner playing with the bangles around a very pretty instep, desired to go away into the town. We professed to detain the begums merely for their own safety, and of course we could not recognize the institution of slavery. The young lady, whom we declared we did not want to keep, was a slave, and it was our business to set her free; but, on the other hand, we knew she would not improve her condition by her liberty, and the begum to whom she belonged argued that we had no right to deprive her or let her be deprived of her property.

Thus we learn how very shallow is the influence of our government in India. It does not penetrate the institutions of the people. A domestic slavery is common which is not affected by our laws. At every step some little incident like this comes to light, which convinces me that in many parts of India our government is purely political, and that it is not social or deep searching.

I left the begums without reluctance, and as the heat was too great to permit me to write, I rode over to Banks' bungalow, where General Outram was busy sending out the Proclamation of the Governor-General with a rider of his own, which seemed to mean "don't mind the Governor-General; his bark is worse than his bite; come in at once to me, and I'll make it all right for you and your lands."

As he was going to visit Mrs. Orr and Miss Jackson,

who were in the ruins of an adjoining bungalow, I was happy to accompany him and Dr. Ogilvie (who is the kind and anxious guardian of the two ladies), not in any spirit of vulgar curiosity, but to pay my respects to two of my countrywomen, who had suffered so long and so heroically. Alas! their appearance showed that they had suffered much. It was an interesting and, to me, an affecting interview, and I retired sadly away; but I had the satisfaction of inducing them to accept the use of my gharry to take the air they so much required.

Whilst returning from it across the compound, we heard the guns which saluted Sir Colin Campbell in the Maharajah Jung Bahadoor's camp, whither he had gone to pay a visit of ceremony ere the departure of the latter for Nepaul.

March 23rd.— McNeil, one of the deliverers of Mrs. Orr and Miss Jackson, who commands a brigade of Goorkhas, dined with me to-day. He says Jung is really a very clever man, active in mind and body, "bloody, resolute, and cruel," but as brave as steel. His officers, many of whom are related to him, are by no means so indifferent to danger or prodigal of blood, and they have no influence over their men, who will only follow courageous leaders. There was a little state dinner at Sir Colin's as General Outram came over to meet Lieutenant-Colonel Stewart, the military secretary of the Governor-General, who has arrived in the Head-Quarters' camp.

March 24th. — Part of the Goorkhas marched to-day for Fyzabad, on their way home. I remained in my tent all day writing. In the afternoon young Gore of 7th Hussars, son of Mrs. Gore, called on me with letters, and with a message from poor Bankes of the same regiment, who was so desperately wounded the other day, to request I would go over and see him. I promised to do so, and engaged my friend Tice, who is senior Surgeon in charge of the whole of the Infantry here, to come with me. A horrid row, bursting the captured guns all day. The poorer sort of people are returning to the city, but we hear with regret that the women are sometimes ill used, and Hindoos commit suicide when they are dishonoured. Captain C. Johnson, who has been in charge of the parties employed to bury the dead, who are found all over the town, has told me some very affecting stories of the distress and misery he has witnessed.

March 25*th*.—Dr. Tice, who has managed to "rise a buggy," called for me early, and we started off for the Moosabagh, but had not got as far as the Muchee-bawun, when we came upon a corps of Goorkhas marching out with baggage, camels, and hackeries. Fortunately our syces had led our horses after us, and so we mounted, and with much difficulty made our way through the dusty crowd of armed men. The detention exposed us both to the full rays of the sun, which, with the dust, proved very fatiguing. As we passed by the Hosseinabad, the Bengal Fusileers were just sitting down to breakfast in the arched gateway, and right glad were the doctor and myself to join them at a cool clean repast of curry and claret-cup. After a short halt proceeded slowly in a blazing atmosphere out to the camp of the Moosabagh. The tents of 7th Hussars were pitched on a meadow near the Goomtee. I entered poor Bankes' tent, and found him awake and listening to the news which the

Rev. Mr. Waterhouse was reading for him at the bedside. His eyes looked clear and bright, but his injuries are of a frightful description. One leg lopped off above the knee, one arm cut off, the other leg nearly severed, the other arm cut through the bone, and several severe cuts on the body. A band of Gazees, who issued out of an old mud fort and charged the guns and the party of the 7th Hussars covering them, had got the lad down and hacked at him in that cruel way till he was rescued by his comrades. It is pefectly astonishing to witness his cheerfulness and resignation. "If I get over this, Russell," he said, "they tell me I'll be able to go yachting, and that's all I care about. We'll have many a jolly cruize together." "If it please God," he added, after a moment.

I sat about an hour with him. Tice examined his wounds, and then we left him alone with the good clergyman. In another tent we found Slade and Peter Wilkin, of the same regiment, laid up with wounds received in the same charge and on the same day. Their wounds were not dangerous. Stewart took us over to the Mess-tent, where were Colonel Hagart and Sir William Russell, the latter of whom I now met for the first time, though I had heard before that he was esteemed a good officer. He is a very tall, powerfully built man, with a fine black beard. Seidlitz used to say no man could lead light cavalry who weighed more than 160 pounds, and if so, the gallant Baronet (who by the bye is *lié* to India by his ancestors), and a good many other Hussars, will be found over weight. Turned into the Moosabagh and visited Brigadier Stisted, who has his quarters there, and thence back to camp through suburbs full of corpses in a most disgusting state of decomposition.

March 26*th*.—Writing for the English Post. General Outram is going to Calcutta at his own request as soon as possible, inasmuch as he does not feel himself able to carry out the Governor-General's policy. Although the General will be well placed at the council-table, I regret that he does not remain in Oude, where his name is well known, and where he has many personal acquaintances among the great chiefs; but if he has not the support and confidence of the Governor-General in the discharge of his high duties, it is out of the question to expect a man like General Outram to retain a post in which he is called upon to carry out a policy of which he disapproves. It is strange that in the course of a few years the man who, as resident at Lucknow, recommended the annexation of the kingdom, should now, as commissioner of the revolted British province, feel himself obliged to force on the consideration of the supreme Government the claims of the rebels to more liberal treatment than Lord Canning is disposed to offer them. His Excellency has, indeed, made some concessions, but his general policy, as regards Oude, is looked upon by all men here, political and military, as too harsh and despotic. In the abstract, and as a question of principle, I think Lord Canning may be right, with this single exception —he assumes that the fall of Lucknow has been followed by the submission of Oude, and that he is in a position to confiscate all the lands of the province; but the fact is, that we are very far from such a consummation. So far the threat is mere *brutum* *fulmen.* Though it may be the bolt will fall some time or other, we cannot hurl it now. Mr. Montgomery is on his way to relieve General Outram.

March 27th.—Rode out before breakfast, and visited Sir William Peel, whom I found in the same room with Gloster of the 38th Regt., who was shot right through the abdomen, and is nevertheless progressing fast towards convalescence. Peel looked thin and feverish, but he says he is much better, and is only waiting till he is strong enough to get down to Cawnpore on his way home. He is as much opposed to the Proclamation as any one I have spoken to. Dined at General Outram's mess. In the evening Mr. George Campbell, financial commissioner for Oude, arrived, preceding Mr. Montgomery, who is expected in a few days. General Outram and he did not at all agree in the policy which should be adopted towards the rebellious native chiefs and others. The former is for a large and generous and general amnesty, except in the cases of actual murderers; the latter is for the most vigorous prosecution and punishment.

March 28th.—Palm Sunday.—The heat quite overpowering. Hope Grant is going out with a force to sweep away sundry collections of sepoys in the east of Oude, notably one headed by the begum at a fort on the Gogra, called Bitowlee.

March 29th.—Rode over to Banks' bungalow, and saw part of the column which is going under Lugard to clear the Azimghur district of the band under Koer Sing, on their way out. They have fifteen marches to make ere they reach the scene of their operations. Sir James Outram has received permission from Lord Canning to offer more liberal terms than are contained in the Proclamation to any of the great zemindars who show a disposition to surrender. From the bungalow rode with Morland through part of the city, and visited Luff, 23rd, and others in their quarters, near the Hosseinabad. The worst portion of the inhabitants have evidently returned to the city.

March 30th.—Remained in my tent all day writing, with the perspiration streaming from every pore; had a ride of half an hour; to dinner and to bed.

March 31st.—Lieutenant Hope Johnstone came in to me this morning, by order of the general, with a telegram announcing the defeat of the Palmerston Ministry on their *entente cordiale* Bill. The news did not cause much sensation in camp. To Indians such events have really a great deal of the character of local politics. As it is becoming a physical impossibility to write during the day in such a tent as I have, I accepted with pleasure the kind proposal of General Outram, that I should go over and establish myself in one of the empty rooms at Banks' bungalow. I unfortunately slept there out in an open verandah, where some half-dozen charpoys were laid for as many guests. The mosquitoes devoured me, and I was in a perfect fever when the morning dawned.

April 1st.—After breakfast this morning, I was rather amused at a little scene which took place. We were sitting at a table smoking and reading the papers, when a chuprassee came in and announced that Munoora-ood-dowlah, formerly a man of great rank in Oude, an ex-minister, and related to the Royal family, craved an audience of the Chief Commissioner.

He was ordered to walk in. A very old and venerable-looking gentleman entered, followed by two or three attendants, and salaamed all round to us, whilst he and his chief secretary paid us many compliments, expressive of delight at seeing us.

First Aide.—I say, you speak the old chap's lingo better than I do. Tell him the General is busy, and that he must wait.

Second Aide.—No, you tell him yourself. Confound me, if I do your business.

All this time Munoora is standing. After a little further controversy, the second aide tells him to sit down, and he and his attendants shuffle into broken chairs, and balance themselves with evident uneasiness.

First aide whistles, with his legs on the table; second aide draws assiduously a fine bold sketch on a sheet of blotting-paper. Munoora-ood-dowlah, after a long pause, begs to know whether the burra sahib bahadoor knows he is waiting, and is likely to see him.

First Aide.—I say now, it's your turn to go in to Sir James. I don't want to be bored by this old humbug.

Second Aide.—Well, hadn't we better say Sir James won't see him?

First Aide.—No, hang it; he's been a faithful old swell, and all that; and Sir James might be angry, as they were chums long ago.

Second Aide exit.—You are one of the laziest——

After a time in came Sir James; but in the interval Munoora was the very type of misery; for to an Oriental of his rank all this delay and hesitation about an audience were very unfavourable symptoms. He had really been our friend, and had undergone the greatest misery, privation, loss, and insults at the hands of the rebels. In former days he was noted for his hospitality to the English, for his magnificent sporting parties, and for his excellence as a shot at both large and small game. He had upwards of one hundred rifles of the very best English makers in his battery, and his greatest pleasure was to lead a chickar for his friends. Sir James gave him rather a kindly reception, and sent the old man away in better spirits. (But he never recovered the ignominy to which he had been subjected by the rebels, and he died soon afterwards.)

Good Friday.—April 2nd.—Our camp was moved to-day from the Martinière to the enclosures around the Mess-house and the Tara Kothie, or the observatory, in the latter of which are some rooms available for the Chief, and for the officers of the heads of departments. My tent was pitched close to a well at an angle of the Mess-house, which had a very offensive smell. Indeed, the air of Lucknow is thoroughly tainted.

In the course of some conversation with Sir James Outram to-day, I happened to mention that a Russian general, speaking in condemnation of Menschikoff's position on the Alma, stated that a river formed the worst defence that could be relied on, that a daring enemy could always cross it; that the army which was attacked was always beaten, and that there was no remarkable instance in history of a river being converted into a successful line of defence, whereas

THE CHIEF COMMISSIONER OF OUDE. 367

many of the most celebrated battles had been won by armies which had forced the passage of rivers in order to win them. Sir James combated that view with ability, and at much length; and in doing so evinced a remarkable knowledge of famous military operations.

April 3rd.—Mr. Montgomery, the Chief Commissioner of Oude, arrived to-day, to relieve General Outram, under a salute, and I was introduced to him. He is a man of peculiar smoothness of manner and appearance—a large vigorous head, a clear, good eye, and great firmness of mouth and lip. He is understood to have obtained permission from Lord Canning to modify the menaces of the Proclamation, and to offer considerable concessions to the rebels in Oude. Indeed, it is felt by all who know anything of the country and of the circumstances of the case, that the zemindars of Oude require more consideration than the chiefs in other parts of India who have revolted against us. Mr. Montgomery has a grand task before him, but he is believed to be suited to the work, and the glory of accomplishing it will be great as the labour. At present all Oude may be regarded as an enemy's country, for there are very few chiefs who do not still hold out, and defy the threats of the Proclamation. The capture of Lucknow has dispersed the rebels all over the country, and reinforced the hands which the rajahs and zemindars have collected around their forts. The few friendly landowners as excepted from the Confiscation Clause, with the addition of those who have tendered their submission, are not large or powerful enough to give us a *nucleus* for the restoration of our rule. All our machinery of government is broken and destroyed. Our revenue is collected by rebels. Our police has disappeared utterly. Oude is to be conquered. Before it was only "annexed." When it has been completely subjugated, the labours of the civil officers to establish law and order, finally begin.

April 4th.—Easter Sunday.—Sold my palkee and horse (and coachman, as before, with his wife and family) to the Chief Commissioner, who literally had nothing to go about in. On going over to Banks' bungalow after breakfast, I found a regular levée of officers taking leave of Sir James Outram, who starts for Cawnpore, on his way to Calcutta. It was 2 o'clock ere he got away. The horses of himself and staff were at the door, and I was glad to be able to join the cavalcade and ride out part of the way with him. Sir James led us himself by the road he took on coming into the town, and by the Charbagh, over the bridge, pointing out every locality which was remarkable for any incident during his advance towards the Residency, as we moved on towards the Alumbagh. With him went Colonel Berkeley, late chief of his staff (on his way to take command of H.M.'s 32nd), Cooper, Hargood, Denison, Money, and Olpherts (Chamier, being unable to travel, was left behind at Lucknow).

I never was out in a hotter day. Sir James had given distinct orders that there was to be no escort; but, on reaching the well at the Alumbagh, we saw a clump of spears on the horizon, which Cooper admitted, after some hesitation, might belong to a few cavalry. We argued the question whether, as the enemy were all about us, it was not as well to take an escort. "Suppose you met a party of sowars, Sir James," said I, "what would you do?"

"Why, I'd ride over the rascals, and knock them down with this stick" (a pretty stout one) "like ninepins," replied he. And I'm very certain he would do his best, at all events, to keep his word.

When we got two miles beyond Alumbagh we halted, and, with much regret, I bade the General good-bye, carrying back with me feelings of respect and regard for him which time cannot alter. He rode on without his escort. Olpherts and I returned to Lucknow, and we arrived in time to dine together at our mess.

April 5th.—Easter Monday.—I was fortunate enough to secure a corner in a room of the Messhouse to write in—a room! rather say, a walled enclosure full of holes. The walls are covered with doggerel verses, with charcoal sketches of the Nana in torture, in the early manner, with "Hurra for Tim Flanagan, of the gallant 53rd!"—"Down with tyrant Magee!"—"Three cheers for the 42nd Highlanders who took Lucknow!"—"Six cheers for the 53rd who took the Mess-house and slawtered the sepoys!"—and such little historical notes.

Colonel Pakenham has one room, or part of one; the Post-office is up-stairs. Colonel Keith Young, our excellent advocate-general, has another den. Dr. Brown and Douglas have an office in a fourth compartment. C. C. Johnson and Allgood work at their plans and reports in another. Macpherson, the quartermaster-general, gives me a bit of his premises; and lying on a charpoy in the same room as his gallant brother, who was wounded the other day whilst displaying the greatest bravery. We had a dust-storm as a foretaste of what we must expect in the height of the hot weather. I cannot conceive anything hotter than this day. The air was like a furnace blast.

Colonel Kelly, H.M.'s 38th, dined with me at mess. We were routed ignominiously after dinner by an alarm of a must-elephant, which got loose, and charged through the garden close to our tent. Had it rushed at the tent some of us would have lost the number of our mess, for we must have been crushed by the poles and kanauts. The beast was chased by an army of mahouts, with spears and shouts, and we heard him trumpeting in the distance after he had swam, or forded, the Goomtee below us, and set the whole camp in an uproar.

Easter Tuesday, April 6th.—It is resolved to form a corps of observation, combined with a corps of occupation, for Lucknow. To constitute the first, certain regiments are warned to have companies ready to start at signal for a common rendezvous. These will be under Hope Grant, and are to act against any body of rebels who may assemble near Lucknow. The rest of the troops are to remain in garrison in the Mucheebawun Fort, and in the strong places commanding the bridges. Walpole, at the head of a magnificent little army,—the Highlanders, a regiment of Punjaub Rifles, cavalry, and artillery, field and heavy,—marches to-morrow for the west of Oude, which he is to clear towards Rohilcund, in a line parallel to the course of the Ganges. We are surprised that Sir Colin trusts his Highlanders to Walpole. I dined with Olpherts and the officers of his troop, B.A., at the Kaiserbagh.

April 7th.—Went over to visit Bankes. Alas! he has passed a very bad night, and I did not see him; the surgeon said it would be imprudent to disturb him.* Returned, and wrote all day in a vapour bath.

April 8th.—Sir Colin, in the course of some conversation to-day, mentioned that he was going to start that night for Allahabad, in order to see the Governor-General about Rohilcund. Whilst I was in his room, he sent for Biddulph, a young artillery officer, and told him "to send on relays of artillery horses for a particular friend of his who was going to travel to Cawnpore that night in all haste." But of little avail are all these precautions. When I was at mess to-night I heard one say, "The Chief is going to start for Allahabad to-night, as he can't get any decided replies from Canning, and he is taking Bruce with him."

April 9th.—At six o'clock this morning went over to the Kotwallee, where the sales of property captured in Lucknow are going on, under authority of the prize-agents for the benefit of the troops. I saw nothing of any value, and it struck me that the things which were sold realised most ridiculously large prices.

April 10th.—The result of Sir Colin's visit to Allahabad is tangible to-day in a general order just issued, that we are to march for Cawnpore at 2 A.M. to-morrow morning. General Grant starts

* He died shortly afterwards.

with his column for Bitowlee also, and I bade him farewell this evening. As I was over with General Mansfield about 5 P.M., another telegram arrived, announcing that the Chief was on his way from Allahabad to Cawnpore. The Chief of the staff at once issued an after-order to countermand our march. Sir Colin arrived in camp from Allahabad about midnight.

CHAPTER XXIII.

My last days in Lucknow.—The soldier's goods and chattels.—
A palpable obstruction.—A night of great pain.—A melancholy
mode of progression.—Lord Clinton ill at Cawnpore.—The
whole art of war.—Welcome repose.—A drive through Cawnpore.—Death of Adrian Hope.—Discomfort of night-marches.—
Joy to reach the camping-ground.—The lost tent.—The ruins
of Kunouj.—Futtehguhr.—Brigadier Seaton.

AT last the time arrived when we were to leave Lucknow. Had the change been more advantageous, it would have been hailed by us all with delight. Even as it was, there was universal satisfaction, although we were only about to substitute one phase of camp-life for another, and were merely to pass from passive to active warfare. The sun had become so fierce, that it threatened to strike down any European who encountered it in the daytime; but, nevertheless, we looked forward with positive pleasure to the campaign in Rohilcund, which it was considered necessary to make before the rains set in. The fall of Lucknow had by no means effected the subjugation of Oude. In that province, and in the adjoining country of Rohilcund, the rebels were either paramount by force of a majority, or were altogether masters of the soil, and revenue, and government of the country. On the west, in Goruckpore, an old chuckledar of Oude, Mehndie Hoosein, was at the head of formidable forces, and Koer Sing's career of conquest had not yet been brought to its close. Bundelcund was also more or less hostile, and Sir Hugh Rose had not made his triumphant march to Calpee. My last days in Lucknow, and inglorious mode of departure from it, will be best exemplified by extracts from my diary.

April 11*th.* (*Low Sunday.*)—Very hot; the well next my tent smells abominably. I suspect decaying pandies are at the bottom of it. In the evening, Torrens and Duff (Welch Fusileers) came to see me. The latter brought over the case of my telescope, which I left at the Iron bridge, the day of Outram's *reconnaissance.* A sergeant of the regiment had found and kept it for me. Stewart, of 7th Hussars, also came over from his camp to say good-bye. He starts with Hope Grant's force to-morrow, "to scour the country" towards Roy Bareilly and the southeast of Oude. Pretty "scouring" with the thermometer at 100° in the tents already! It is an ill wind that blows nobody good. Kelly, of the 38th Regiment, sent me over a "splendid assortment" of chicks and purdahs for tent-doors, chairs and tables, which he took out of his quarters. This is one of the small miseries of a soldier's life. He heaps up riches, prepares his quarters for a life-long residence, and lo! there cometh the route, and another steps into fruition of his labours. It was only this evening that, in the course of my ride, I was admiring his snug arrangements, complimenting him on his candlesticks, mirrors, and carpets.

Hume and I rode over to the big Imambarra, and visited Slade, Wilkin, and others, who were lying wounded there; found some of them very jolly in the open cloisters of the buildings near the mosque, talking of England, which is now the prevalent cry; nor was claret-and-water quite neglected. There were some there, alas, who would never live to reach their promised land! I observe an immense increase of people in the city — some murderous, scowling scoundrels among them. The coolies returning from work made such a dust that it was really with difficulty I could make my way back to my tent in order to dress for dinner. I did not think it would prove strong enough to deprive me of that said dinner; but it turned out that it did. I had been engaged to dine with Forsyth, secretary to the Chief Commissioner, who lived in a bungalow off the road from our camp to Banks' bungalow, to the right of the Begum Kothie. I set out on horseback, and got into the Huzrutgunj, which was thronged with thousands of coolies and many hundreds of bullocks, hackeries, and camels, so that it was scarce practicable to get through them, and I felt as though I were breathing soup or an atmosphere of puff-powder. Still, by keeping close to the wall, and by the aid of the lights of the torches and lamps on the bazaar-sheds, I got somehow as far as the Begum Kothie, where the dust became a real palpable obstruction; my eyes were filled, my ears crammed, my mouth and nose choked up. No London fog (and I have seen some good ones) could be so dense or so disgusting. I literally had to turn round my horse and to ride back through the crowd, up the Huzrutgunj to the bridge of boats, and so into camp, where I arrived ere mess was over. This fact will give some notion of the dust. I suppose the stratum was about fourteen or fifteen feet high. The natives whom I met had covered up their mouths and noses with pieces of linen; and all the Punjaubees had carefully swathed their beards and luxuriant whiskers to protect them from the contaminating dust.

Monday, April 12th. — This morning awoke very seedy; violent sickness and headache. Went into Mess-house, and saw D——, who administered a dose of peppermint, which I took, though I knew he might as well have given me a mouthful of air. Grinning with pain, and rubbing my stomach, and getting worse all day. Laid down in Macpherson's room. Sir Colin came in and told me a good deal of his plans. He seems to regret, now, that Campbell did not do his duty, and display vigour in pressing after the rebels.

Tuesday, April 13th. — A night of great pain. Clifford came in to see me, and pronounced that I had an attack of dysentery. This is pleasant, considering the Head-Quarters march to-night, and I must go with them. Clifford says there is no alternative but to take a dooly, as I am quite unfit to travel on horseback. Such a way to begin a campaign! But, please God, I'll be able to get into the saddle ere the fighting begins. I am to eat nothing but arrow-root, and to drink nothing but congee-water, which is water in which rice has been boiled, said to be very antidysenteric. Lay in my tent, suffocating with heat, and in much pain all day, drinking congee-water, for which my repugnance increases at every draught. Could get no sleep, and yet I must start.

Wednesday, April 14th. — At a quarter past 2 o'clock this morning, my dooly was brought up to my tent. I was now so weak from the effects of the dysentery and diarrhœa, that I had to be carried into the pleasant vehicle. In consideration of my weight, I have an extra supply of bearers, so there are eight instead of six coolies to carry me. They light me into the dooly with flaring torches. Simon fills it with supplies of congee-water, puts sword and pistols handy by my side, as, says he, "There plenty budmash as mastar pass through little streets of city." We have only a handful of men as escort, and the members of our mess have started just as they pleased, some on elephants, some on horseback, some in buggies, and the sick in doolys. I was too much fagged to observe more than the picturesque effect of the torchlights moving in the distance. Soon we were in the deserted lanes of the huge city, and frequently we came upon families returning to their homes, who had selected night for a secret return, and were surprised by the torchlights. *Ay de mi*, Lucknow. I'm quite convinced it was the dust which made me ill. We went out of the city by the Charbagh, passing the Alumbagh on our way to Cawnpore. This is a melancholy mode of progression—so sad and solitary; no one to speak to; smothered, if you open the purdahs, by dust, and by heat if you keep them shut. At last sleep came, and the divine Oneirus made merry with me, and told me I was travelling in a first-class carriage to Thurles, where, somehow or other, I was obliged to go in regard of my episcopal functions; that I never was better in my life; that it was not fast-day, and that the cardinal and my brother prelates had ordered a very fine banquet, and an uncommon fine tap of claret for 5 "P.M. sharp," and that in ten minutes we should be at the station. *Ay de mi*, again! I awake under the shade of a tree in our old camping-ground at Buntheerah, now inexpressibly nasty, owing to the frequent detachments which have rested here. They are measuring out the ground. Beside me there rests another dooly; a thin hand is stretched out, and draws the curtains. A pale face rises languidly from the pillow. "What, Russell! you in a dooly? Why I thought nothing would upset you. What's the matter?" "Why, my dear Sir William, if a man lives over graves, drinks bad water, and breathes powdered pandies, he must give in at last."

It was poor Peel, who looked, I thought, weak and ill, but he says he is getting stronger, and is looking with great pleasure to getting home with his ship. We had a long chat this morning. He expressed great uneasiness about young Lord Clinton, son of the Duke of Newcastle, who belongs to his ship, and is now very ill at Cawnpore—a nice lad, who is liked by all that know him. He is delighted that the Ministers are out on the French Bill, and said, "Well, after all, the House of Commons is national, and has honest instincts. I'm glad that Ministers who could propose to truckle to France in that way should be turned out. But it would put us in an awkward relation with the Emperor." We then began to talk of the chances of a war with France, which he seemed to consider very likely; and we had a good deal of conversation about Cherbourg, which I had visited when the "President" Louis Napoleon reviewed the French fleet there. Of both man and fleet it might be well said, "*Quantum mutatus ab illo!*" He told me he had a plan of attacking Cherbourg by floating batteries, strongly parapetted and "gabioned" which he was sure would succeed. It was about seven o'clock when the tents were up. Clifford forbad animal food, and insisted I was better. I hope he is right; but I, who ought to know best, don't feel at all improved.

April 15*th.* — Buntheerah to Nuwabgunj. — At 2 this morning marched from Buntheerah, and arrived at Nuwabgunj, and encamped at the usual hour. Our wits sharpened all night by reports that the enemy are hovering on our flanks as we march. We see nothing of them, but Simon announced that one of my camels had suddenly bolted off in the dark with my chairs, and the best part of my camp outfit on his back, and says, "Budmash sowars will catch mastar's chairs." There is a brave old custom of always encamping on the same ground, which secures you the reversion of the smells of your predecessors, and something more. Peel had some papers to lend me, and I was able to read some of them, but the pain is still very great, and the disease obstinate.

April 16*th.* — Nuwabgunj to Oonao. — Marched from Nuwabgunj at 3, and arrived at Oonao at 7 A.M. Was kept awake last night by a very talkative picket near the watch-fire, close to my tent. An Irish corporal was instructing his hearers in the art of war. "It all depinds," said he, "on where you hit yer inimy. Suppose I offered to hit you, Hollman, on the head, ye'd have yer two hands ready for me, and I wouldn't hurt you a bit; but suppose I gev you a sthroke in the stomach; bedad, I'd do for you. That's what we calls a vinerable part, and that's the whole art of war to find it out, and do it clane and cliver. It's Sir Colin finds out the vinerable part; it's their flanks or their sides he comes down on, and thin they turn their backs in a minit, for they 're 'cute enough to know whin they 're bate, anyhow; and sometimes they discovers it afore it happens, the poor craytures."

April 17th. — Oonao to Cawnpore. — Left Oonao, which is famous as the scene of one of Havelock's fights, at 3 o'clock A.M. No graves to be seen. It is likely that Havelock lost very few in his early actions. The enemy were not so bold then as they are now. They were almost surprised at their own temerity in daring to stand before white-faced infidels. At about half-past 6 crossed the bridge of boats to Cawnpore, which was steaming hot in the sun, to Sherer's, where I found — oh, luxury! — a clean charpoy ready for me, clean sheets, tea, fresh milk, a dark room, punkahs, and repose. Sherer was out, but a competition wallah, whose manners were by no means indicative of his merits and attainments, received me, and my excellent friend made his appearance soon afterwards, fresh from his morning ride. The civilian mess still holds on here; the necessaries of life are more abundant; got fairly desperate at the smell and sight of dinner; dashed away the bumper of congee-water and the dish of arrowroot, and went madly in for claret and currie; saved my life by this stroke of genius. All the civilians are open-mouthed against the Lucknow management, and declare Sir Colin has "botched" the whole affair, whereupon I contend against the civilians. They say that Oude is swarming with the budmashes, and that if matters had been well managed we ought to have killed twenty thousand of them! Woke much better after my nap *post prandial*, and was quite able to appreciate

Sherer's moonshee, a young gentleman who is twenty-two years of age, and weighs twenty-two stone—an oily rogue, who feasts on ghee, and sugar, and sweets, and seems sorely perplexed with the official necessity incumbent on him to get up a proper amount of indignation against the budmashes, which he fears may impede his digestion. Sherer is intent on levying a fine on the Cawnpore people, who are said to have great quantities of European property concealed in their bazaar. As a matter of general policy I doubt the utility of fines inflicted in that general way. I drove through Cawnpore, and found the place swarming with people; and Sherer took me to the native kotwal, who is a most magnificent-looking fellow, of great stature, and prodigious abdominous dimensions. The European kotwal, a big English, or Anglo-Indian, official, is almost worthy to compete with the Mahomedan mayor. He is married to Mrs. Byrne, whose husband was killed in the mutinies, and whose life was saved by the Nuwab of Furruckabad, who knew her and her mother, and received them into his zenana. The ruins around the fort are nearly cleared away; all the trees have been cut down to give free play to the guns; the bungalows have been partially repaired, but the church is just as the mutinies and the fight at Cawnpore left it. Had we desired to mark indelibly our sense of the wrong inflicted upon us, we could have transferred the station and cantonments to some spot above or below the present site; but the railway terminus now fixes the British settlement.

April 18*th.*—Sir Colin and Mansfield have arrived, and evil news has come with them. I have just seen a telegram, from which it appears that Walpole has been repulsed in an injudicious attack on a body of rebels under Nirput Sing, posted in a mud-fort called Royca or Rooca, near Rhadamow, and that Adrian Hope has been killed in the action. A gentler, braver spirit never breathed—a true soldier, a kind, courteous, noble gentleman in word and deed; devoted to his profession, beloved by his men, adored by his friends—this is indeed a loss to the British army! A sad fate for such a one as Adrian Hope, who would have shone in the grandest battle-fields, or have done himself honour in the greatest of European campaigns by the exhibition of courage and of skill, to be shot down in a ditch by an ambushed ruffian in an obscure Oude jungle-fort. The Chief is greatly grieved. But who is not? Walpole seems to have made the attack in a very careless, unsoldierly way, as far as we know at present. Poor Bramley is killed, and so is Douglas. The 42nd and the Sikh regiment engaged have lost more than 100 men killed and wounded.

A sepoy, caught by Maxwell, who is watching the Calpee rebels, was brought in just as we were going to dinner. He was cool and collected, though he knows his doom. It being Sunday, he was not hanged, but early to-morrow the wretch will swing, for he was taken with arms in his hands. Two Eurasian ladies, drummer's daughters, came into Cutcherry to complain of great rudeness on the part of European officers last night. These poor creatures had been carried off by the mutineers, and had escaped worse than death by ready compliance with the worst. They were quite willing to speak about their misfortunes. Neither of them was sixteen years old.

April 19*th.*—Cawnpore to Chowbeypore.—I got up perfectly well this morning, and feeling all the better for my little rashness, so that I am quite up to the mark for our march. Our camp moved out yesterday to the Subadar's Tank. I went on to Chowbeypore this morning. Sir Colin did the two marches in one. In the evening my good kind host, Sherer, drove part of the way towards camp in his mule-gharry, which he had lent to carry me out, and we took leave on the road-side, where he had saddle-horses waiting for his return. It was dark ere we got near the camp, which was pitched some way off the road-side, and I had great difficulty in finding my way across ploughed fields to the watch-fires.

April 20*th.*—Chowbeypore to Poorwah.—Oh, Sir Colin, this is very severe! At 2·15 this morning we we were on our way to Poorwah, thirteen miles. The fatigue and monotony of these slow, long marches in the dark, are indescribable. You can see nothing. Unrefreshed by sleep, only half-awake, every moment you catch yourself just going over the horse's shoulder. You must look out lest you ride over soldiers or camp-followers who throng the road, mingled with flocks of goats, sheep, tats or ponies, camels, bullocks, begum-carts, all shrouded in dust and darkness. At last dawn comes, very slowly, no glory in it, no clouds— on the horizon there is a dim fog of dust, a haze which hides the sun. There is no colour, no atmosphere. The moment the sun shows above the haze, he burns you like fire. As you pass through the villages, ghostlike figures clad in white rise from their charpoys, which are laid out in the street, stare at you for a moment, and sink to sleep again. Early marches, how I hate you! and yet you must be, for the men must be got under cover ere the sun is long out. It is joy indeed to come up to the camping-ground, and to find the mess-dooly already established in full play under some fine tree, to join the group which is lying on the ground among the ants and dried leaves—alas! there is no grass—and to get the first gulp of refreshing tea. I have hired two bullock-hackeries which come along very nicely with my effects, and Sherer gave me two splendid black jenny-goats on starting from Cawnpore, which set me up every morning with abundance of delicious milk.

April 21st.—From Poorwah to Urrowl, thirteen miles. Started at 2.15 A.M. I go on ahead with Allgood and C. C. Johnson, the Quartermaster-General, who precede the column, and mark out the ground for the camp. This gets us out of the dust. In India the Government camping-ground is reserved at certain stages all along the road, and is marked off by stone pillars. The great object is to get the men under the shade of the trees, the Commander-in-Chief of course getting the best place. Whilst Allgood and Johnson gallop to and fro with the camp, the kotwal and colour men were laying down the cords for the streets of tents. I fasten up my horse if the syce is not up, and take a sleep with one eye open for the mess-camels. One by one the staff come in. Sir Colin and the chief of the staff are generally some time behind us. Then comes their escort, a handful of cavalry; next the interminable line of tent-camels and elephants, then the cavalry in the centre of a cloud of dust, and at last, "rub-a-dub-dub, rub-a-dub-dub," and the infantry, hot and fagged, and white as bakers, trudge up; then more baggage; then the rear-guard, and three miles of stragglers, and bazaar people. We have the 80th with us, fine soldierly-looking fellows, with a cruelly bad band.

April 22nd.—Left Urrowl at 3·15 and marched to Meerun-ke-serai, ten miles—a decided improvement as to time and distance. As I came up to camping-ground, passed a disconsolate-looking Englishman on the roadside who had got out of his gharry, and was looking for the troops. It turned out to be Ross of the 93rd, formerly adjutant-general at Balaklava, and I directed him to our tope. Dined with Sir Colin, and after a long talk with him and with General Mansfield, who was also one of the guests, I made for my tent. For the life of me I could not find it. I wandered about among the trees in the dark, and at last was forced to shout out "Simon" at the top of my voice, no doubt receiving kind wishes from the inmates of the tents. There were plenty of fellows sleeping out in the air on their charpoys, as it was cooler than in the tents. No Simon answered. At last, quite savage, I made over to a charpoy, and shaking the sleeper, said, "Who's here? Can you tell me where my tent is?" It was Sir Colin himself, who, wide awake in a minute, gazed at me with some wonder. I apologized and told him my story; he laughed, and said, "Well, take a fresh departure from this point now, and you must come upon your tent down that street." I did so, and next distinguished myself by walking in upon Mansfield, who was sitting up reading. After disturbing all the camp I got to my own tent at last. The position of it had been changed owing to the arrival of Colonel Percy Herbert and others at Head-Quarters. We were near the famous ruins of Kunouj to-day, the great Hindoo city and seat of empire. An old man who sold rose-water and preserved tamarinds, and who told us he had been guide to Lord Lake, promised to come in the evening and conduct us to the place, but he did not keep his word, and so I missed seeing those very wonderful remains, which are, however, only appreciable by one who is better versed in Hindoo antiquities than most of us are. Only one or two officers went; and they came back, declaring it was a "do—a sham, nothing but old bricks and rubbish."

April 23rd.—Meerun-ke-serai to Gooshaigunj near the Ganges. Slaughtered some fine peacocks under our tope, and saw some deer; but the heat was so intense I dared not stir out to stalk them. Sir Colin pushed on straight to Futtehguhr, where he has summoned General Penny to meet him, and the latter will have a ride of sixty miles ere he can keep the appointment. This morning Sir Colin gave me a good idea of the Rohilcund operations. Penny is to cross the Ganges and to clear the Budaon district, which is full of rebels, and then he is to join Sir Colin, who will pass over at Futtehguhr, and take command of Walpole's column, now on the Ramgunga, where Walpole gave a large body of the enemy a defeat, after his check before Royea. Meanwhile, Jones and Coke will march down from the north-west towards Bareilly; Khan Bahadoor Khan and all the Rohilcund rebels are there in force; but I fear they will slip through our fingers; we are very short of cavalry.

April 24*th.*— From Gooshaigunj to Kamalgunj. Left at 2 A.M., arrived at 6·15; road villanous to a degree. Passed the Kalanuddee by the suspension-bridge, at the place where Sir Colin beat the Nuwab of Furruckabad and the Futtehguhr rebels on the 2nd January. They had a very strong position, and had they destroyed the bridge altogether, they would have caused us serious inconvenience; but they only took up the planking! It is a very strange, and to me an unaccountable fact, that the rebels have never yet thoroughly destroyed a bridge, or cut up roads, or impeded communication. At Delhi, they left portions of the drawbridges down at the Cashmere and other gates. Here the cavalry, under Hope Grant, got on their flanks, and Hodson gave them a glorious hunt. The consequence of our success was, that Futtehguhr and Furruckabad were abandoned without a struggle. The village bears mark of our shot still.

April 25*th.*—Marched into Futtehguhr this morning at 6·15. Passing through a city of ruins, desolated bungalows, and burnt station, came to a high and spacious mud-fort. Passed through gateways up to a compound inside, and found Alison and Baird and others drinking tea in front of a large bungalow. These were the quarters of Legeyt Bruce, who was acting as superintendent of the gun-carriage department here, and to whom I was armed with letters of introduction. To my immense delight, he offered me part of a room. Before breakfast we went down to the ruins of Maharajah Dhuleep Sing's park, garden, and palaces, where there is a most delicious swimming-bath, in which we had an invigorating tumble. Dined with Sir Colin in the evening, where I had the pleasure of meeting Brigadier Seaton, a very intelligent, smart, gentlemanly man, and in look and manner quite bearing out the reputation he has gained for decision, dash, and soldierly qualities.

CHAPTER XXIV.

Dhuleep Sing's bath.—A savage, beastly, and degrading custom.—
The column filing off.—Told off to an elephant.—Fields strewed
with skeletons.—Junction with Walpole.—An Indian storm.—
—A short but grateful sleep.—Difficulty of keeping Highlanders
back.—Sir William Peel no more!—An English soldier and his
"presner."—Desperate kick from a horse.—Mounted on a
tumbril.—A day of drowsy pain.—More dooly travelling.—
General Penny killed.—Disaster at Kukrowlee.—Halt near
Shahjehanpore.—Ride through the city.—Sea of mango groves.
—Conflicting reports from Bareilly.—Bamboo backsheesh.—
Expected engagements.

April 26th.—We returned this morning from the Maharajah's bath, to breakfast in a small pagoda or mosque inside a large serai, which is used by our officers as a kind of club. How the natives must be disgusted at our use of the holy places! I was very much shocked to see in this court-yard, two native servants, covered with plaisters and bandages, and bloody, who were lying on their charpoys, moaning. On inquiring, my friend was informed by one of the guests, they were So-and-So's servants, who had just been "licked" by him. It is a savage, beastly, and degrading custom. I have heard it defended; but no man of feeling, education, or goodness of heart can vindicate or practise it. The sobs of the poor woman, the wife of one of the men, who sat by the charpoys, were most affecting; but not a soul went to comfort or say a kind word to her. The master who had administered his "spiriting" so gently to his delinquent domestics, sat sulky and sullen, and, I hope, ashamed of his violence, at the table; but he had no fear of any pains or penalties of the law.

I had a day of cool work, in a cool room, in which the thermometer was only 88°. Bruce brewed mighty beakers of claret-cup; Mylne sent us in bottles of craftily-constructed and scientifically-refrigerated milk-punch. And lo! round comes the Adjutant-General's chuprassee with the orders. And they are very distressing. We march at 12 to-night, and cross the Ganges into Rohilcund, which is one great rebel ant-hill. At dusk, Bruce and myself rode over to our camp, which was pitched in a tope about a mile outside the fort of Futtehguhr, and dined at our mess. After dinner, I was obliged to return to the fort to see my tent packed. It was bright moonlight, and the little plateau inside, in front of the bungalow, presented a curious sight, for the tents were already down, and the few inhabitants of this quarter were in the open. Sir Colin was fast asleep in his chair, in the open air; Mansfield was writing at a small table under a tree; Crealock copying letters and despatches on his knees. Having seen my goods and chattels off, I returned to camp, where our elephants were to be in readiness at midnight. It was resolved to use those useful creatures for the first part of the march. On my way back, I met the vast column filing off towards the bridge. Some of the rear-guard begged that I would take measures to prevent a drunken artilleryman, who had tumbled into a hole, from coming to harm. They were obliged to hurry on after their comrades. All tents were down in camp, and the officers were lying asleep in their cloaks. I made out Macpherson, the Quartermaster-General, who was placidly reposing on his charpoy, and reported the artilleryman's case to him. "If it's from drink," quoth he, "the man will be all right by morning." The noble Highland sagacity of the sentiment won my instant assent, and so I laid me down on the ground beside my much-esteemed friend, and slept as well as the jackals would permit me.

April 27th.—From Futtehguhr across the Ganges into Rohilcund.—We started from our camp soon after 1 o'clock this morning. The Chief left the fort on his elephant at 1·30; Mansfield, ditto, ditto, at the same time about. Colonel Macpherson, the Quartermaster-General; Major Stewart, Assistant Adjutant-General, and Mackinnon, formerly of the 42nd, who has joined the Staff as surgeon to the Lord Sahib, in lieu of Clifford, gone to Landour, and myself, were told off to an elephant, which had something like the body of an Irish jaunting car placed on its back for our reception. I own that I mounted with trepidation, and had some doubts of the *équilibre* of the howdah. We passed out from the trees to the plain, which was peopled by ghosts flitting along in the moonlight. The scene was theatrical and strange-looking. The old fort of Futtehguhr towering above the silvered flood of the Ganges, seemed the work of some grand canvassed Grieve, and it was only the dull roar of the multitude pouring over the bridge of boats which gave its real character to what was around us.

The wretchedness of this morning, this night and morning march! How one's head went to and fro at every jog of the beast in a sleep-compelling manner which was irresistible. With what a jerk one caught himself up just as he was going to plunge head foremost fifteen feet to the hard sand! It was about

4 o'clock when we crossed the Ganges and got into Rohilcund. Then for some hours we toiled over sands till we came to the Ramgunga, a deep stream, which our elephant waded across, so that our feet nearly touched the water. The hathi nearly floated his driver off his neck. Higher up was a bridge of boats made by the rebels, which was taken the other day (23rd, I think) by Walpole, in a smart advance of cavalry and horse-artillery. The Commander-in-Chief was crossing it as we came up. Here our horses should have been waiting, but my syce was invisible, and I had to continue and jog on in the iron embrace of the howdah. For several miles our course lay over fields strewed with horrid bloated skeletons—the men killed in the pursuit from the Ramgunga. Some of those who fell had white gaiters and other articles belonging to the Highlanders and Sikhs who were killed in the attack of Royea, so it is probable they were Nirput Sing's men. The motion of the elephant made Stewart perfectly sick, so that he had to get down and mount Sir Colin's carriage, which was near us at the time. I took up Colonel Pakenham, and Norman, the Adjutant-General, whose elephant would not behave itself, and who were toiling on in the dust and heat of the sun, as their syces were also missing. The heat of this morning was beyond endurance. It seemed as if Tingree, for which we were bound, was inaccessible. At last, thank Heaven, we see our tents pitched, and the bazaar flags flying, though the camp is in a sandy plain. I found every one nearly as done up as myself; our mess-tent not up. Breakfasted in Allgood's tent; thirst, most distressing. Here we effected our junction

with Walpole's force. I found the officers of the 42nd and 93rd in a state of furious wrath and discontent with their general. They told me they were afraid of mutiny, or worse, when poor Hope was buried! Nirput Sing drew off his men in the night, and when Walpole was told next morning the place was evacuated, he said, "Thank God!" He would not take any notice of the information sent round to him by the cavalry at the other side of the fort where there was a jeel nearly dry, and the wall of the fort was so low that a man might have leaped over it. This is strange; for although Walpole had no experience of service before he came out to India, and had chiefly been engaged in staff employ, he showed energy, courage, and conduct at Cawnpore. His manners are unpleasant, and he has managed to make himself unpopular. It would be impossible to give an idea of the violent way in which some officers spoke of him to-day.

As we were at dinner this evening I had the first idea of an Indian storm. Suddenly the sky became jet black and shut out the moon—lightning flashed incessantly. I was going to my tent with Captain Apthorp, the postmaster, when the dust-storm struck us. I was blinded, and all I could do was to keep my hands over my eyes, and shout till some Kelassies came to our aid and led me to my tent. Everything was smothered with dust an inch deep. The storm threatened to blow my tent down, and actually beat the mess-tent and several others to the ground. Bullet-like drops of rain fell, and there were some heavy peals of thunder; but the moon shone out and the clouds were gone in an hour's time.

April 28th.—The force was off before 2 A.M. this morning for Jellalabad on the road to Shahjehanpore. About 3 A.M. we halted, and lay down in our cloaks for a short sleep, which was very grateful. At 3·30 the bugles sounded, and on we went again. Country very flat, but well wooded and highly cultivated. The fields full of dall, sugar-cane, and cotton plant stumps, which are very apt to lame the horses. My best marcher was put *hors de combat* to-day by one of these, which went clean into the frog. Sir Colin also had a horse rendered unfit for work from the same cause. The villages are invariably deserted as we advance. About 5·30 we had another halt, and I remained alongside Sir Colin whilst his pet Highlanders marched by—the 42nd, 79th, and 93rd. I had short chats with old friends and acquaintances, Cameron, Taylor, Hay, and others. Sir Colin evidently did not wish to speak about Royea, but once or twice referring to it and to the Highlanders, he said, "The difficulty with these troops, Mr. Russell, is to keep them back; that's the danger with them. They will get too far forward." The Highlanders are very proud of Sir Colin, and he is proud of them. They look on him as if he belonged to them, like their bagpipes,—a property useful in war. His Excellency gave me a copy of his proclamation on entering Rohilcund, a very useful and sensible document. About 8 A.M. we came in sight of a high mud fort, dominating a large village. Our vedettes said they could make out men inside. Away scampered some cavalry and guns to the fort, and I with them. But the fort was empty, though it had evidently been very recently occupied by a very numerous picket of the enemy. Our camp was pitched some distance outside the village.

Here there is a confusion of dates in my Diary, as I find on this day, "What sad, sad news! Sir William Peel no more!" When at Futtehguhr, I heard he was unwell at Cawnpore, and I at once telegraphed to the Rev. Mr. Moore, the chaplain, to ask how he was. The morning we left Tingree a messenger came out to me with a telegram from Mr. Moore: "Sir William is doing as well as can be expected in a bad case of confluent small-pox." I showed the message to Sir Colin, who evinced anxiety and concern. Dr. Clifford, when he heard Peel was ill of small-pox, said, "He never will get over it. I know him so well; I'm sure he's the worst subject possible." Alas! his diagnosis proved too true. This morning Sir Colin rode after me, after the second halt, and said quietly, "You'll be sorry to hear this bad news. Poor Sir William is no more." There is no use in dilating on one's own feelings. The news went abroad from regiment to regiment, through all the ranks, and all this day and during the march I heard nothing but expressions of regret and deep sympathy. The greatness of our loss we in all probability shall never know.

At breakfast-time Sir Colin was missing. He was hunted for in all directions. Alison set off to look for him in the fort, and I rode with him. On entering over the parapet, we found Sir Colin, sure enough, with Colonel Sterling, going over the place. Again he alluded indirectly to the Royea affair, to the rashness of officers in a subordinate position attempting to blame or judge the acts of their superiors, of the strength of those mud forts, and of the difficulty of restraining the Highlanders. "Look at this fort, and see how easy it would be for a few resolute fellows to pick off a body of men rash enough to run into that ditch. Why, these young gentlemen raised an outcry the other day against that poor fellow, Campbell, because he did not cut up the runaways at Lucknow; but Major Daly, who understands his duty as well as any man, and who was present at the time, told me he did not think Campbell could have done more than he did!" His Excellency did not allude to the heavy guns with the column, or to the easy way into the fort of Royea.

On our way back, met an English soldier unarmed, who had ferreted out a budmash in the village, armed with sword and shield, "took him presner," as he said, and, having tied his arms behind his back with his turban, was conducting him in triumph to the Provost-marshal. In the afternoon I sauntered out on horseback through the delicious groves around us; visited the advanced posts and pickets, all of which had seen sowars in the distance. I had my gun; killed some beautiful mango birds, wood-peckers, bright jays, pigeons, and doves, and had a splendid run after a fox, in which I strained the inner muscle of the thigh, in consequence of a violent shy made by my horse, as he nearly leaped on top of a jackal crouching in a rut amid high grass. I was thoroughly tired when I got back to camp, and could not go out to the 42nd, where I was engaged to dine with Colonel Cameron.

April 29th.—"*Dies carbone notanda.*"—Left Jellalabad for Kanth at the usual early hour, notwithstanding that we were in an enemy's country; but it is moonlight. I rode for some time with Dr. Tice, but, getting tired of his slow pace, I pushed on by the side of the column so rapidly that my syce could not keep up, particularly as the ground was full of sharp stumps. At last I got up to the guns of the advanced guard, just as the halt was called. I gave my horse to a syce to hold, and lay down beside Bunny, and slept by the road side. At last the bugles sounded. I woke up at the " Stand by your horses," and saw that the syce to whom I had given my horse to hold had fallen asleep like the rest of us, so that the other quadruped of which he was in charge had free access to bite, and kick, and fight with the only remaining horse I had available for a long march. All the stallions about us were squeaking and lashing out violently. I ran over to preserve my beast from being eaten alive,—but I was sleepy; my leg was stiff from the strain of the day before,—and, just as I was getting up to the head of my horse, a powerful Arab, belonging to Stewart, ran back to have a last go in at his enemy, and delivered a murderous fling, from which I could not escape, for my own horse was pressing hard against me. I saw the shoes flash in the moonlight. In an instant I was sent flying along the ground under my horse's belly. One heel had struck me just at the lower part of the stomach, but the steel scabbard of the sword I wore broke the force of the blow there, though the shoe cut out a small piece of skin; the other hoof caught me right in the hollow of the right thigh. Several men ran towards me. Ricketts and Bunny picked me up, and helped me to one of Tombs' guns, where I managed to hold on by the tumbril seat. I was in great pain, faint, sick, and burning with thirst. For three hours or so I rumbled along on the tumbril, till we came within about two miles of Kanth, where we were to encamp. An alarm was raised that the enemy were close to our front, and Tombs was ordered to gallop on with his guns and some horse, to reconnoitre. I, of course, had to be helped from the tumbril, and placed on the road side. As I sat there Sir Colin came up, dismounted, and sat down near me; but neither he nor I thought enough of the kick to pay attention to it. Indeed, he was quite absorbed with the case of a native official, who was hanged in our camp by Mr. Money, in virtue of his civil authority. Sir Colin was extremely indignant at the transaction, which he characterized in the severest way. It appears this man had been tehsildar, or head of a revenue police department, in our service, but had gone over with all the rest of his class to the rebels. However, he had recently been in communication with some of our officers; and Captain Carey, on Walpole's staff, had taken it on himself to say that if he surrendered or came in, his life should be spared. The man came in accordingly, but Mr. Money seized him, and yesterday evening he was hanged, loudly invoking with his last breath the honour of British officers and the promise given to him. As Sir Colin says, such conduct will leave rebels no alternative but to hold out to the last. This severity is a premium to resistance. He has spoken to Mr. Money in a sharp and decided tone, which will prevent such occurrences in our camp in future.* Sterling, indeed all the Head-Quarters people, are exceedingly displeased at the occurrence, and declare that the word of a British officer should have been held inviolate.

When our conversation was ended, and the tents appeared ready in the distance, Sir Colin mounted; but my syce was nowhere to be seen, and so I had to walk as best I could beside Sir Colin's horse, leaning with pain on my sword, which was the only support I had. The distress of movement increased at every step, and by the time I had walked to the camp I was all but fainting. Sir Colin has seen too much of pain to think much about it, and said, "You'll be all right after a little rest." After breakfast, Mr. Mackinnon came to my tent, and examined the injury. A large, blood-coloured lump, the size and shape of a horse-shoe, had risen up in the hollow of the thigh, and I was otherwise injured. Cold lotions ordered. I lay on my back all day in good Macpherson's tent, listening dreamily to the hum-drum narratives of the endless spies who were coming in with all sorts of stories about the enemy, generally of a very poetical and unpractical sort. His tent was cool and airy considering the awful heat, and so in drowsy pain I lay all day. To-morrow morning I must take my place in a dooly again. This is a bitter disappointment to me; but I have arranged that I may move with the advanced guard, so as just to keep abreast of the guns; therefore I shall not miss anything that is going forward.

* Lord Canning subsequently approved of Mr. Money's act, as he proved the man was a ringleader in rebellion.

Friday, 30th April.—Kanth to Shahjehanpore.— Unable to mount a horse, I am carried in a dooly. I am to know more of those doolys, it would appear, than I care for. I confess that there is something revolting to my feelings about the mode of progression, though we had our sedan chairs, and were no better than Hindoo notables in our day. It is miserable jogging along by the column. Every one bullies dooly-bearers; therefore, to avoid knocks, and whip cuts and bad language, they go off in the open, and expose one to the risk of being cut up by the enemy's cavalry. They were reported to be strong at Shahjehanpore; and it was not pleasant to find myself at dawn this morning out in a wide plain, with only a cloud of dust in the distance to show where our column was marching. As the bearers, in compliance with a hint from a revolver, were turning towards the line of march, a body of eight or ten native cavalry came upon us out of a tope, shouting like furies, and brandishing their lances and sabres. I gave it up as a bad chance for life, but sat up in the dooly with pistols ready for action, and hoping that if I hit the leader, the others would think better of the matter and retire. The dooly-bearers to my astonishment, instead of dropping me and running for their lives, broke into a canter, but the horsemen soon came up with them; and just as I was about pulling the trigger on the leader, who had his lance point within a yard of the hindmost of the bearers, they swept by us towards our column, leaving two of their number to conduct the delinquent dooly-men to their proper station. In effect, it was a patrol of Mooltanee horse, which had been sent out at night, and was now returning to the troops, and, in execution of their orders, they fell on the dooly, which was out of the line of march, and compelled the men to go to their proper place. Our course lay to Shahjehanpore, where the outbreak of mutiny took place, under circumstances of great barbarity; and as it contained a large fanatical Mahomedan population, it was supposed the enemy would hold it; but our scouts brought us word last night that it was evacuated, though the Moulvie and Nana Sahib were in it up to a recent period, and one of the ladies of the zenana had presented the latter with a son just before our arrival.

As my dooly was brought up to camp, Sir Colin walked up to ask after me, and sat on the ground whilst his tent was being pitched. I saw Mansfield walking rather rapidly over towards us with a despatch in his hand, which he delivered to Sir Colin, saying, " This is from Colonel Jones, sir. General Penny is killed!"

Sir Colin did not express the least surprise, but simply asked the two questions, " When and where?" " At a place called Kukrowlee, the night before last; a sort of ambuscade or surprise it seems."

" Here, Mansfield! Please take the despatch and read it!" And so indeed it was. The gallant old officer was making a loosely-ordered night march; and relying on the information of the civilian who accompanied his column, he believed there were none of the enemy's forces near him, and took no steps to keep his column together, or to send out a proper advanced guard in front. " Googur" Wilson, as he is called, a well known active and courageous civilian, was in charge of the column, which had been sweeping through Budaon, and he directed Penny's march to a place called Oosaite, where a large body of infantry, with guns and some cavalry, were said to have taken up their position. The force consisted of a wing of the Carabineers, under Jones, about 200 strong, 353 of H.M.'s 64th, under Bingham, the Belooch battalion (360), a portion of 2nd Punjaubees, 250 sabres Mooltanee horse, and six heavy and six light guns, about 1,550 in all. Oosaite was deserted. All the natives declared that the enemy had made off towards the north-east, where they would probably endeavour to get into Oude. On this point information was positive.

"Yes," observed Sir Colin, "you find civilians are continually deceiving us, or allowing themselves to be deceived by the natives. They will insist on it that the people are not against us."

Penny directed his march along the Budaon-road, and at a place called the Kukrowlee, from the head of the column where he was riding, some indistinct objects and some lights were seen. It was quite dark, and ere they could ascertain the nature of those appearances, a discharge of grape and musketry threw them into confusion. Penny, whose bridle-hand was probably disabled, seems to have been carried by his frightened horse right among the enemy, where of course he was cut to pieces. In a charge of the Carabineers subsequently they all tumbled on a lot of gazees in a ditch. Forster, Betty, Eckford, Davis, and Graham, were badly wounded, and several of the men put *hors de combat*. The 64th entered the village at the point of the bayonet, after it had been severely shelled, and the enemy got away with small loss as usual. " It is astonishing that an old soldier like General Penny could have been so indiscreet! Poor man!" And yet he was indeed a good soldier, and a very careful leader, who had seen much and various service in India.

In war there is no time for elaborate grief. We passed the entrance to Shahjehanpore in our march by a bridge of boats over the river. The stone gate-house and the houses of the city looked exactly like the entrance to Russian frontier stations. By order of Nana Sahib, all the houses or buildings suitable to shelter troops in the city or cantonments have been destroyed. We were, therefore, obliged to cut to a thick tope outside the city, at the other side of the river, and some of the column were encamped actually in the open under a tremendous sun. Sir Colin told me he would leave a small force under Colonels Hale or Percy Herbert, to keep Shahjehanpore when he moved on to Bareilly.

May 1st.—We halted all day here, principally, I believe, to permit the Engineers to make a very feeble attempt at fortifying our tope, so as to make it an entrenched position for the men who will be left in garrison here. The proceeding was so very imbecile that the tope was abandoned; the day was lost, and our labour thrown away. It was resolved to send Hale's little force to occupy the gaol, which is in tolerable order and preservation, and which dominates part of the city. The tracing of the work provoked immense laughter to-day. Why is it that our Engineers are so ——? It is a melancholy fact, that with all our mechanical skill, and with our immense genius as civil engineers, we have produced no military engineer of any grand genius—no one who has invented a system like Vauban or Cormontaigne, or who has written any original work worth three halfpence. There are highly-respectable officers, such as Bourgoyne, Jones, Gordon, and others, but no one will say we have a Todtleben. In India it is said the best engineers are captains of infantry; but from what I have seen of the Company's Engineers, such men as Robert Napier for example, I think them equal to the best in the Queen's service.

This afternoon I felt so well, after a powerful leeching and blistering of the leg, that I mounted an elephant, and with Goldsworthy and Mr. Donald, a Rohilcund planter, who has come up with our column to look after his property, or the wreck of it, went through the city. The population have fled, a very few ill-looking, scowling fellows prowling about the streets, and some sweetmeat-sellers at the corners. The main street is very clean and neat, being paved with small brick-like tiles, set with the thin edge upwards, and I can readily believe it was, as we are told, one of the most delightful stations in the Northwest Provinces. We proceeded as far as the fine road leading to cantonments, which is lined by magnificent trees, and then returned in time for mess, at which I was present for the first time since my accident. Whilst at dinner I felt a little uneasy about the place where I had been kicked, a throbbing not very painful or violent. When I retired to my tent there suddenly sprang up an excessively sharp and bitter pain in the calf of my leg, which I could only alleviate or endure by placing my foot against the tent-pole high above the level of my head. Here is some new mischief. Doctors now-a-days are content to "watch symptoms as they rise." The heroic treatment is now to be tried — bleeding and blistering, and leeching, and smearing all my leg with belladonna. Our warm weather is beginning to tell on us. Baird has got fever. Alison has small-pox. Both are down on their backs, and must travel in doolys like myself. The Chief is thus left without aides-de-camp, for young Forster is acting as assistant prize-agent at Lucknow. This is rather an inglorious way for us three to go forth to battle.

May 2nd.—In great agony last night; up at 1 this morning, and left Shahjehanpore camp at 2 A.M.; bound for Tilhour, twelve miles distant. In much pain all day ; a large lump forming in the hollow of the thigh, from near the knee to an inch of the hip. The kick is now really serious. Twenty-five leeches were put on the calf of my leg as soon as we halted. Why on the calf? Bleed, and bear, and ask no questions. The country through which we passed is very flat, very fertile—a rich sea of mango groves; but the people have fled from before us. Crops of sugar-cane are abundant, and the system of irrigation appears excellent, and very perfect of its kind. Wells are numerous, and water is readily found a few feet below the surface. Riding about at night is very dangerous, as the mouths of the wells are not raised above the surface, nor marked in any way. Tilhour is a very ancient place, and we saw some fine old houses and mosques near us as we were borne by. The enemy, who were said to have occupied it, were not visible on our approach. Scarcely was our camp pitched when I was carried into my tent, and made an attempt to sleep, in spite of many friends who came in to pay me their visits, but I could not succeed.

As I was speaking to Tod Brown I heard very distinctly the report of guns a long way off. I called his attention to it, and begged that one of them would go and mention it to the Chief. The firing was soon audible to most of us. What an exciting and all-absorbing sensation it produces in war time! Sir Colin, who came in towards evening, decided that it must be at Shahjehanpore. "That rascally Moulvie! —a very clever fellow though, and shows a good deal of skill."

The reports from Bareilly are very conflicting. Some say the enemy are very strong, and confident; others that they are weak, and desponding. Our spies serve two masters.

May 3rd.—Marched from Tilhour to Futtehgunj, or the Place of Victory, where our Indian forces gained a battle in one of our unholy aggressions on Rohilcund. How fortunate Hale and his handful of men were not left in the entrenched tope! The Moulvie was down on them the moment our backs were turned, with lots of cavalry, guns, and some infantry. Hale, however, was strongly posted in the gaol; made excellent dispositions, and with two light and two heavy guns showed a front that held the enemy in check and eventually he pounded them out of their close proximity to his position. The enemy, however, cut up some camp-followers and sowars, and captured hackeries and stores, &c.

There is great indignation expressed around me

against Khan Bahadoor Khan, the rebel chief of Rohilcund. He is, it is true, a pensioner of ours, and a retired native judge, or sudder ameen; but he is also descendant and representative of Hafiz Hushmut Khan, the chief whom we slew in the battle which led to the overthrow of his rule in Rohilcund. We conquered the province for the Nuwab Vizier of Oude, and now we have swallowed up Oude and the kingdom we gave the Nuwab. When he got an opportunity he grasped at what he believed to be his own, and he did so in a way which no one can approve of, for his ways were treacherous and bloody. According to the lights of his faith and civilization, the acts of which he has been guilty are not much worse than our own. He was appointed to his place years ago on the ground that, though unfitted for it, he could not, consistently with policy, be permitted to wander about before the people of India in a state of destitution.

A spy came in to-day from Bareilly with news that there are 30,000 foot, 6,000 horse, and 40 guns there. Another reported that he had just come in from Furreedpore, and that there were no guns, sowars, or infantry there; but as some other emissaries had given information of an opposite character, the quartermaster-general ordered his eyebrows, beard, and head to be shaved, and a plentiful allowance of bamboo backsheesh to be administered to him. It turned out that the man's story was quite true!

In great pain all day. Twenty more leeches on my leg.

May 4th.—On arriving at Furreedpore this morning, after a long and tedious and hot march all night from Futtehgunj, we found the place deserted, and encamped without opposition. Our pickets saw plenty of sowars capering about in our front. Again, this morning at dawn on looking out of my dooly I discovered that the doolys, with Baird and Alison inside, were the only portions of our force visible for miles. As I have resolved not to be cut up without a fight for it, and giving myself a chance, I had up my syce this morning, and warned him, under terrible pains and penalties, to lead my best horse always close to my litter, ready for mounting, with one revolver loose in the holster. I shall have a very miserable time of it. I am very weak, owing to starvation diet; to constant leeching and blistering. To-day a huge strong blister is applied from my knee to my hip, inside the leg. The heat to-night was very great. Sir Colin came in to my tent to see how I was, and told me, "Those fellows will fight to-morrow. All our reports declare they will stand. I'm sorry you're not a little better able to be with us; and there's Baird and Alison unfit for duty also." The fact is, we must get this work over, or the sun will become very deadly.

END OF VOL. I.

www.ingramcontent.com/pod-product-compliance
Lightning Source LLC
Chambersburg PA
CBHW051733300426
44115CB00007B/546